D0893352

Software
Engineering

VOLUME 2

Software Engineering

COINS III

VOLUME 2

Proceedings of the Third Symposium on Computer and Information Sciences held in Miami Beach, Florida, December, 1969

Edited by

JULIUS T. TOU

Center for Informatics Research
University of Florida
Gainesville, Florida

Academic Press   New York · London · 1971

ACADEMIC PRESS, INC.
111 Fifth Avenue, New York, New York 10003

United Kingdom Edition published by
ACADEMIC PRESS, INC. (LONDON) LTD.
Berkeley Square House, London W1X 6BA

LIBRARY OF CONGRESS CATALOG CARD NUMBER: 76-127707

PRINTED IN THE UNITED STATES OF AMERICA

Contents of Volume 2

Computer-Assisted Documentation of Working Binary Computer Programs with Unknown Documentation

EDMUND C. BERKELEY

Quality Control in the Publishing Process and Theoretical Foundations for Information Retrieval

MANFRED KOCHEN

ISL—A New Programming Language for Information Retrieval

R. T. CHIEN, S. R. RAY, AND F. A. STAHL

On the Role of Exact and Nonexact Associative Memories in Human and Machine Information Processing

NICHOLAS V. FINDLER

On Syntactic Pattern Recognition

K.-S. FU AND P. H. SWAIN

Grammatical Inference Techniques in Pattern Analysis

THOMAS G. EVANS

Linguistic Analysis of Waveforms

T. PAVLIDIS

A Grammar for Maps

AZRIEL ROSENFELD AND JAMES P. STRONG

A Software Engineering Approach to the Space Information System of the Future

T. P. GORMAN

An Efficient Program for Real-Time Assignment of Jobs in a Hybrid Computer Network

I. T. FRISCH AND M. MALEK-ZAVAREI

An Algorithmic Approach to Sequential Automata Design

CHESTER C. CARROLL, WILLIAM L. OLIVER, JR., AND WILLIAM A. HORNFECK

List of Contributors to Volume 2

Numbers in parentheses refer to the pages on which the authors' contributions begin.

Berkeley, Edmund C.,* *Information International,* Inc., Boston, Massachusetts (1)

Berkowitz, S., Naval Ship Research and Development Center, Washington, D.C. (119)

Carroll, Chester C., Electrical Engineering Department, Auburn University, Auburn, Alabama (265)

Chien, R. T., Coordinated Science Laboratory, University of Illinois, Urbana, Illinois (55)

Evans, Thomas G., Air Force Cambridge Research Laboratories, Bedford, Massachusetts (183)

Findler, Nicholas V., State University of New York, Buffalo, New York (141)

Frisch, I. T., Network Analysis Corporation, Glen Cove, New York (253)

Fu, K.-S., Purdue University, Lafayette, Indiana (155)

Gorman, T. P., Gorman Computer Systems, Inc., Bowie, Maryland (241)

Hornfeck, William A., Electrical Engineering Department, Auburn University, Auburn, Alabama (265)

Jackson, D. M.,† Cornell University, Ithaca, New York (71)

Kochen, Manfred, University of Michigan, Ann Arbor, Michigan (19)

Kuhns, J. L., The Rand Corporation, Santa Monica, California (89)

Malek-Zavarei, M.,‡ University of California, Berkeley, California (253)

*Present affiliation: Computers and Automation, Newtonville, Massachusetts.
†*Present affiliation:* The Ohio State University, Columbus, Ohio.
‡*Present affiliation:* Bell Telephone Laboratories, Inc., Holmdel, New Jersey.

Oliver, William L., Jr., Electrical Engineering Department, University of Illinois, Urbana, Illinois (265)

Otten, Michael,* International Business Machines, Inc., Bethesda, Maryland (105)

Pacak, Milos G., National Institutes of Health, Bethesda, Maryland (105)

Pavlidis, T., Princeton University, Princeton, New Jersey (203)

Ray, S. R., Coordinated Science Laboratory, University of Illinois, Urbana, Illinois (55)

Rosenfeld, Azriel, University of Maryland, College Park, Maryland (227)

Stahl, F. A., Coordinated Science Laboratory, University of Illinois, Urbana, Illinois (55)

Strong, James P., National Aeronautics and Space Administration, Greenbelt, Maryland (227)

Swain, P. H., Purdue University, Lafayette, Indiana (155)

Wilcox, Richard H., Executive Office of The President, Washington, D.C. (285)

*Present affiliation: Corporate Headquarters, International Business Machines, Inc., Armonk, New York.

Preface

The COINS-69 which was held in Miami Beach on December 18–20, 1969 is the third International Symposium on Computer and Information Sciences. The first was organized by Northwestern University and the Office of Naval Research in 1963, and the second was cosponsored by Battelle Memorial Institute, the Office of Naval Research, and the Ohio State University in 1966. The COINS symposia were formed to provide a forum for promoting communication among scientists, engineers, and educators in the computer and information science field and to act as a catalyzer for stimulating creative thinking within the community of information processing.

The theme of this COINS symposium is software engineering. This theme has been selected because software is emerging as the core of computer and information science. In the study of computer design problems, language processing problems, pattern recognition problems, information retrieval problems, and artificial intelligence problems, software plays an important role. During the past several years, the computer and information science field has made remarkable advances in software engineering. In organizing the symposium we attempted to fit thirty-nine technical papers into three days, reporting new developments in many aspects of the field. The authors of these papers came from various parts of the United States and from Canada, England, France, and Japan. The COINS-69 featured a banquet speech by Congressman Roman C. Pucinski.

The papers contained in this book were presented for discussion at the symposium. The material is published in two volumes. The first volume contains papers concerning computer organization, systems programming, and programming languages; and the second volume is devoted to information retrieval, pattern processing, and computer networks. In order to maintain coherence between the papers and to help the reader locate items of particular interest, the papers in both volumes are arranged in logical groups and indexes are provided. It is recognized that many other eminent research workers have made significant contributions to the understanding of software engineering. Unfortunately, the omnipresent tyranny of time and space prohibited the inclusion of their work in the symposium. We sincerely hope that their papers will be presented at the next COINS symposium.

Acknowledgments

Credit for any success in this symposium must be shared with many people who contributed significantly of their time and talents. In organizing the symposium the chairman, Julius T. Tou, received considerable help from the symposium committee, including Wayne H. Chen and William R. D. Nickelson of the University of Florida, James E. Norman and Yale N. Patt of the Army Research Office, Gordon Goldstein of the Office of Naval Research, Milton E. Rose of the National Science Foundation, and Robert R. Johnson of Burroughs Corporation. Much credit is due to our invited reviewers of the symposium papers. My best thanks are also due to G. Jack Lipovski and Mrs. Grace Searle of the University of Florida and several members of the Research Technology Division of the Army Research Office at Durham, North Carolina, for their valuable assistance in preparing announcements, programs, and badges, and in arranging and conducting the symposium.

It is the authors of the individual papers whose contributions made possible the symposium and the subsequent proceedings. The participation of Chancellor Robert B. Mautz of the Florida State University System and Representative Roman C. Pucinski of the U.S. Congress significantly enhanced the stature of the symposium. To all of them, and to Academic Press, the editor wishes to express his heartfelt appreciation.

The Challenge for the 1970s in Information Retrieval

Roman C. Pucinski

HOUSE OF REPRESENTATIVES
WASHINGTON, D.C.

As we embark on the new decade of the 1970s, we can envision some of the huge opportunities and challenges which face us as a result of our phenomenal and ever-increasing growth. It is a measure of our time that, whereas it has taken our nation 195 years to reach a gross national product of one trillion dollars, projections of our growth rate predict a total of two trillion dollars in the short period of the next ten years. There is even reason to believe that, by the time of the twenty-first century, a total of four trillion dollars will have been reached. Computer capability has been and will continue to be a vital force in this increasing growth. It is my belief that this nation has always had the vision for such achievement but, until the advent of the computer, lacked the tools for full implementation of that vision.

As early as 1929, Dr. Robert Goddard suggested a formula for a propulsion system which would lift man and his rockets free of the earth's gravity. In the ensuing years, scientists developed many ideas and much of the machinery which could have placed a team on the moon years before the great American achievement of 1969. It was the lack of the unifying force of the computer sciences which held back earlier success in this venture. And just as the transistor revolutionized electronics, so has the computer revolutionized the entire application of science by bringing together its disparate branches through the medium of information retrieval and exchange. As the coming years bring ever greater problems to mankind, the computer industry will have the opportunity for an ever greater role in the solution of those problems and the making of a better life on this world. Since we in the United States have had the good fortune to develop this unique industry more effectively than any other nation, it is incumbent on us to accept this great challenge and to find the most effective means for applying the whole complex of science data processing and information retrieval to the needs of not only the 1970s and 1980s, but as far as we can project into the twenty-first century.

It is encouraging to note that many of our leaders in government, industry, and university life have designated data processing and information retrieval as a high national priority and a potentially significant contribution toward the solution of many of our most crucial problems. Indeed, information retrieval is well on its way to becoming a basic industry employing millions of people and adding a new dimension to our growth.

All of you are well versed in the staggering statistics on the proliferation of scientific data as well as the hopeless task our scientists are faced with in attempting to find pertinent information from flowing torrents of scientific documents. We are caught in a vice on one side of which is the force of over 100,000 technical journals, over 130,000 research and development reports, and countless other books and periodicals published each year. On the other side is a physical limitation of the human capacity to absorb knowledge. The eminent neurologist, Dr. Grey Walter, has stated:

> During the last two generations, the rate of accumulation of knowledge has been so colossaly accelerated that not even the most noble and tranquil brain can now store and consider even a thousandth part of it. Humanity is in a critical state compared with which the constitution of the dinosaur and the community of the Tower of Babel were triumphant.

Dr. Vannevar Bush, the great American scientist, characterized the urgency of the problem with the following grim note: "Science may become bogged down in its own products, inhibited like a colony of bacteria by its own exudations." Indeed, Dr. Wassily Leontief, the distinguished Harvard University economist, pointed out recently: "If all pure research now were stopped, it would take 10 years to incorporate what we have."

Basically what we have is knowledge: scientific and technical information. This is the heart of the problem and these are some of the many reasons why we must be deeply concerned about the future direction of our national effort in the area of data processing and information retrieval. It is imperative that our mounting investment in research be, in fact, for new and expanded work and not for duplicate effort contained in documents drowned in an ocean of inaccessible information. In addition, unless our scientists are given better, faster, and more accurate information wherever needed, their valuable training and creative energies will be substantially impaired. Clearly the first step in the undertaking of a research project is the study of prior art. At the present time, it is practically impossible to assure that such a study will be thorough and exhaustive. Physical limitations are such that the average person reading 12 hours a day for 50 days, at the most could read about 16,000 technical books in his lifetime. Compared to the resources of over 30 million books in the world today, man's capacity to absorb information appears to be limited indeed.

Just how important is this? Let me give you a few examples. The single, most important product responsible for our remarkable progress in automation, and the seed of the electronic revolution, is the transistor. However, an interesting fact has recently been uncovered. It appears that almost a quarter of a century before the Bell Laboratories' discovery, a scientist by the name of Lielienfeld had discovered substantially the same idea.

Dr. Virgil E. Bottom, Professor of Physics and Chairman of the Department of Physics and Mathematics at McMurry College, Texas, had this to say about Mr. Lielienfeld's discovery:

> His devices operate on the basis of conductivity modulation by minority carrier injection in semiconductors, which is the basis of operation of the modern transistor... he invented and used solid state amplifiers identical in principal with the modern transistor nearly a quarter of a century before it was rediscovered and made into a practical device.

The loss of money, material, and manpower resources from waste and duplication is overwhelming. But what is perhaps less known is that these losses are not confined merely to money and material but to lives as well. Let me give you one example: in 1916, Dr. Peyton Rous and Dr. F. S. Jones developed an important method for using tissue cells in studying viruses. In 1954, almost a half-century later, the same method was rediscovered by Doctors Dulbecco and Vogt, leading to vaccine production and treatment of virus diseases. I am told that millions of lives could have been saved had the earlier method been readily available to our scientists.

These are some of the problems. But what are some of the solutions? During the past several years it has been a rich experience for me, as a member of the Ad Hoc Subcommittee on a National Information System, to learn a great deal about some of the problems and solutions associated with DPIR. I had the privilege to hear testimony on the subject of information handling from many outstanding scientists representing universities and industry from all over the United States. Without exception, witnesses appearing before our committee agreed to the need for cooperation and coordination. The creation of a national information system is one solution which would serve to coordinate all the various information centers throughout the country and the world. The proposed system would serve in the capacity of a switching network between all the independent sources of information, thus making it possible for individuals to participate in the efforts of many. Each of our hundreds of specialized documentation centers has an important function and would be the major lifeline and source for a national information system. In addition, many of the problems besetting each center would tend to diminish because of coordination and cooperation for a common purpose.

There is an extraordinary opportunity for the art of microelectronics to pioneer and help realize the future promise from the wealth of scientific and technical information. Through miniature devices, a scientist's own laboratory may be able to utilize the full range of computers, teletype equipment, closed circuit television, and whatever new means the electronic industry may develop, to become in effect its own word storehouse of knowledge. Such a storehouse would provide ideas and information not only from a man's own field but from other disciplines as well. In addition, a great contribution could be made to underdeveloped countries by providing "instant libraries" of technical information, possibly via satellite communication.

The full significance of the startling breakthrough we have witnessed in recent years becomes readily apparent when we recall that only 130 years ago people were still counting on their fingers, over 25 years ago atomic energy was a speculation, 20 years ago computers as we know them today were dreams, and now even the moon has succumbed to man's ingenuity.

Today we are on the threshold of another great revolution in exploration of the vast wealth of scientific and technical information at our disposal. I am fully aware that the establishment of a national information system is a major undertaking. I am also aware that there are some who doubt its feasibility or necessity, procrastinate, and, thereby, risk forsaking the future. To these skeptical prophets, let me read the editorial of the *New York Times* about space exploration written in 1920, almost half a century ago:

A SEVERE STRAIN ON THE CREDULITY

As a method of sending a missile to the higher, and even to the highest parts of the earth's atmospheric envelope, Professor Goddard's rocket is a practicable and therefore promising device . . . . It is when one considers the multiple-charge rocket as a traveller to the moon that one begins to doubt.... For after the rocket quits our air and really starts on its longer journey, its flight will be neither accelerated nor maintained by the explosion of the charges it then might have left. Professor Goddard with his "chair" in Clark College and the countenancing of the Smithsonian Institution, does not know the relation of action to reaction, and of the need to have something better than a vacuum against which to react—to say that would be absurd. Of course he only seems to lack the knowledge ladled out daily in his schools....

To build a meaningful world community, we need men of vision and courage, of dedication and understanding. The achievements of the community of scientists working in software engineering strongly indicate that there are many such among you and that much of our future lies in your hands.

Contents of Volume I

List of Contributors to Volume I

Numbers in parentheses refer to the pages on which the authors' contributions begin.

Anceau, F., University of Grenoble, Grenoble, France (179)

Barbe, Penny, PROBE Consultants, Inc., Phoenix, Arizona (151)

Barton, R. S., Department of Computer Science, University of Utah, Salt Lake City, Utah (7)

Bemer, R. W., General Electric Company, Phoenix, Arizona (121)

Campbell, G., Brookhaven National Laboratory, Upton, Long Island, New York (79)

Creech, B. A., Burroughs Corporation, Pasadena, California (29)

Detlefsen, G. D., University of Manchester, Manchester, England (17)

Fuchel, K., Brookhaven National Laboratory, Upton, Long Island, New York (79)

Heller, S., Brookhaven National Laboratory, Upton, Long Island, New York (79)

Knowlton, Prentiss Hadley, * Harvard University, Cambridge, Massachusetts (225)

Kuck, D. J., Department of Computer Science, University of Illinois, Urbana, Illinois (45)

Lawrie, D. H., Department of Computer Science, University of Illinois, Urbana, Illinois (45)

Liddell, P., University of Grenoble, Grenoble, France (179)

Maurer, W. D., University of California, Berkeley, California (139)

Present affiliation: University of Utah, Salt Lake City, Utah.

Mermet, J., University of Grenoble, Grenoble, France (179)

Morris, D., University of Manchester, Manchester, England (17)

Payan, Ch., University of Grenoble, Grenoble, France (179)

Poole, P. C., Culham Laboratory, UKAEA, Abingdon, Berkshire, England (167)

Ross, Douglas T., SofTech, Inc., Waltham, Massachusetts (91)

Rossiensky, Jean-Paul,* Compagnie Internationale pour l'Informatique, Les Clayes sous Bois, France (205)

Sammet, Jean E., International Business Machines, Inc., Federal Systems Division, Cambridge, Massachusetts (103)

Tixier, Vincent, Ecole Nationale Superieure de l'Aeronautique, Paris, France (205)

Tou, Julius T., Center for Informatics Research, University of Florida, Gainesville, Florida (1)

Waite, W. M., University of Colorado, Boulder, Colorado (167)

**Present affiliation*: Cegos Informatique, Puteaux, France.

Computer-Assisted Documentation of Working Binary Computer Programs with Unknown Documentation

Edmund C. Berkeley†

INFORMATION INTERNATIONAL, INC.,
BOSTON, MASSACHUSETTS

I. Introduction

A. SUBJECT

The subject of this paper is the documentation of computer programs with the assistance of a computer. We are primarily interested in the discovery and the development of powerful methods and principles by which a computer program that has no documentation or very little can be easily and quickly documented by a human programmer with the assistance of a computer.

B. DEFINITIONS

Documentation here means giving enough information about a computer program so that a reasonably trained computer programmer who is not familiar with the program can understand it adequately, and can modify it to fulfill new objectives.

Computer-assisted here means applying the power of a computer to assist a human programmer in finding out how a computer program actually operates, and how to modify it.

C. AN EXAMPLE

Let us give an example. On one occasion a member of our company Edward Fredkin) was employed as a consultant by a manufacturer of digital computers to rescue a compiler. This compiler was in the form of a working binary program only. It had been sold to the manufacturer by a software firm under a contract, and delivered.

† *Present affiliation: Computers and Automation*, Newtonville, Massachusetts.

At that point the manufacturer and the software firm had disagreed—about what was to be delivered under the contract, about its value, about the price, and to whom belonged the ideas in the compiler.

After further argument, it was agreed that what fully belonged to the manufacturer in exchange for the existing price was a working binary program for the compiler plus zero documentation; and this was the settlement.

Fredkin took the working binary program for the compiler and made a computer program to simulate the computer, to analyze the program, and to control and operate the program in segments. He determined the subroutines and their functions, and the key registers. He determined each branch of the program and exercised it. He produced a working symbolic program with adequate documentation. The compiler he produced was the first one of the series of compilers provided by that manufacturer.

Although this kind of business situation is unusual, it does highlight what actually happens with many computer programs: The creator of a program goes on to other duties, or other employment, or other geographical areas, etc., and leaves a complicated computer program in a state in which it is extremely hard to understand.

D. LIMITATIONS

The documentation of computer programs is a large territory. Consequently the particular area chosen here for beginning the present research is the following:

1. Working binary programs, which do not have equivalents expressed in a general-purpose programming language such as FORTRAN or COBOL;
2. Small programs, those with not more than about 2000 instructions in machine language;
3. Programs in which the instructions for operating are known and the program will actually operate;
4. Programs written in the machine language for the PDP-9 computer made by Digital Equipment Corporation.

We are making the assumption that the methods and principles, once discovered and developed for this class of programs, can be extended in the future without too much difficulty to many other classes of computer programs.

II. Cryptanalysis of a Portion of a Computer Program with Unknown Documentation

The first topic that we shall talk about is cryptanalysis of a portion of a computer program with unknown documentation. Methods of solving cryptograms—in other words, methods of discovering the meaning of strings of numbers—were applied to decipher the meaning of some 500 registers contained in a working binary program. The particular working binary program was one of those called DDT. Let us explain a little about DDT.

A. DDT, DYNAMIC DEBUGGING TOOL

Here DDT stands for dynamic debugging tool or dynamic debugging tape, and programs like DDT have probably been in existence since about 1960. They enable a programmer while he is on-line with a computer to examine the program he is trying to make run, and to run it partially or completely on various kinds of test cases. He uses the commands of DDT to insert or alter instructions or symbols, to insert patches and try them out, to test subroutines on sample cases, and so on. In this way a programmer can track down an obscure error and determine the coding change which will remove it.

Apparently, DDT programs were first worked out about 1960 at the Massachusetts Institute of Technology and in its circles of influence; DDT has since become a fairly standard piece of operating software for many computers. After a programmer has become accustomed to using DDT to debug a program, he finds it an almost indispensable tool for rapid correction and improvement of his programs in the future.

B. THE DOCUMENTATION OF DDT

The documentation of a given version of DDT is often incomplete or missing. It is true that sometimes there is a documentation of a DDT in the form of a symbolic program from which the binary program was assembled. But program comments, the meanings of the mnemonic symbols, and other information are regularly lacking. For example, in one DDT symbolic printout a couple of years ago I found the mnemonic ZORCH; but I have not yet found a meaning for it. A number of inquiries to various programmers who might have known has not revealed what ZORCH stood for.

The historical reasons for the lack of documentation for DDT's is clear. These programs have been worked on from time to time by various clever programmers; then they have moved on to other jobs. Either they did not leave behind explanations of what they did, or else the explanations they left have become inaccessible because there is regularly fairly rapid change to a "new and better" DDT.

The effect of various factors is to make the documentation of many DDT's basically unknown, except that (1) there has been no deliberate intention to conceal (just as in ancient writing); (2) what DDT does, and how it can be operated, is usually explained in an accompanying programming manual;

consequently, all the programming subroutines for accomplishing the functions should certainly exist somewhere in the DDT program.

To begin on computer-assisted documentation of a particular DDT, let us consider one of the versions of DDT.

C. OLD 16K DDT

Consider that version of DDT called "Old 16K DDT." It is expressed in a working binary program that apparently has no symbolic version extant. This DDT was probably devised in 1966. Its commands are largely (but not completely) described in a set of operating instructions called "DDT Program Description," which is available.

Using the computer and DDT operating upon itself, we can report the contents in each register of this DDT. In this way, we can more easily produce a full description of the binary program.

This DDT begins at Register 14505, the lower limit of DDT, and goes up to Register 17777, the upper limit of this DDT, and the last register in core.

A part of this description, the part from register 14505 to register 15546, a little over a 1000 (octal) or 500 (decimal) registers is the part which contains what is called the "permanent symbol table" of DDT. This is the region of DDT which recognizes the standard mnemonics for the PDP-9 machine language commands, such as LAC (load the accumulator with . . .), ADD (add the contents of . . . into the accumulator), and so on. This symbol table we shall here seek to analyze and understand.

D. THE PERMANENT SYMBOL TABLE OF DDT

If we look at the printout given by DDT for itself we see at the beginning:

14505/	AND I 654	:	520654
14506/	0		
14507/	ROF	:	724604
14510/	AND I 614	:	520614
14511/	0		
14512/	RON	:	724602

What does this signify? In the first line, the first expression (14505) is the octal name of a register in core. The slash (/) is a command to DDT to print the contents of the register. The second expression (AND I 654) is the contents of the register, stated in DDT's usual language (AND, 500000; I, 20000; remainder, 654). The colon (:) is a command to DDT to express the previous machine word as an octal number. The third expression (520654) is the translation of the second expression as an octal number.

E. Deciphering the Coding of the Symbols
   in Part One of the Printout

What is happening here? In the first place, clearly these are not instructions but something else, because:

1. The only meaning of 0 is CAL 0, a "subroutine call" to a subroutine starting at register 20. And there is no subroutine at register 20, or for that matter anywhere in core below register 14505.
2. The sequence of machine words AND I 654, 0, ROF, AND I 614, 0, RON makes no sense at all as a sequence of instructions.

As we look through the rest of the printout up to 15034, we see almost the same patterns, in threes; and in a great many cases the middle register contains 0, but not always. At 15035 we see

15035/	ISZ	12202	:	452202
15036/	0			
15037/	HLT		:	740040

Looking up the instruction HLT on the PDP-7 instruction list we find:

$$\text{HLT} \quad 740040$$

So it appears that the actual machine instruction as a symbol and in octal notation is expressed in the third of each triple of registers. It is easy to confirm that this is the case.

Page 15 of the operating manual for DDT states "The DDT-7 tape . . . contains the following symbols in its permanent symbol table." So it is easy to deduce and confirm that registers 14505 to 15422 constitute a first part of the "permanent symbol table" of DDT.

F. The Coding of the Symbols

It is reasonable to guess that the gibberish in the first two registers of each triple of registers may express the alphabetic characters which specify the symbolic name of the octal word in the third register. For example, in registers 14505 to 14512, it is reasonable to guess that ROF may be coded 520654 and that RON may be coded 520614, in which R is represented as 52, O is represented as 06, F as 54, and N as 14.

If we tally the instances of supposed coding for registers 14505 to 15422, (and omit a few discordant cases, which may be due to errors in the program), we find the pattern shown in Table I.

TABLE I

Use of the OR Feature

	First Letter			Second and Later Letters	
Letter	Code	No. of Instances		Code	No. of Instances
A	7∅	5		6∅	26
B		∅		46	8
C	56	11		34	26
D	62	15		44	16
E	6∅	2		4∅	6
F	66	4		54	19
G	53	2			∅
H	45	1			∅
I	54	7		3∅	12
J	72	2			∅
K	76	2		74	2
L	51	18		22	35
M	47	19		16	15
N	46	3		14	18
O	43	4		∅6	13
P	55	7		32	1
Q		∅		72	22
R	52	14		24	21
S	64	14		5∅	48
T	41	4		∅2	14
U		∅		7∅	4
V	57	2		36	8
W		∅		62	9
X	67	5		56	5
Y		∅		52	4
Z		∅		42	4

We now lack only the following codes: first letter, B, Q, U, W, Y, Z; and later letters: G, H, J.

Is there some relation between the octal code for the first letter and the octal code for a later letter? All the octal codes for later letters are even. Is each one twice the octal code for its corresponding first letter, omitting the first digit?

     A: $2 \times 7∅ = 160$,   C: $2 \times 56 = 134$,   D: $2 \times 62 = 144$.

This conjecture is true.

G. Deciphering the Coding of the Symbols

We now want to determine the codes in use for registers 15426 to 15546. For example, we have

15426/	DZM M$ 1235	:	157∅14
15427/	TAD 1245	:	341245
15430/	JMP M$ 1554	:	617333

M$, according to page 7 of the DDT manual, has a meaning; it holds "the mask used in word searches." (The remaining printout of DDT shows that register 15557 is M$ and at the outset it contains LAM which is 777777). So JMP M$ 1554 (in the register 15430) is a reasonable command.

Translating 70 14 34 12 45, using Table I for "later letters," we have U N C H and something unknown for 45. U N C H makes us think of PUNCH. Page 11 of the manual shows the command "PUNCH$." Apparently, here is the place where the symbol for that command is recognized. And M$ 1554 could very well be the start of the subroutine called. And here the code for P as a first letter is 15.

For another example, in registers 15431 to 15432, we have for "later letters" 32 70 02 45, which translate into I N P U T $. So 14, the first code, stands for I, clearly. INPUT$ is another DDT command stated in the operating instructions.

In this way, using the manual and the printout we derive the deciphering shown in Table II.

Clearly, the new first letter codes are 40 less than the old first letter codes, and therefore every one can be deduced.

TABLE II

USE OF THE AND FEATURE

New First Letter Code	Letter	No. of Instances	Old First Letter Code
01	T	1	41
03	O	1	43
06	N	1	46
11	L	1	51
12	R	1	52
14	I	1	54
15	P	1	55
16	C	1	56
22	D	1	62
24	S	2	64
30	A	2	70
31	W	1	71
36	K	1	76

III. The Simulator Analyzer

A. THE SIMULATOR ANALYZER

We shall now consider a concept which we previously called a simulator analyzer (SA). This is a computer program which: takes in a working binary program (to be documented), controls the working binary program as it operates on sample problems, simulates the operation of the computer on the working binary program, analyzes the working binary program by operating it completely or partially, and obtains various pieces of information about what the working binary program is doing.

The particular simulator analyzer that will be discussed at this point is one which we call Model 10, since it is the tenth one in a series of actually working programs, ranging from simple with few capacities to sophisticated with many capacities, which have been implemented.

The location of the working binary program input to the SA may be any part of core outside of the registers occupied by the SA.

B. Acceptance of All Instructions of the PDP-9 Computer

Model SA-10 accepts all the kinds of instructions that occur in the PDP-9 computer. SA-10 also accepts memory reference instructions that are either directly or indirectly addressed, recognizes which is which, and determines the effective memory address.

C. Recording

SA-10 has five recording buffers. In these it records (if the mode "record" is specified):

NU—The sequential number of the instruction as the program is operated

PC—The name of the instruction (the contents of the program counter)

MB—The instruction itself (the contents of the memory buffer)

MA—The effective memory address (the address in the instruction if it is directly addressed, and the address contained in the address of the instruction if it is indirectly addressed)—provided the instruction is a memory reference instruction

IMA—The contents of the effective memory address (if the instruction is a memory reference instruction)

D. Conditions for Recording

The recording mode, when turned on, arranges recording only if two conditions are met. One of these conditions is that the sequential number of the instruction executed is more than a specified lower limit and less than a specified upper limit. The reason for this is that frequently one only wants to know the sequence of operations for maybe 10, 15, or 20 instructions.

The other condition is that the pattern of successive instructions executed is *not* a repeating pattern of exactly the same instructions X, Y, X, Y, X, Y, and so on. The reason for this is that signals between the central processor and an I/O device pass through a buffer, and the buffer waits for the device to operate or to be ready to operate before it transmits a signal to or from the central processor. So the computer program contains a loop of two instructions which causes the computer to wait for a flag to be changed from "not ready" to "ready," in order to transmit a signal. For such waits, many hundreds of exactly the same pair of instructions may be executed. To record all these instructions would produce "nauseous repetition." So a part of the program in SA-10 eliminates such recording.

E. Option: No Recording

The mode "no recording" may be called instead of the mode "record." When the mode of no recording is in effect, the program may be operated for thousands and even millions of instructions. This is convenient for finding out if a working binary program being analyzed by the SA actually does perform a function which it is supposed to perform.

Even in the mode "no recording," the total number of instructions executed is recorded in the counter NU. Also the last four instructions executed are recorded in the four registers MB4, MB3, MB2, and MB1.

F. Test: Add–Subtract–Omit Machine

To illustrate the behavior of SA-10, suppose we deal with the following problem:

Problem. Given a certain working binary program with no documentation. It has the following operating instructions:

1. In registers 1000 to 1007 may be stored (octal) numbers. In registers 1100 to 1107 may be stored signals, one corresponding to each number. The signals are 1 for add, 2 for subtract, and 3 for omit. According to the signal in each signal register the machine will add, subtract, or omit the number in the corresponding number register. For example, four numbers may be 6, 5, 15, 22; the four corresponding signals may be 1, 2, 1, 3. The total then is $6 - 5 + 15 + 0 = 16$.

2. The answer is provided in register 1242.

3. The starting address for the program is 1227.

The working binary program, before it is operated, is shown in Table III.

The task of this problem is to understand and to document this working binary program.

Solution. Using DDT (which already contains some useful properties of simulator analyzers), we can at once take a most useful step: converting each octal number into the sum of two parts, where one part is the command, if any, contained in the octal number, and if there is a command, the command

TABLE III

1000/	3
1077/	3
1100/	3
1177/	3
1200/	201100
1201/	541244
1202/	601210
1203/	541245
1204/	601214
1205/	541246
1206/	601221
1207/	616000
1210/	201242
1211/	301000
1212/	41242
1213/	601221
1214/	201000
1215/	740001
1216/	301242
1217/	41242
1220/	601221
1221/	441211
1222/	441214
1223/	441200
1224/	441243
1225/	601200
1226/	616000
1227/	141242
1230/	201247
1231/	41211
1232/	201214
1233/	201250
1234/	41214
1235/	201251
1236/	41200
1237/	201252
1240/	41243
1241/	601200
1242/	3
1243/	3
1244/	1
1245/	2
1246/	3
1247/	301000
1250/	201000
1251/	201100
1252/	777767

TABLE IV

7/	1253
1000/	6
1001/	5
1002/	15
1003/	22
1077/	3
1100/	1
1101/	2
1102/	1
1103/	3
1177/	3
1200/	LAC 1104
1201/	SAD 1244
1202/	JMP 1210
1203/	SAD 1245
1204/	JMP 1214
1205/	SAD 1246
1206/	JMP 1221
1207/	JMP 16000
1210/	LAC 1242
1211/	ADD 1004
1212/	DAC 1242
1213/	JMP 1221
1214/	LAC 1004
1215/	CMA
1216/	ADD 1242
1217/	DAC 1242
1220/	JMP 1221
1221/	ISZ 1211
1222/	ISZ 1214
1223/	ISZ 1200
1224/	ISZ 1243
1225/	JMP 1200
1226/	JMP 16000
1227/	DZM 1242
1230/	LAC 1247
1231/	DAC 1211
1232/	LAC 1214
1233/	LAC 1250
1234/	DAC 1214
1235/	LAC 1251
1236/	DAC 1200
1237/	LAC 1252
1240/	DAC 1243
1241/	JMP 1200
1242/	16
1243/	LAW 17773
1244/	1
1245/	2
1246/	3
1247/	ADD 1000
1250/	LAC 1000
1251/	LAC 1100
1252/	LAW 17767

LAW 17767: 777767

LAW 17773: 777773

TABLE V

1000/	6
1001/	5
1002/	15
1003/	22
1100/	1
1101/	2
1102/	1
1103/	3
1200/	LAC 1104
1201/	SAD 1244
1202/	JMP 1210
1203/	SAD 1245
1204/	JMP 1214
1205/	SAD 1246
1206/	JMP 1221
1207/	JMP 16000
1210/	LAC 1242
1211/	ADD 1004
1212/	DAC 1242
1213/	JMP 1221
1214/	LAC 1004
1215/	CMA
1216/	ADD 1242
1217/	DAC 1242
1220/	JMP 1221
1221/	ISZ 1211
1222/	ISZ 1214
1223/	ISZ 1200
1224/	ISZ 1243
1225/	JMP 1200
1226/	JMP 16000
1227/	DZM 1242
1230/	LAC 1247
1231/	DAC 1211
1232/	LAC 1214
1233/	LAC 1250
1234/	DAC 1214
1235/	LAC 1251
1236/	DAC 1200
1237/	LAC 1252
1240/	DAC 1243
1241/	JMP 1200
1242/	16
1243/	LAW 17773
1244/	1
1245/	2
1246/	3
1247/	ADD 1000
1250/	LAC 1000
1251/	LAC 1100
1252/	LAW 17767

TABLE VI

(1)	(2)	(3)	(4)	(5)	(6)
1	1227	DZM 1242	3	SM5 1/	ADD 1000
2	1230	LAC 1247	ADD 1000	SM5 2/	ADD 1000
3	1231	DAC 1211	ADD 1000	SM5 3/	LAC 1000
4	1232	LAC 1214	LAC 1000	SM5 4/	LAC 1000
5	1233	LAC 1250	LAC 1000	SM5 5/	LAC 1000
6	1234	DAC 1214	LAC 1000	SM5 6/	LAC 1100
7	1235	LAC 1251	LAC 1100	SM5 7/	LAC 1100
10	1236	DAC 1200	LAC 1100	SM5 10/	LAW M$ 2210
11	1237	LAC 1252	LAW M$ 2210	SM5 11/	LAW M$ 2210
12	1240	DAC 1243	LAW M$ 2210	SM5 13/	1
13	1241	JMP 1200	LAW M$ 2210	SM5 14/	1
14	1200	LAC 1100	1	SM5 17/	6
15	1201	SAD 1244	1	SM5 20/	6
16	1202	JMP 1210	1	SM5 22/	ADD 1001
17	1210	LAC 1242		SM5 23/	LAC 1001
20	1211	ADD 1000	6	SM5 24/	LAC 1101
21	1212	DAC 1242	6	SM5 25/	LAW M$ 2211
22	1213	JMP 1221	6	SM5 27/	2
23	1221	ISZ 1211	6	SM5 30/	1
24	1222	ISZ 1214	6	SM5 31/	2
25	1223	ISZ 1200	6	SM5 33/	5
26	1224	ISZ 1243	6	SM5 35/	6
27	1225	JMP 1200	6	SM5 36/	1
30	1200	LAC 1101	2	SM5 40/	ADD 1002
31	1201	SAD 1244	2	SM5 41/	LAC 1002
32	1203	SAD 1245	2	SM5 42/	LAC 1102
33	1204	JMP 1214	2	SM5 43/	LAW M$ 2212
34	1214	LAC 1001	5	SM5 45/	1
35	1215	CMA	LAW M$ 2213	SM5 46/	1
36	1216	ADD 1242	1	SM5 50/	1
37	1217	DAC 1242	1	SM5 51/	15
40	1220	JMP 1221	1	SM5 52/	16
41	1221	ISZ 1211	1	SM5 54/	ADD 1003
42	1222	ISZ 1214	1	SM5 55/	LAC 1003
43	1223	ISZ 1200	1	SM5 56/	LAC 1103
44	1224	ISZ 1243	1	SM5 57/	LAW M$ 2213
45	1225	JMP 1200	1	SM5 61/	3
46	1200	LAC 1102	1	SM5 62/	1
47	1201	SAD 1244	1	SM5 63/	2
50	1202	JMP 1210	1	SM5 64/	3
51	1210	LAC 1242	1	SM5 66/	ADD 1004
52	1211	ADD 1002	16	SM5 67/	LAC 1004
53	1212	DAC 1242	16	SM5 70/	LAC 1104
54	1213	JMP 1221	16	SM5 71/	LAW M$ 2214
55	1221	ISZ 1211	16	SM5 74/	1
56	1222	ISZ 1214	16	SM5 75/	2
57	1223	ISZ 1200	16	SM5 76/	3
60	1224	ISZ 1243	16		
61	1225	JMP 1200	16		
62	1200	LAC 1103	3		
63	1201	SAD 1244	3		
64	1203	SAD 1245	3		
65	1205	SAD 1246	3		
66	1206	JMP 1221	3		
67	1221	ISZ 1211	3		
70	1222	ISZ 1214	3		
71	1223	ISZ 1200	3		
72	1224	ISZ 1243	3		
73	1225	JMP 1200	3		
74	1200	LAC 1104			
75	1201	SAD 1244			
76	1203	SAD 1245			
77	1205	SAD 1246			

is expressed in symbolic form. The other part is the remainder, which will often be an address, provided the number supposedly expressing the address falls within the range of the beginning and the end of the working binary program, in this case 1000 to 1252.

The result of this step is shown in Table IV. Because of the idiosyncrasies of this DDT, in some cases the octal number is separated into two or more parts, and the meaning of the separated parts is different from the sum of one instruction and one address.

Examining this sequence of instructions we can see clearly some of the structure of the program, i.e., the places where it separates into meaningful pieces, following either a single jump instruction or a pair of consecutive jump instructions. These separations are shown in Table V.

We shall now apply the simulator analyzer Model 10 to this working binary program, with the given example, so as to reveal the operation of the program.

Table VI shows the results. In columns 1–4 are shown, respectively, NU—the consecutive number of the instruction executed (contents of buffer SM1); PC—the identification of the instruction executed (contents of buffer SM2); MC—the instruction executed (contents of buffer SM3); AC—the contents of the accumulator after the instruction is executed (contents of buffer SM4). Column 6 holds the contents of the effective memory address IMA.

TABLE VII

Consecutive number (octal)	Instruction names	Function
1–13	1227–1241	Initialize the program.
14–16	1200–1202	Select addition for the first signal 1.
17–22	1210–1213	Add the first number 6 to 0.
23–27	1221–1225	Index the appropriate addresses for the next case.
30–33	1200–1204	Select subtraction for the second signal 2.
34–40	1214–1220	Subtract the second number 5, producing the total 1.
41–45	1221–1225	Index the appropriate addresses for the next case.
46–50	1200–1202	Select addition for the third signal 1.
51–54	1210–1213	Add the third number 15 producing the total 16.
56–61	1221–1225	Index the appropriate addresses for the fourth case.
62–66	1200–1206	Select omission for the fourth signal 3.
67–73	1221–1225	Index the appropriate addresses for the 5th case.
74–77	1200–1205	Find no signal 1, 2, or 3, and accordingly jump out to DDT (16000).

Column 5 names the register in simulator buffer 5 which holds that contents. (The DDT being used here omits any line for which IMA is zero; consequently, the information in this column is not aligned with the other information. This format defect will be corrected in a later model of the simulator analyzer.)

What is happening in this program when it is operated on this example is now completely clear as expressed in Table VII,

Looking back at the program stated in Table IV, we can put in comments as in Table VIII.

TABLE VIII

Registers	Comment
1000–1007	Data–Numbers
1100–1107	Data–Signals
1200–1207	Multiple switching subroutine
1210–1213	Add subroutine
1214–1220	Subtract subroutine
1221–1226	Indexing subroutine
1227–1241	Initializing subroutine
1242	Cumulative total
1243	Counter
1244–1252	Constants

A later simulator-analyzer will enable the programmer to tell the computer to enter these comments for him.

In addition, we can symbolize the octal starting addresses of various parts of the program having particular functions with mnemonic symbols which bring to mind the function of that part of the program. For example, we could assign symbols to octal registers as in Table IX.

TABLE IX

Octal register	Mnemonic Symbol	Meaning
1000	GIVC	Given data, program C
1100	SGNC	Given signal, program C
1200	SWR	Multiple switching routine
1210	ADR	Add routine
1214	SBRC	Subtract routine
1221	IXR	Indexing routine
1227	INITC	Initializing routine, program C
1242	CUM	Cumulative total
1243	CTRC	Counter, program C
1244–1251	various	Constants
16000	DDT	Starting register of DDT

TABLE X		TABLE XI

```
GIVC/        3
GIVC 77/     3
SGNC/        3
SGNC 77/     3
SWR/         LAC SGNC
SWR 1/       SAD C1CC
SWR 2/       JMP ADR
SWR 3/       SAD C2CC
SWR 4/       JMP SBRC
SWR 5/       SAD C3CC
SWR 6/       JMP IXR
SWR 7/       JMP DDT
ADR/         LAC CUM
ADR 1/       ADD GIVC
ADR 2/       DAC CUM
ADR 3/       JMP IXR
SBRC/        LAC GIVC
SBRC 1/      CMA
SBRC 2/      ADD CUM
SBRC 3/      DAC CUM
SBRC 4/      JMP IXR
IXR/         ISZ ADR 1
IXR 1/       ISZ SBRC
IXR 2/       ISZ SWR
IXR 3/       ISZ CTRC
IXR 4/       JMP SWR
IXR 5/       JMP DDT
INITC/       DZM CUM
INITC 1/     LAC CADC
INITC 2/     DAC ADR 1
INITC 3/     LAC SBRC
INITC 4/     LAC CSBC
INITC 5/     DAC SBRC
INITC 6/     LAC CSGC
INITC 7/     DAC SWR
INITC 10/    LAC CM10C
INITC 11/    DAC CTRC
INITC 12/    JMP SWR
CUM/         3
CTRC/        3
C1CC/        1
C2CC/        2
C3CC/        3
CADC/        ADD GIVC
CSBC/        LAC GIVC
CSGC/        LAC SGNC
CM10C/       LAW DDT 1767
```

```
MACH ADSUBOMIT ED 1 VS 4 4/7/69
GIVC=1000   SGNC=1100   DDT=16000
GIVC,        3              /DATA NUMBERS
GIVC 77/     3
SGNC,        3              /DATA SIGNALS
SGNC 77/     3
SWR,         LAC SGNC       /MULTIPLE CONDITION
             SAD C1CC
             JMP ADR
             SAD C2CC
             JMP SBRC
             SAD C3CC
             JMP IXR
             JMP DDT
ADR,         LAC CUM        /ADD SUBROUTINE
             ADD GIVC
             DAC CUM
             JMP IXR
SBRC,        LAC GIVC       /SUBTRACT ROUTINE
             CMA
             ADD CUM
             DAC CUM
             JMP IXR
IXR,         ISZ ADR 1      /INDEXING ROUTINE
             ISZ SBRC
             ISZ SWR
             ISZ CTRC
             JMP SWR
             JMP DDT
INITC,       DZM CUM        /INITIALIZING
             LAC CADC
             DAC ADR 1
             LAC SBRC
             LAC CSBC
             DAC SBRC
             LAC CSGC
             DAC SWR
             LAC CM10C
             DAC CTRC
             JMP SWR
CUM,         3              /CUMULATIVE TOTAL
CTRC,        3              /COUNTER
C1CC,        1              /CONSTANTS
C2CC,        2
C3CC,        3
CADC,        ADD GIVC
CSBC,        LAC GIVC
CSGC,        LAC SGNC
CM10C,       LAM-10
START DDT


/:50
```

TABLE XII

Mnemonic symbol	Octal register	Meaning
ADR	121Ø	Addition subroutine
CADC	1247	Constant for initializing addition subroutine
CM1ØC	1252	Constant register holding minus ten
CSBC	125Ø	Constant for initializing subtraction
CSGC	1251	Constant for initializing signal recognition
CTRC	1243	Counter for counting number of steps
CUM	1242	Cumulative total register
C1CC	1244	Constant register holding 1 (for addition)
C2CC	1245	Constant register holding 2 (for subtraction)
C3CC	1246	Constant register holding 3 (for omission)
DDT	16ØØØ	Starting address of dynamic debugging program
GIVC	1ØØØ	Given data, numbers
INITC	1227	Initializing routine
IXR	1221	Indexing routine, for handling the next case
SBRC	1214	Subtraction routine
SGNC	11ØØ	Given data, signals
SWR	12ØØ	Multiple condition switching routine

This DDT can at present assign symbols in this way. The result of assigning symbols in this way is shown in Table X.

At this point we can make use of the symbolic editor, and produce a symbolic version of the program. This is shown in Table XI.

This version can be assembled to be located anywhere in storage. In this form it can be readily modified by a programmer to provide for changes in purposes of this program. In addition the assembler can produce a table of the symbols in alphabetic order, with their octal locations; and a programmer can write opposite each symbol its mnemonic definition. This is shown in Table XII. This substantially completes the documentation of this unknown working binary program.

Of course, larger and more intricate programs need to be dealt with. Many of the operations described here which are performed by a person, or by changing from one piece of software to another, need to be transferred to the computer. Also, various kinds of searches, and of independent operation of various subroutines need to be provided for. But at least a part of the problem of computer-assisted documentation has been successfully solved.

The details of Model 10 of the simulator analyzer are given by Berkeley [1].

In the working binary program of this example, we can notice two programming defects, although they do not interfere with the operation of this program. One defect is that the number of registers assigned for data and the similar number assigned for signals is 100 (octal), although the problem only calls for 10 (octal). The other defect is the presence of an unnecessary instruction LAC 1214 at address 1232; it could be dropped and the program patched with a NOP instruction, and before the program is next assembled, this instruction could be deleted from the symbolic. But these defects revealed by the documentation, do not interfere with the operation of the working binary program. They may be corrected by the programmer at the same time as he makes other modifications in the program to fulfill other purposes.

IV. Concepts and Principles of the Simulator Analyzer

Finally let us consider the concepts and principles of the simulator analyzer.

We have been doing some thinking about the sorts of properties that would be desirable in a simulator analyzer, a program which would simulate the computer and analyze an unknown working binary program, and we have made a list of the properties that seem desirable. They are

1. *Simulator.* The SA should be able to simulate, under the SA's own control, every instruction of the computer, and operate the working binary program under the SA's control.

2. *Analyzer.* The SA should be able to analyze every specifiable aspect of the working binary program.

3. *"Exercising" Segments.* The SA should be able to run segments of the working binary program (WBP), assigning starting values and producing calculated final values, thus "exercising" every segment of the WBP.

4. *Relocation.* The SA should be able to relocate a WBP from one area of core to another. Then it should be able to test whether the contents of any register should or should not be changed by the relocation difference.

5. *Subroutine Calls.* The SA should be able to tag every register called as a subroutine.

6. *Return Addresses.* The SA should be able to tag every register called as a return address.

7. *Pointers.* The SA should be able to tag every register used as a pointer.

8. *Counters.* The SA should be able to tag every register used as a counter (which is initialized with a negative number, indexed from time to time, and which produces a jump out of a loop when the contents of the counter becomes zero).

9. *Other Register Types.* The SA should be able to tag every register of a type that can be identified by the occurrence of a pattern of instructions or operations.

10. *Breakpoints.* The SA should be able to operate a working binary pro-

gram up to a certain instruction, insert there a "break-point," and later continue the operation of the WBP from that point on. (This enables the examination of a working binary program in midstream.)

11. *Comments.* The SA should be able to provide for inserting comments opposite instructions in the WBP.

12. *Patches.* The SA should be able to insert patches in the WBP.

13. *Read-in Buffer.* The SA should have a correctible read-in buffer for its commands, so that individual characters may be rubbed out, and the whole command or series of commands can be edited before it is issued.

14. *Stacked Commands.* The SA should be able to be given a series of commands, which can be executed one by one, with a fail-safe provision.

15. *"Magnifying-Glass" Property.* When a break-point occurs, the SA should be able to show the contents of: the program counter; the accumulator; the memory buffer; the effective memory address; the sequential number of the instruction executed; and the contents of such other registers as may be specified.

16. *Value-Change Tag.* The SA should be able to tag any register which has had its value changed by the operation of the WBP.

17. *Symbolic Names.* The SA should be able to assign symbolic names to the contents of registers in the working binary program.

18. *Inventory of Branches Run.* The SA should be able to keep track of those branches of the WBP which have been exercised and those that have not been exercised, and thus lead the programmer to devising means for exercising every branch of the program.

19. *Interaction.* The SA should be able to interact in many ways in real time with the programmer, and thus help him arrive at appropriate instruction names, comments, and modifications of the WBP.

In addition, there is good reason to expect that many other procedures frequently used by the operator can be programmed and delegated to the automatic portion of the system, the simulator analyzer in the computer.

ACKNOWLEDGMENT

The work reported here was performed under Contract No. N00014-68-C-0268 from the Office of Naval Research to Information International, Inc. for the purpose of investigating computer-assisted documentation.

REFERENCE

1. Berkeley, E. C., Research in Computer-Assisted Documentation of Computer Programs, Vol. 1, First Year Annual Report under Contract N00014-68-C-0268 from the Office of Naval Research to Information International Inc., Boston, Massachusetts, 1969. Copies of Reference 1 may be obtained (while they last) from Edmund C. Berkeley, *Computers and Automation*, 815 Washington St., Newtonville, Mass. 02160.

Quality Control in the Publishing Process and Theoretical Foundations for Information Retrieval

Manfred Kochen

UNIVERSITY OF MICHIGAN
ANN ARBOR, MICHIGAN

I. Introduction

Information retrieval, as usually understood, is performed by retrospective document search systems, like MEDLARS [1] or current awareness systems, like SDI [2]. To evaluate such systems, the following two quantities are usually given:

1. h, that is, the ratio of the average number of "relevant" documents retrieved for (or disseminated to) a user to the total number of "relevant" documents that user should have received (called recall ratio or *h*it rate).
2. a, that is, the ratio of the average number of "relevant" documents retrieved (or disseminated) to the total number of documents he received (called precision ratio or *a*cceptance rate).

For example, if there are 200 "relevant" papers on "spacesuits for lunar exploration" and an interested user is sent 235 papers of which he judges only 120 to be "relevant," then $h = 120/200$ and $a = 120/235$. Quite typically, $h = 0.60$ and $a = 0.52$ [3]. But these quantities are neither operationally nor conceptually very well defined, and even if they were, they would at best characterize indexing quality.

Rational design and evaluation of information retrieval services require conceptualization of such key notions as relevance. Maron and Kuhns [4] proposed to measure "relevance" by a real number in the interval [0, 1], which represents the probability of a document satisfying a given request. Swets [5] and Pollock [6] have used a similar notion in developing their proposals for evaluating information retrieval results. Cleverdon [7] used as an operational measure of relevance the relation between a question and its

19

answer in a document from which the question was selected for retrieval experiments. Swanson [8] objected to the source–document concept because it created a "biased" relationship between the question and the course document. Hillman [9] felt that relevance must be defined independently of any system, that it must be dealt with in terms of "relatedness of topics and concepts."

In one of the first attempts to explicate "relevance" more mathematically, Goffman [10] defined relevance as analogous to "a measure of effective contact between a susceptible and an infective." In information retrieval this becomes a measure of contact between a query and the document. He also added the important element of "previous contacts," thus introducing the concept of "level" (of sophistication).

Rees and Saracevic [11] recognized that relevance is a relation established by a judgment between system responses and the user–judge. Such judgments are often subjective, inconsistent, and restricted by the type of user, his purposes, his environment, the time, the subject area, etc.

Most recently, Cuadra and Katter (see Cuadra *et al.* [12]) have gone further in explicating "relevance." By introducing the idea of relatedness between judges, needs, documents, situations, and scales, they have opened the path for studies to measure these variables and their components more precisely.

But such explications are still far from providing adequate theoretical underpinnings. One of the major obstacles to progress has been the view of a document as relevant to a user (in a specified situation, at a given time, for a particular purpose) if he says that it meets his information need. The concept of need and the behavioral measures for ascertaining that it has been met are less clear than relevance or pertinence was in the first place. Furthermore, most publications—even those judged to be relevant—are of very marginal utility to users. In the solid-state-physics literature, for example, Herring [13] estimated that, at publication time, a small proportion of papers are wrong, a larger proportion have zero value, while a majority are positive contributions. Within 5 years about half of these regress to zero value, as do eventually almost all.

Either the users' information needs are not very dire or only a small fraction of the current literature can meet important information needs. The latter bias is often expressed in articles with titles like "Is the Literature Worth Reviewing?" [14]. Much of the contemporary scientific literature also appears to serve more as a forum for authors than a service to readers. The referee of this paper made an important point about the potentially pernicious influence of page charges on standards, which would be determined more by what people will pay to print than what people will pay to read. The editors' clearinghouse, he proposed, would uncover those journals consisting mainly of rejects from more prestigious journals.

Of all the stages in the process of generating, controlling, and using documents, few are more responsible for subsequent difficulties in meeting the information needs of intended users than the refereeing process. Few are more vulnerable to change and more critical in influencing improvements in the quality of publications and of meeting users' needs. If we can represent a manuscript submitted for publication—or even more fundamentally, a research proposal—so well that we can select the most appropriate referees, we can achieve a higher level of publications. Carefully selected referees would be more able to judge the quality of the paper assigned to them, thus ensuring that only the most significant, valid, novel, and clear papers are actually published. Furthermore, if we can choose the most appropriate referees for a certain paper, we can also select the readers most likely to benefit from reading it. These processes are just as important as the later process of locating the document and disseminating it.

Here is a key problem: seeking the properties of a viable system for grading each new document and locating it rather precisely in our voluminous literature. We can only read so much, and we cannot afford merely relevant and good documents. If there is, somewhere in the world's libraries or information stores, a document which would be just right for a particular user just now, then ideally he should get it, even if he does not know of its existence nor even how to request it with very great precision.

Indexing papers long after they are published is not the way to solve this problem, even (or, perhaps, especially) with current automatic indexing. Once the decisions have been made to publish an article, in what final form, and in what journal, certain basic relevance and quality judgments have already been implicitly made. If there are too many useless papers—either because they are irrelevant to most people's needs or because they are insignificant, erroneous, redundant, or unclear—a good place to apply corrective or preventative measures is in the publishing process. Perhaps an even better place is in the proposal screening process, which is very similar to the process of refereeing manuscripts submitted for publication.

The first step taken by an editor on receiving a manuscript is to select referees. This is also the first time a relevance judgment is made. Thus, studying the publishing process may not only bear fruit in leading to the introduction of quality control procedures, but may shed light on some fundamental problems underlying the design of systems for information retrieval and dissemination as well. However, conceptualization has not yet matured sufficiently far so that high level mathematics can be brought to bear. This is especially true for the most basic concepts like "needs," "significance," "relevance," "novelty." Nonetheless, considerable progress toward a clear explication of these notions is achieved by focusing on the refereeing process, and some mathematical analyses of idealized models are possible.

II. Conceptualization: Informal Discussion

A. ON THE UTILITY OF DOCUMENTS

Many a parent with an autistic child may find some use for a document demonstrating a successful treatment of infantile autism. Many intelligent people would consider a *Scientific American* article on wound healing valuable enough to buy and read. How useful, under what circumstances, for what purposes, when, and to whom, is (a) an article arguing that we can design genetic change, to make diabetics no longer dependent on insulin injections for survival, or (b) an article proving that every even number is the sum of two primes?

We focus our investigation on a particular document user p who has a question q in mind: the father of an autistic child who is desperate to try anything that may help and is anxious to know of any successful treatments of autistic children. To be useful to him, a document d must: (1) address itself to question q or to a related question q', (2) if to q', then q' must be of comparable concern to p, (3) contain a valid answer to q, (4) which is new to p, and (5) which p can understand.

The first requirement is that of *relevance*. If a document d is entitled "Behavior Modification of an Autistic Child" and q is as in the above example, then d is very probably relevant to q for p. If, further, d contains explicitly the question "Are there any successful treatments for autistic children?" then the hypothesis of relevance is further confirmed. A problem arises in recognizing whether q' is related to q; by that we mean that a valid answer to q either logically implies an answer to q' or helps in the search for an answer to q'. We view the set of all questions which are closely enough related to one another in this sense as constituting a topic. A document is relevant to a topic if it deals with a question on that topic.

The second requirement is that of *significance*. Significance is a property of a question in relation to those concerned with it. A question q is very significant for p if a valid answer to it directly implies an answer to other questions, some of which are themselves meaningful for p. If q is significant for p, then p knows with considerable clarity the precise nature of the ignorance he seeks to supplant. Significant questions reflect a great deal of understanding. A good scholarly journal often requires that papers acceptable for publishing deal with, above all, questions that are highly significant to most of its readers.

There is a third requirement that a useful or high-quality document must meet: that the answer to q be valid in its relevant topic according to the conventionalized norms of methodology and fact.

Fourth, the answer contained in the document should be novel to its readers. Readers with questions on a certain topic are very familiar with what is known in that topic. However, nonspecialists in a certain topic might find it novel. Quality control of tutorial or review papers that are aimed at helping a wider, more general readership differs from quality control of original research papers addressed to colleagues. This paper being restricted to the latter is not meant to deny the great importance of quality control for publications that serve a more general public. Indeed, it is the author's major thesis (developed in [14a]) that such publications or their computer-aided equivalents are urgently needed.

Referees, then, should obviously be readers concerned with the same type of questions. If the referees accurately represent other readers who are equally concerned, then their judgment of novelty is also representative.

Finally, and perhaps most necessarily, there must be literacy on the part of p and clarity in d for the answer to be comprehensible to p. In sum, document d is useful to p on question q if (1) d is *relevant* to q, (2) d contains a *valid* answer to q, (3) q is *significant* for p, (4) d is *new* to p, and (5) d is *clear* to p.

The relevance of a manuscript is first judged by the editor, through his choice of referees. Its validity, significance, novelty, and clarity is judged by the referees. As we will see, relevance and significance are intertwined. A good referee should not only be *concerned* about the question dealt with in a manuscript; he, being a reader also, must be deeply concerned and have an intense need for the answer, rather than merely a casual, general interest.

B. On Questions, Topics, Relevance, and Indexing

By a question we mean a well-formed sentence in a formal, English-like source language [15, 16]. Harrah [17] has logically classified questions into (a) "n-place whether" questions, like "Is it raining or snowing?" for $n = 2$, and (b) "which questions," like "When did Shakespeare write *Othello*?" or "What are even numbers?"

Two questions like "Is there a largest prime?" and "Is the set of primes infinite?" are certainly related. An answer to one implies an answer to the other. (Indeed, this relation is the basis of Euclid's proof.) A question like "Is the set of twin primes [e.g., (2, 5), (11, 13), (17, 19)] infinite?" is clearly also related, but not as closely. (The answer is still unknown.)

Finding such a relation, especially one that is subtle, can rank as a major contribution in its own right. We are proposing that specifying a set of questions, together with known logical connections among them, may begin to capture the essence of a "topic." In another paper we develop this idea more completely. We relate it also to the notion of a paradigm in the sense discussed by Kuhn [18]. This is a set of concepts, rules for writing these concepts, procedures for laboratory and theoretical work and styles of publishing which, for a time, guide the beliefs and action of a community of practitioners.

In order to pick relevant documents to send to a reader, we must consider the variables which describe the concerns of the readers or referees. Silverman and Halbert [19] proposed the user's sophistication as one such variable. They suggested calculating a degree of sophistication for documents by comparing their profiles with those of each related document, to indicate how uncommon it is in its subuniverse. In retrieval, the user's need profile (representation of the query) would be compared with document profiles, weighting each pattern by its commonality. Users would not only accept or reject documents as irrelevant, but reject them as being too easy or too difficult as well.

Many research projects begin with a proposal to a sponsor which usually states the long-term problem concerning the researcher. He thus invests considerable intellectual effort in formulating a question which is sufficiently complex as to require a program lasting 1–5 years. Almost necessarily, the question thus formulated, though highly significant, is not sufficiently detailed and specific to lead fruitfully and efficiently to a valid answer. Hence the researcher analyzes this long-term question into highly specific short-term problems that he almost certainly can solve, each within a few days. These problems by themselves are seldom sufficiently significant by his own standards. But a collection of such problems can be significant if these are so connected that their solutions also solve a larger problem which, in its turn, contributes significantly to answering the long-term question. We might call such a problem, which falls between the insignificant but directly solvable 3-day problem, and the very significant but directly unsolvable 3-year problem, the 3-month problem. It is this which is solved and reported in a scientific publication.

The wording of the question with which a scientist is concerned for the long run may well contain the terms needed to name the topic of the research. The topic of the 3-month question (named by the title which the author assigned to the paper in reporting his answer) is quite likely to contain an index term which may appear as a subject heading in book catalogs or even as an entry in the index to a general book. If it occurs in an index for a large segment of the journal articles in the field, it will undoubtedly be broken down into several subheadings with many document numbers posted under each.

C. INDEXING: REPRESENTATION OF USER NEEDS AND DOCUMENTS TO MATCH THEM

An index term such as "superconductivity" names not only the topic of a 3-year question like "Can we have superconductivity at room temperature?"

but of 30- or 300-year question like " What accounts for all the phenomena of superconductivity?" One scientist's concern with the first may be much deeper than with the second question. Perhaps a discussion of superconductivity in a general book on advanced quantum physics would be of utility, perhaps not. A section in that book or a whole book headed " superconductivity at room temperature" is at least highly relevant for him, and especially useful if it contains valid information that is comprehensible and new to him.

If we consider in addition to "superconductivity," "cryogenics" as a second index term, then the Boolean conjunction (superconductivity) AND NOT (cryogenics) may be the name for a more *specific* topic containing the 3-year question. Documents so indexed should be more relevant (and if valid, new, and clear, also more useful) than documents indexed merely under "superconductivity." Most relevant would be documents indexed under the most specific name of the 3-day question's topic. Such a name would be even more specific than the title of an article. Documents approximately indexed under such names are very unlikely to exist.

Conventionally documents are represented by a conjunction of index terms [20–23]. By "index term," which we intend to be generic for "subject heading," we mean an entry in a dictionary-like directory. Index terms often occur in the text of the documents they refer to (on pages in the case of a book). Quite generally, an index term is a word or phrase of some natural language, plus technical terms and proper names, which we find in indexes.

Let us call such a surrogate for the document an *indexing expression*. By an indexing expression, we mean a set of well-formed strings generated according to formation and transformation rules of a special grammar [24].

If an indexer assigns to a document an indexing expression, he judges that the document deals with a question on a topic that is suitably named by his indexing expression. If the indexing expression is much less specific than would be appropriate for the question posed in the document, then a reader for whom this question is insignificant may be led to this paper. To compensate for this, a reader for whom this question turns out to be highly significant, but who has in mind another significant question which is related by virtue of belonging to the same topic, can be led to this paper. Of course, the likelihood of the match between the document, as represented by an indexing expression, and a reader's question depends on the indexing expression he uses to represent his question.

As an example of a very special indexing language, consider the set of all strings producible by the following two rules starting with the symbol I:

1. $I \to N/(N)\,(N)/(I)\,(\text{and})(I)$
2. $N \to$ file/structure/search/content/analysis/strategy/maintenance/user/ information/needs. (The slashes denote " or.")

The first rule actually consists of 3 subrules; it states that from I can be generated either the string N *or* a string with which has a left N concatenated with a right N, *or* a string consisting of two I's joined with "and" between them. The second rule has 10 subrules, the first of which states that from N can be generated "file." That is as far as we can go in applying rules (1) and (2) starting with I. But rule (1) could be applied repeatedly, as in $I \rightarrow (I)$ (and)$(I) \rightarrow (N)(N)$(and)$(I) \rightarrow$ (file)(structure)(and)$(N)(N)$(and)$(N)(N) \rightarrow$ (file)(structure)(and)(content)(analysis)(and)(user)(needs).

The resulting eight-word string, with parentheses removed, is an indexing expression in the sense of being one of the well-formed strings generated by our illustrative "grammar." It is sufficiently specific to serve as the title for a document. The individual words like "file," "structure," etc. are index terms, though they need not have been single words; "edge notched card" or "graph theory" could, for example, be index terms produced by N. Not all the well-formed indexing expressions, e.g., (structure)(maintenance), would be useful in this hypothetical indexing language.

A good indexing language should permit theoreticians to logically structure topics in useful and penetrating ways. Indexing, in its deeper sense, is an intellectual task of the first magnitude. It calls for the location of documents, topics, and people within an organized intellectual structure based on rather deep understanding of the substantive and logical relations with all other documents, topics, and people. Such "Cartesian" indexing languages may not be adequate.

It should be kept in mind that the above type of indexing language, though widely used, is very elementary. Its short-term practicality may be deceptive.

D. The Refereeing Process

For each manuscript submitted for publication to a particular journal, the editor must eventually decide whether or not to accept it. To take a broader view, we can envisage an editor of the future deciding, for each manuscript, not only whether to accept or reject it for his journal, but where it best fits into the entire literature.† At present, he uses a decision procedure for his journal which we shall assume aims at maximizing the utility of accepted papers for his readership, while keeping the effort to do so within bounds or at a minimum. If he has no data to represent the needs of his readership, he makes assumptions about their tastes, familiarity with the topics, literacy, competence, technical level, etc.

† The referee of this paper, deploring the practice of a poor article rejected by one journal being sent almost unchanged to another journal, suggested setting up an "editor's clearinghouse" to exchange referees' reports. The experimental refereeing form in the appendix provides a mechanism for trying this.

It may be plausible to assume that the intellectual leaders in a field of knowledge can not only select long-range questions of significance to them and to most of the other leading practitioners in that field, but appropriate short-range questions as well. If an editor assumes the readership of his journal to consist of the intellectual elite of his field—generally accepted and potential leaders only—then the referees should be recruited from this elite.

This is not to say that, because an author reflects good taste in his publications, in selecting significant problems, competence to solve them, originality, and clarity of expression, he is also a good judge of this in the work of others except for the above-mentioned qualities of taste in selecting and recognizing significant problems. Nor, conversely, does it follow that if a person is a good judge of significance, validity, novelty, and clarity in the work of others, that his own work will also possess these qualities. Nor does a referee's ability to judge the utility of a document to himself always imply his ability to judge its utility for others, or conversely.

The most reliable response from a referee is probably his judgment of a document's utility to *him*. In choosing a referee, then, it is important that (1) he be well qualified to judge the utility of papers to himself, (2) the questions of concern to him be representative of those that concern the readers. To meet the first criterion, the editor can choose a generally recognized or potential leader. To meet the second condition, the editor must have accurately represented the paper by an indexing expression and chosen referees concerned with questions that are represented by matching indexing expressions.

The central problem of analysis is to evaluate such a procedure, with specific methods of assigning indexing expressions to documents and readers, of matching them, and of obtaining utility judgments and decision functions. This evaluation takes into account the extent to which the basic function of this process is implemented: to provide a service of disseminating and providing access to published documents and their content to optimize utility for the users.

E. RETRIEVAL, DISSEMINATION OF INFORMATION, AND QUESTION ANSWERING

Given a document d and a user p for whom it is likely to be useful, there are four major modes of use to be pointed out in this discussion.

a. p wishes to read the document a second time or for the first time after he has learned from a reliable source of d's existence; he needs to be able to locate d based on what he recalls about it.

b. p does not know of d's existence, but is searching a corpus through a subject index, for old or new documents such as d, which are both good and relevant to a topic of great concern to him.

c. p has a standing request for all documents meeting his need as he represents it, and, as soon as d is published, he is informed of that.

d. p has a specific question in mind, and he is provided with an answer that is extracted from d, or deduced from something extracted from d, either at the time the question is asked or when d is first analyzed.

The following is a fifth mode, which, though important, is outside the scope of our discussion: p uses d to get new ideas, as a source of stimulation for new questions and new ideas.

The first two modes (a and b) of use are known-item and retrospective searching, respectively; the third mode (c) is maintenance of current awareness. The fourth and fifth (d and e) are aids to question answering and question asking (research), respectively. If we can assign representative indexing expressions to documents at the time they are generated, usage in all five modes can be greatly improved.

Let $e(d) = v_1$ & v_2 denote an indexing expression, a conjunction of two index terms, assigned to d: "autism" and "children" is an example. A person p with a standing request represented by v_1 & v_2 will receive d or at least a notice that d exists. Assuming that this indexing expression accurately represents the topic of his need, if it also accurately represents d, then d should be relevant for p. If d is also good for p—significant, valid, new, and clear to p— and if d is disseminated to p as soon as it is published, then the current awareness function (c) has been improved. Among many selective dissemination services that do this, a most recent one is called MOS (Mathematical Offprint Services) by the American Mathematical Society [25]. This does indeed attempt to provide notices of papers still in galley-proof stage. Similar systems have been tried stressing prepublication notification with the engineering literature, and, of course, the idea of disseminating separates has had a long history of critical discussion [26] and trial [27, 28].

Similar remarks hold for a person searching an index for all documents with the indexing expression v_1 & v_2. Most of the operational systems perform in mode (b).

The assignment of representative indexing expressions can help in known-item searches, mode (a), as well. If the searcher cannot recall title and author of an item, he may be helped by searching for the known item through a subject index. Although it is rare† that a searcher starts the search for a known item through the subject-heading approach, this approach becomes predominant when he has failed in locating author and title of the item [29].

For mode (d), more sophisticated systems are required. Here the key question, and the claim to its answer, is extracted from a document and translated into a formal language suitable for logical processing. This might be

_____

† A recent study in which the author participated shows this to be about 5%.

done by the author, by the referees, or may perhaps even be automated [30]. For example, from a paper claiming to prove that every even number is the sum of two primes would be extracted a logical proposition in something like an applied predicate calculus: "It is false that there is an even number n and two numbers x, y such that either $x + y \neq n$ or x is not prime or y is not prime" or some logical equivalent. Such sentences constitute a structured data base which is searched in question answering. Thus, if a whether question in the same formal language (for example, corresponding to q being "Is it true that every power of 2 is the sum of two primes?") is posed, it is possible to find an answer by computer, based on the resolution principle [31]. There is now a complete proof procedure for the first-order predicate (and propositional) calculus, and operating programs of increasing efficiency have been developed [32] and are being improved. There are also designs for programs [16] for translating statements, such as "Is it true that there are no primes between 25346 and 25493?" from an English-like source language into computer programs that can couple into theorem proving programs and search data bases for answers. Of course, a good index or its equivalent to the stored questions and answers is essential. This index will resemble closely the index to the documents that explain these questions and answers.

A good analytic procedure for evaluating the performance of a system capable of operating in all five modes can apply to evaluating a refereeing system. It is to the development of such an analytic procedure that we turn next. We focus this on a model of the refereeing process because of its central role.

1. *A Model for Cost Minimization*

Consider an idealized model which stresses our central point of optimizing the benefit–cost ratio by appropriate referee selection. Suppose there are N readers. Imagine them divided equally into M classes of experts named by M index terms $v_1, \ldots, v_M$ with N/M experts in each group. Assume that each reader is correctly characterized by just one of M index terms: $v_1, \ldots, v_M$. What we seek to investigate are the consequences of readers being misclassified.

Let β be the conditional probability that an expert is classified under one term, given that he ought to have been classified under that term. The probability of misclassification is $1 - \beta$.

Let A denote the event of a randomly chosen paper d being accepted, and $\overline{A}$ its rejection. This time the acceptance criterion is, for mathematical convenience, the unanimous approval of each of n referees.

Let G denote the event that d is significant, valid, novel, and clear to those able to appreciate it and who are concerned with it. (G is mnemonic for "good" and denotes a set.) Let ρ denote the probability of $\bar{G}$, that d is not in G, i.e., that d is of poor quality. The only thing we consider nonrandom about d is that it *should* go to the N/M readers in class K of experts correctly named by index term v, and that it is correctly indexed under the single term v. It will be refereed by n readers chosen from K and, if accepted, disseminated to all the members of K. What is the expected cost of processing such randomly chosen documents?

The expected cost C has five components:

1. The expected cost C_1 of failure to get d to all of K.
2. The expected cost C_2 of sending d to members of groups other than K.
3. The expected cost C_3 of publishing if d is accepted.
4. The fixed costs of refereeing and indexing C_4 and C_5 respectively.

We have shown that

$$C = c_1(N/M)\{\beta(1-\rho)[1-(\beta D+(1-\beta)B)^n]+(1-\beta)(1-\rho)[\beta D+(1-\beta)B]^n\}$$
$$+ c_2(N/M)\{\beta\rho(\beta a+(1-\beta)b)^n+(1-\beta)(1-\rho)[\beta D+(1-\beta)B]^n\}$$
$$+ c_3\{(1-\rho)[\beta D+(1-\beta)B]^n+\rho[\beta a+(1-\beta)b]^n\}+c_4 n+c_5.$$

Where c_1 is the penalty in dollars per document per intended user of his not getting a document he should have received, c_2 is the penalty in dollars per document per intended user of his getting a document he should not have received, and c_3 is the cost in dollars per document of editing, printing, and distributing a paper it if is accepted.

To simplify the resulting formula and sharpen our focus on the effect of β, let us take $D = 1$, $a = 0$, $b = B = 0.5$, and $\rho = 0.2$. Then,

$$C = c_1(N/M)\{0.8\beta[1-((1+\beta)/2)^n]+0.8(1-\beta)((1+\beta)/2)^n\}$$
$$+ c_2(N/M)\{0.2\beta((1-\beta)/2)^n+0.8(1-\beta)((1+\beta)/2)^n\}$$
$$+ c_3\{0.8((1+\beta)/2)^n+0.2((1-\beta)/2)^n\}+c_4 n+c_5.$$

If $\beta = 1$, then $C = 0.8c_3 + nc_4 + c_5$, and clearly picking just one referee would minimize cost. If $\beta = 0$, then

$$C = [0.8(N/M)(c_1+c_2)+c_3]2^{-n}+c_4 n+c_5.$$

In this case of maximum possible misclassification, there is an optimum value of n; for $N/M = 100$, $c_1 = 50$, $c_2 = 1$, $c_3 = 300$, and $c_4 = 10$, this value of n is about 8. The classification of readers is mostly confused rather than being systematically wrong (e.g., every *Playboy* reader predictably gets *Harper's* and vice versa) when $\beta = 1/M$. In that case, if we take M to be large and $n \geq 3$, then

$$((1 + \beta)/2)^n \doteq 2^{-n} e^{n/M} \qquad \text{and} \qquad ((1 - \beta)/2)^n \doteq 2^{-n} e^{-n/M}$$

so that

$$\begin{aligned} C \doteq \; & c_1(N/M)\{(0.8/M)(1 - 2^{-n+1} e^{n/M}) + (0.8)\, 2^{-n} e^{n/M}\} \\ & + c_2(N/M)\{(0.2/M)2^{-n} e^{-n/M} + 0.8(1 - 1/M)2^{-n} e^{n/M}\} \\ & + c_3\{(0.8)2^{-n} e^{n/M} + (0.2)2^{-n} e^{n/M}\} + c_4 n + c_5 . \end{aligned}$$

If we take figures like the above, with $M = 40$, and noting that $2^{-n} e^{n/40} = e^{-0.668n}$, then

$$\begin{aligned} C = \; & 100(0.02c_1 + 0.76c_1 e^{-0.668n}) + 0.78c_2 e^{-0.668n} + 0.005c_2 e^{-0.718n} \\ & + c_3(0.8e^{-0.668n} + 0.2e^{-0.718n}) + c_4 n + c_5 . \end{aligned}$$

The value of n for which this is least is about 9.

The numbers given here are not unrealistic: page charges of up to $50 per page to defray publication costs are not uncommon, while actual publication costs may go as high as $100 per page, of which $50 is for printing alone. A typical 5- to 10-page article may thus easily incur a cost of $c_3 = \$300$. This figure is, however, dominated by $(1 - \rho)(N/M)(c_1 + c_2)$, with c_1 and N/M most critical because the penalty c_2 for a false drop is generally negligible in comparison to the penalty c_1 for a miss. Both are, of course, hard to estimate in the absence of behavioral (preferably economic) data, but $50 may be a reasonable guess, even if the actual figures would vary from $5 to $500. Refereeing and indexing costs are usually lumped into the publication cost and the figure of $c_4 = 10$, which we used, is undoubtedly an underestimate.

That a journal's field of coverage should be characterized by $M = 40$ topic names is not unreasonable for a fairly specialized journal. The value of $N/M = 100$ implies that the journal's total readership is about 4000, which is a typical circulation figure for successful scientific journals, and it implies that any article gets read by about $\frac{1}{40}$ or 2.5 % of the readership [33].

The probability that referees and users are correctly classified may be comparable to the probability of documents being correctly indexed. If that is so, then β may be approximated by the hit-rate (or recall ratio) h defined in the beginning of this paper. This was

E(Nr(retr and relev))/E(Nr of relevant papers)

$$= \text{Prob}(d \text{ is retrieved} \mid d \text{ is relevant}),$$

where E denotes the mathematical expectation operator; if a relevant paper *should* have been indexed under index term v, then h is the conditional probability that it was so indexed.† From data like that of MEDLARS, with $h = 0.6$, we can estimate $\beta = 0.6$.

With $c_1 = 50$, $c_2 = 1$, $c_3 = 300$, $c_4 = 10$, $M = 40$, $N/M = 100$, we have $C = 10n - 528(0.8)^n + 72(r)^n + 2400 + c_5$, which is least if $n = 1$. If, instead of the above, $c_1 = 40$ and $c_2 = 10$, then

$$C = 10n - 80(0.8)^n + 180(0.2)^n + \text{constant.}$$

This function of n is least when $n = 2$.

Toward greater realism, we now briefly sketch several avenues of needed investigation. These explore the consequences of weakening the various assumptions made so far.

2. Representation of Topics with More than One Index Term

We assumed that a person's concern, as well as a document, is represented by an indexing expression consisting of just one index term. Even if each reader could be classified into just one of M subject classes, it is unlikely that each class would have exactly N/M members. Some subjects are more popular than others. This would be reflected in the varying populations of the subject classes. Similarly, the number of documents per topic would reflect the popularity of that topic with authors. The distribution of population over these M topic classes is then used to modify the formulas for cost developed in the last section. Suppose now that each reader is concerned with and qualified to judge papers in more than one class namable by an index term. Let $c(p, v)$ denote potential referee p's concern with and competence in topic v. Given a matrix of such values of $c(p, v)$ for all the potential referees and all index terms in V, we can ask how to assign the p to the v. This is now related to the von

---

† The acceptance rate a (called precision ratio) is defined as

$$\frac{E(\text{Nr(Retr \& Relev)})}{E(\text{Nr retrieved papers})} = \frac{\text{Prob (Retr|Relev) Prob (Relev)}}{\text{Prob (Retr \& Relev)} + \text{Prob (Retr \& Irrel.)}}$$

$$a = \frac{hr}{hr + c(1 - r)},$$

where r is the probability that randomly chosen document is relevant and $c = $ Prob (Retr|Irrel.), which is analogous to the probability of misclassification. Given h and a we are free to assume $h = \beta$ and $c = 1 - \beta$ by computing an appropriate value for r, namely

$$r = \frac{a(1 - h)}{a(1 - h) + h(1 - a)}.$$

A better definition of h and a, suggested by Segur (Mental Health Research Institute, University of Michigan, Ann Arbor, Michigan) is to take the expectation of the ratio rather than the ratio of the expectations. This would avoid biasing the calculation against searches with a small number of relevant papers. But this is mathematically more complicated and is left for other studies.

Neumann assignment problem [34], which seeks to optimally assign N men to N different jobs by minimizing the sum of the N applicable performance ratings given to the N^2 man–job combinations.

This would be applicable if documents were indexed under just one topic term, though readers were concerned with several topics in varying degrees. But documents, too, are relevant to several topics in varying degrees. We are faced with a generalization of the assignment problem. A simplest formulation is to consider a document–index term relevance matrix with $r(d, v)$ indicating the degree of relevance of the question in d to the topic named by v. Then seek those (d, p) pairs which maximize $\sum_v r(d, v)c(p, v)$. This gives the same weight to a document with a very concerned reader in an only slightly relevant topic as it does to an only slightly concerned reader in a very relevant topic. Probably the reader's concern with a topic should be given greater weight than the relevance of the topic.

Note that this generalized assignment problem is analogous to the problem of assigning employers to employees. Each employee may be characterized by his score on a battery of tests, and each employer may represent his personnel requirements by a vector of desired scores on that same battery of tests. What is an optimal correspondence of employees to employers?

3. On the Significance of Questions

One of the key attributes of document quality a referee judges is that of significance. We propose that significance is a property of questions. The significance of a question varies with the person asking it, his circumstances, purpose, and the time. It varies above all with how much the questioner knows about the logical relations of question q to all the other questions that might be asked. If this knowledge were perfect—and other factors constant—there is still an important sense in which some questions are logically more significant than others. In this sense, we could assign to each question q a number $s(q)$ in $[0, 1]$ which expresses how central a place q occupies in its logical relation to other questions.

Consider as an example a (trivial) topic of four questions q_1, q_2, q_3, q_4 related by

$$q_1 \to q_2, \quad q_1 \to q_3, \quad q_2 \leftrightarrow q_4, \quad q_3 \to q_4,$$

where "$q_i \to q_j$" stands for "the answer to q_i implies the answer to q_j." Intuitively, q_1 is most central; the answer to q_1 implies the answers to more questions than does the answer to q_2, q_3, or q_4. Assume that $s(q_i)$ is proportional to the number of questions, the answer to which is implied by the answer to q_i, weighted by the significance of the implied questions. Formally

$$s(q_i) = (1/\lambda) \sum_j s(q_i)a_{ij},$$

where $(1/\lambda)$ is the constant of proportionality. Here let A be the incidence matrix of implications, with $a_{ij} = 1$ if $q_i \rightarrow q_j$, 0 if not. Letting $\mathbf{s}$ denote the column vector corresponding to $(s(q_1), s(q_2), \ldots)$,† we have

$$\mathbf{s} = (1/\lambda)A\mathbf{s} \quad \text{or} \quad (A - \lambda I)\mathbf{s} = 0,$$

where I is the identity matrix. This is an eigenvalue problem and there is a nonzero solution for $\mathbf{s}$ if the determinant $|A - \lambda I| = 0$. In the example given above

$$A = \begin{pmatrix} 0 & 1 & 1 & 0 \\ 0 & 0 & 0 & 1 \\ 0 & 0 & 0 & 1 \\ 0 & 1 & 0 & 0 \end{pmatrix}$$

with the proviso that $a_{ii} = 0$ for all i. The characteristic equation is

$$\begin{vmatrix} -\lambda & 1 & 1 & 0 \\ 0 & -\lambda & 0 & 1 \\ 0 & 0 & -\lambda & 1 \\ 0 & 1 & 0 & -\lambda \end{vmatrix} = 0 = \lambda^4 - \lambda^2 = \lambda^2(\lambda^2 - 1),$$

and $\lambda = 1$ is a double real root. Corresponding to this eigenvalue, we have $s_1 = s_2 + s_3$, $s_2 = s_4$, $s_4 = s_2$, from which it follows that $s_1 = 2s_2$; $s_2 = s_3 = s_4$. If we arbitrarily select $s_2 = s(q_2) = 0.1$, then $s_1 = s(q_1) = 0.2$.

Generally, a topic, as known at any time, is characterized by a graph or relation matrix specifying the known logical relations among questions. From this we could, in principle, compute the significance of each question and select the key questions.

But, of course, this graph changes with time. Indeed, each significant question that is validly answered (for the first time) may well lead readers to pose questions they did not think of before and, more importantly, to recognize logical relations between the new question and older ones.

4. On the Qualifications of Judges

Success in assigning referees to papers depends on how the qualifications for the task of potential referees are defined and measured. It is not enough to assume that a matrix of values like $c(p, v)$ is given which reflects p's concern with and competence to judge the significance of questions relevant to topic v, as well as to assess validity, novelty, and clarity of the answers claimed in a document. It should be possible to grade readers according to whether their

† In the example this vector has four components, corresponding to the weights for q_1, q_2, q_3, and q_4; these are denoted by s_1, s_2, s_3, and s_4.

qualifications to judge significance, validity, novelty, and clarity in a subject are low, average, or high. The following are some plausible desiderata for a measure to grade readers in this way.

a. A reader's qualification to judge significance of questions on topic v might be measured by the number of times his papers on v have been cited for posing key problems. Here "key problems" are those acknowledged by most practitioners in v to have opened a fruitful new line of investigation or whose answers help answer many other "key problems." Concretely, this may be done by scanning the papers citing the potential referee for appropriate laudatory adjectives; the citing papers could, in turn, be weighted by qualifications of their authors to judge significance.

b. A reader's competence to assess validity may be estimated from his prior record as a referee or reviewer of papers on this topic. A count of the number of errors or violations of procedural norms, that the author acknowledged as such, which a referee submits in his report could be used.

c. A reader's ability to detect novelty depends on his familiarity with the field, among other factors; this may be measured by how much of his time he spends in communication—reading, meeting attendance, etc. It also depends on how well he has assimilated and retained all he knows, so that he can spot redundancy quickly and accurately. Of course, the judgments of novelty, significance, validity, and clarity are very often so intertwined that attempts such as these to dissect the factors are very difficult. Nonetheless, his communicativeness, plus his record as a referee in pointing out genuine redundancies, may be a good index.

d. An index to a reader's literacy in a topic v may be provided by the breadth of his vocabulary of v. If we count all the less common and technical words ever used by this reader in his own publications and rank these in order of decreasing frequency of use, $r = 1, 2, 3, \ldots$, with $f(r)$ being the frequency with which he used the word of rank r, then $f(r)$ may be approximated by $\alpha r^{-(1+\alpha)}$. If α is close to 0, he uses many different words; if α is near 0.5, he tends to use relatively few words over and over. Thus, α may be an index to his literacy in one technical sense. So may the number of papers he has published. Surely, neither vocabulary nor the number of stylish words used by an author measure literacy in the full sense, and there seems to be no generally accepted measure of a reader's literacy in a topic.

5. On Document Quality and Its Judgment

Documents are not intrinsically good or bad according to an absolute standard. Yet, a document containing a false claim is not as good as one with a valid answer to the same question, regardless of whether the error has been detected by most readers. But erroneous documents do not necessarily have negative utility. The detection of an error in a document has led to new avenues of scientific exploration, which perhaps would have been missed had not an error drawn attention to it. Moreover, some scholars may be concerned with the study of erroneous documents as such. Deviances of this kind could cast light on the study of the dynamics of knowledge growth.

We cannot escape defining the quality of a document as a referee's judgment, even if certain objective measures of quality can set bounds on that judgment. We can regard this judgment as a random variable, the distribution of which depends on the qualifications of the judge and the quality of the document being judged either in terms of an objective scale or as a consensus among the judgments of other readers. The following assumptions can help specify the nature of these random variables reflecting quality judgments.

a. If a judge's qualifications to assess significance on a topic are average and the document is clear to him, then his judgment is, on the average, "accurate." This means that his assessment of significance is representative of the assessment of the readership, present or future. But if the judge is exceptionally well qualified and if d is not only clear but very novel, then he will tend to underestimate its significance, for he will tend to be conservative, to uphold the prevailing paradigms that a very novel paper might threaten. An underqualified judge may also underestimate the significance of a clear, novel paper because of bias against fields other than his own.

b. If the judge is highly qualified to assess the validity of a document in his field and d is clear to him, then his judgment is, on the average, "accurate." If he is underqualified, he will fail to detect errors and thus overestimate validity.

c. If the judge is highly qualified to discriminate between redundancy and novelty, then he will, on the average, judge accurately. Otherwise, he will overestimate novelty.

d. To judge clarity, a reader must of course be literate in both the topic and the language of the document. A judge need not be highly literate to assess clarity but should, rather, represent the literacy level of the readership.

e. While very good or very poor documents are easy to spot, the majority in between are not. The variance of a referee's judgment of any of the above four attributes of quality could be assumed to vary as $g(1 - g)$, where g is the quality of the document. If the document is either very poor in some attribute ($g = 0$), or very good ($g = 1$), then the variance is close to 0 and the judge is highly certain of his judgment.

It seems also that the "academic affiliation, doctoral origin, and professional age" of the author and judge are important for the judging process. The more the judge and author have in common in these areas the greater seems to be the ability of the judge to understand and appreciate the work of that author [35].

6. Referee Selection as Mappings into Partitions of the Readership

A clearer explication of the algebraic nature of three basic sets representing the readers, questions, and documents is also desirable. Call these sets P, Q, and D, respectively. Let $\prod(P)$ denote the set of all ordered partitions of P. For example, if $P = \{p_1, p_2, p_3\}$, then

$$\prod(P) = \{(p_1 \mid p_2 p_3), (p_2 \mid p_1 p_3), (p_3 \mid p_1 p_2), (p_1 p_2 \mid p_3), (p_1 p_3 \mid p_2), (p_2 p_3 \mid p_1),$$
$$(p_1 \mid p_2 \mid p_3), (p_2 \mid p_1 \mid p_3), \ldots\}.$$

Consider a mapping c of D into $\prod(P)$. This function might assign, for example, to document d of set D, the partition $c(d) = (p_1 \mid p_2 \mid p_3)$. We interpret this as follows: The three possible readers of d, p_1, p_2, or p_3, are grouped so that d reaches p_1 most directly, p_2 with second priority and p_3 with lowest priority. A two-way partition, like $(p_1 \mid p_2 p_3)$, is interpreted as specifying only two orders of priority: d is sent to p_1 but not to p_2 or p_3. The partition $(\varnothing \mid p_1 p_2 p_3)$ means that d is sent to no one ($\varnothing$ denotes the empty set); on the other hand, $(p_1 p_2 p_3 \mid \varnothing)$ means that d is sent to everyone.

It is well known that all the two-way partitions of P form a simple lattice such as shown in Figure 1.

FIGURE 1

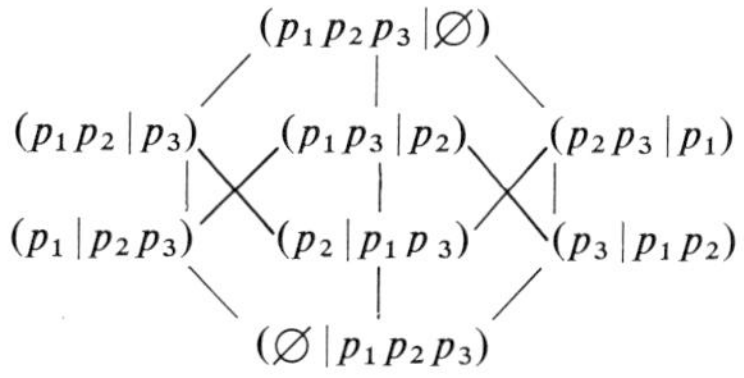

Corresponding to c, which we can suggestively call a circulation function on D because it specifies for each document d to which readers in P it circulates (and with what priority), there is a dual mapping c' from P to $\prod(D)$. We interpret this as a notification function, which assigns a partial ordering of D to each reader $p \in P$; thus

$$c'(p) = (d_1 d_2 \mid d_3 d_4 d_5 \mid \cdots)$$

states that both d_1 and d_2 are definitely sent to P for his urgent attention; $d_3 d_4 d_5$ may not be sent or are sent to p after others have seen them, etc.

These two functions c and c' must meet consistency conditions. Suppose, for example, that $P = \{p_1 p_2 p_3\}$ and $D = \{d_1 d_2 d_3 d_4\}$ and

$$c'(p_1) = (d_1 d_2 \mid d_3 d_4), \qquad c'(p_2) = (d_1 \mid d_2 d_3 d_4), \qquad c'(p_3) = (d_4 \mid d_1 d_2 d_3).$$

Then we have

$$c(d_1) = (p_1 p_2 \,|\, p_3), \qquad c(d_2) = (p_1 \,|\, p_2 p_3), \qquad c(d_3) = (\varnothing \,|\, p_1 p_2 p_3),$$

and

$$c(d_4) = (p_3 \,|\, p_1 p_2).$$

A circulation function c^* is ideal if the ordering on P that c^* assigns to P is such that those people to whom the d is most useful appear on the left-most position, those to whom d is less useful appear on the second position, etc. If d is an article published in a journal, and P is its readership, then $c(d) = P$. All the readers receive it with equal priority. This is far from ideal if d is useful to only a small fraction of the readership. If an ideal circulation function were known, then actual circulation functions could be compared with it, and good publication decisions can be made when d is a submitted manuscript. The distance between two circulation functions c_1 and c_2 could be measured by the length of the smallest path on the lattice of all partitions which connect c_1 and c_2. Given a manuscript d for which referees are to be selected, a circulation function is chosen as a first approximation, and it is used to select as referees those p's who are left-most in the partition. The referees' reports are then used to select another circulation function as a second approximation, and this is, hopefully, closer to the ideal circulation function than was that chosen first. Now the improved circulation function is used for second-stage referee selection. Their reports are to result in a third choice of circulation function. If this procedure converges sufficiently well, a publication decision is computed; if not, steps are taken to guarantee convergence.

There are many strategies for refereeing other than the one we have discussed here. All of them aim at publishing documents of maximum utility to their readership at lowest cost to them. This means not only making good publication decisions, but making sure that each publication reaches all the readers to whom it can be useful.

IV. A Refereeing System

What follows is a description of one way of implementing a refereeing process. It differs in some major ways from that currently used by many journals [36]. We would like to show that these proposed innovations are likely to improve performance of the refereeing process in its objective of screening for documents of greatest expected utility to its readers relative to cost. For ease of exposition, we will trace the flow of a single manuscript after it reaches the editorial office.

This entire discussion is predicted on the actualization of current trends toward automation in publishing. We envisage that more and more authors will, in the near future, have access to the variety of source recording devices existing today. To mention but three, Datatext [37], MTST [38], and Astrotype [39] are commercially available services which provide the author (or his secretary) with a typewriter-like terminal which generates a machine-readable, stored (on magnetic disks or tapes) by-product of the typing process, and allows editing as well. Such digitally encoded data can be displayed, on demand, on inexpensive alphanumeric graphic terminals (like the Sanders 720) or as hard copy by means of a high-speed printer or copier tied to the CRT display.

There is little reason why proposals and manuscripts should not reach editorial offices in the form of magnetic tapes with or without a hard copy. Better yet, such documents can be forwarded over digital communication channels—e.g., "slow" telephone lines at 2000 bits or about 50 words per second (3 minutes of transmission for a typical manuscript)—for storage in the auxiliary memory of the editorial office's computer system. Smaller editorial offices may rent storage facilities of larger ones and use only terminals with access to a computer network. To say that a manuscript reaches the editorial office is to say that transmission has been completed, and a file for the document in the system of the editorial office has been created. Subsequent processing begins after this time, scheduled by a supervisory program in the editorial system, in the following steps:

1. *Gross screening.* The manuscript is displayed to an editor and examined for gross violations of the rules set by the editor; for example, language (non-English?), length (more than 100 pages?), technical detail (too many, too few formulas, data?). If obviously unsuitable, it is returned to the author and processed no further; nor is there any record of its receipt.

2. *Logging in.* If it passes gross screening, it is assigned an identification number. We shall call it d. This initiates creation of an editorial record which shall be used, and added to, during subsequent processing. It is essentially a string of data elements, the first of which is d. The second data element is $t(d)$, the time the manuscript was logged in. At that time there is initiated the automatic creation and mailing of a form letter to the author, acknowledging receipt. He understands that he has, at this time, disclosed his findings for public scrutiny. The next three data elements adjoined to the first two are title, authors, affiliation, and corresponding address. Having identified the paper we would recognize it if it were encountered again, at least if title and authors are both unchanged.

3. *Verification.* A biographic data base, if available, is now searched (by computer, where possible) to verify the author's name and affiliation, and to retrieve prior bibliographic and biographic data about him. This includes

reviews of the author's prior articles. The author is then assigned a tentative rating on a scale like: leader in his field, major contributor, unknown with great promise, unknown or known of average accomplishments, marginal contributor, likely to discredit journal. Authors in the first category (and possibly a few in the last) will generally be known to the editor by name. This step is skipped for them. Some papers may be rejected at this step. In all cases a decision about the extent and priority of further processing is made. This priority assignment is the sixth data element.

4. *Document analysis.* This proceeds iteratively. First, an attempt is made to assign to d an indexing expression (preferably by computer) using only the title, and biographic data about the author. The result is checked against an author-supplied indexing expression that should have accompanied the manuscript. If it did not, it is now solicited by telephone. If the fit is adequate, the indexing expression is adjoined to the editorial record as the seventh data element. If the fit is inadequate, there is further processing (also preferably by computer) using more and more material in the paper. If the paper was received in machine-readable form, the entire text is, in principle, available for this purpose though the processing cost increases with the amount of text beyond the title which is used. Otherwise, data must be converted. How much is converted depends on (a) how much is needed for adequate indexing and (b) the priority assigned to d in Step 3.

After the use of titles, as analysis makes use of more text, would be the use of an author-provided aphorism, an author-provided abstract (both solicited and edited if necessary), the references cited in the paper, the introduction or first paragraph, the last paragraph and selected portions of the text in between. We have not considered various indexing procedures. The simplest permuted title indexes [23], supplemented by the use of a growing thesaurus [40] to pass from words in titles to index terms of a (growing) authority list, are surprisingly effective in comparison with more elaborate methods based on the full text, some employing syntactic analysis procedures [41–44].

Formally, let VT be the set of words to be looked for in titles. Let VI be the authority list of index terms, which will also be used to represent readers. Let VW be a list of all words and phrases *not* in VT nor in VI, which can be used to bridge connections between words in VT to words in VI. A thesaurus, then, is formally a subset of

$$(VT \times VI) \cup (VT \times VW) \cup (VW \times VW) \cup (VW \times VI)$$
$$= (VT \cup VW) \times (VI \cup VW).$$

Viewed as a directory, only VT contains entry points, and the elements of VT may be ordered alphabetically. The most important aspect of this is that all vocabularies can be added to. Special provisions are made for documents on questions that are so new that they cannot be adequately represented by any available indexing expression. How can we encourage authors to report work on very novel ideas? The editor could advertise to prospective authors that the more difficulty he is likely to have in indexing their papers with existing indexes, the better the chances of acceptance, other factors being equal, or rather that they need not worry if their paper does not fit the categories. The order of difficulty would be the editor's subjective judgment.

The final result of the work in Step 4 is an indexing expression to represent the document. That is the eighth data element.

5. Using the indexing expression assigned to d, we now search (by computer, preferably) a file of all readers for whom there are "profiles" or indexing expressions, for that set of readers whose profiles match that of the document beyond a certain degree. In the simplest system, data for the readers' profiles may be extracted from their official titles, the titles of their current projects, the titles of their publications. This file certainly contains all previous authors of the given journal and possibly some nonreaders serving as referees. If the indexing expressions are all simple conjunctions of index terms, this file is an alphabetized list of all the index terms of VI, with all the concerned readers posted on each; where available, an estimate of the degree of concern is posted as well.

The author may have solicited reviews from referees of his choosing and may submit their reports with his manuscript. Such reports will be used if these referees' profiles meet the same criteria as do those of the referees that would have been, or are, chosen by the system.

This is, of course, what every editor does in his head. He selects referees on the basis of personal or professional acquaintance, from hints in the paper's references, etc. to the extent he recalls those during his first reading of the manuscript. What is gained here is access to *all* of a growing pool of potential referees of far greater size and more up to date than any person can keep in mind, as well as more accurate matching. The latter is critical both for quality control and for subsequent utilization in dissemination and retrieval.

6. The set of potential referees' profiles thus retrieved is screened for those most concerned (and qualified to judge), and most available for refereeing. There is at least one system [45] using computers for referee selection. The sample of referees should be representative of the readership and may include not only readers who are themselves authors but students and nonauthor users of the documents as well. After preliminary contact with those potential referees thus selected to secure their agreement to referee, the manuscript and other pertinent records are forwarded to each of the n referees who accepted. Some of the other pertinent records include cited papers in the same journal†

---

† Because it is costly, it would be done rarely. Expert referees may seldom require it. But, once enough articles are economically accessible from an automated repository network, this option should be provided.

and parts of the editorial record, available to the referee on demand (perhaps via teletype or LDX). Some of the more obscure references, if very important in judging the paper, may have been supplied by the author with his paper. The referee's responses themselves are either delivered on a form as shown in the appendix or over a communication channel in a store–and–forward mode, or through on-line interaction with the editorial office. The procedures used by *Science*, as described by Goudsmit [36], is one of the best in current use. None are as yet on-line. On-line interaction can have much more branching than indicated on the form in the appendix.

Shown in the appendix is a sequence of five questions which apply only to original papers; another sequence of questions would replace these for tutorial papers, another for surveys, another for news reports or announcements, etc. With an on-line system, switching from one set of questions to another would be immediate. Also, to reduce costs, referee–editor (as well as editor–author) interactions can take place at mutually agreed upon, predesignated hours. Normally, such an exchange would be initiated by the referee, but if by a deadline he has not communicated the editorial office would initiate it or prompt the referee automatically.

The result is a judgment about acceptance, rejection, or revision. These are the next n data elements, one judgment for each of n referees. Other data (both subjective and behavioral) from each referee report which is pertinent to improving his profile would consist of new names to add to the pool of potential referees and new words to update the sets VW and VI. (The set VT will be updated with newly arriving documents.) The referee is encouraged to submit a conventional essay-type review, as well as comments marked right on his copy of the manuscript, in addition to completing the questionnaire. The referee should return the top, quick-tear sheet immediately on receipt. If he elects not to read the paper, he should return the manuscript and questionnaire form at that time also.

7. To combine the judgments of n referees, it is necessary to normalize their responses. Different referees might rank an article differently not because they judge its quality differently, but because they respond differently to the scales. If one referee *consistently* ranks all papers submitted to him low on a certain scale, and another one *consistently* ranks all papers high on that scale, their judgments should be weighted according to their bias to arrive at a balanced aggregate.

A final publication decision is now made. If d is rejected, another journal for which it is better suited may be recommended. If the author concurs, his paper would be submitted for him. This journal would be one of a group of cooperating journals who have agreed to pool some of their resources (e.g., referees, indexing methods and programs, dissemination and retrospective search programs, etc.). The recommending referee's report would be forwarded.

If d is to be revised, the author is provided with assistance. This takes several forms: referees' comments (which could be edited with computer aid) which are forwarded to the author over a communication channel; computer-aided analysis and editing of his text, prior to automated typesetting, photocomposition copying, and distribution; storage in a central digital repository from where it can be accessible on demand in hard copy or display.

Many passes of "conversation" on various points of dispute between author and referee are made possible by rapid switching and forwarding of the referee's specific comments and questions on substantive points in the paper. This is done through the editorial office's services as a switch and store–and–forward memory to keep the referee unknown to the author, unless he divulges it and establishes direct communication.

It is essential to conduct referee–author communication in such a way that the referee can remain anonymous if he wishes. Yet, this communication must be convenient, fast, accurate. The referee, for example, should be permitted—even encouraged—to write comments right on the manuscript as they spontaneously occur to him during his reading, for forwarding to the author. More futuristically, this might be done on a graphic display console with a light pen.

If d is accepted, it is "published" as above. In addition, its title and abstract are sent to each reader whose profile matches the document's indexing expression. This would precede the circulation of conventional printed issues. Continuation of this service is necessary to (a) maintain adequate profiles for potential readers in the file, (b) minimize the cost of handling too many separates, and (c) provide ready access in the form of bound volumes for conventional (and convenient) access in retrospective library searching and browsing.

As an incentive to the referee, he may (a) have his name published as such, (b) publish portions of his review in the same issue containing the article if accepted, (c) receive complete copies of *all* articles matching his profile from all the cooperating journals, as soon as they are published with top priority, (d) use freely what he learns from the articles he reviews, whether these are finally published or not, and (e) possibly receive economic compensation for his time.

Some of the reasons why this system is likely to be better than current methods are as follows:

1. Referee selection is a very critical factor in successful quality control and use of the literature. It is usually still done fairly well by a good editor who knows most of the key practitioners. Such good editors are becoming increasingly scarce. Often it is a very part-time occupation for the increasingly busy leaders of a field. More importantly, the number of potential readers

doubles almost every decade. This makes it as difficult for even a modern renaissance-type scholar to utilize fully all these available resources as it was for him to keep up with all the literature in his field before World War II. In Newton's time it was possible, but it has been impossible since World War II in most fields; hence, the vigorous activity since then on information storage and retrieval. A typical editor can keep the names of a few thousand potential referees in his mind. But when selecting referees, he is likely to recall only a small fraction of all those he knows who are appropriate. In the proposed system, he has access to a vastly larger, more accurately indexed file of potential referees. Moreover, the process of continually checking and revising referees' profiles against their behavior as referees lowers the likelihood of misclassification. We saw the importance of maximizing β in minimizing costs in the last section.

2. If we select referees well, we can disseminate and retrieve papers just as well because this will reflect that at least a good indexing expression has been assigned to the paper. The references of each paper will have been stored too, making available the very effective and promising alerting systems based on citation indexing. Both alerting and retrospective search via citation matching can be coupled with subject searches.

SDI systems based on profiles of subject heading will certainly be an easy by-product. A number of such systems are operational today, typified by the one at Northwestern since October 1965. In 1967 it was available to faculty at the cost of computer time, about $2.25 per month for each user being provided with a listing of about 100 articles. About 20 journals are covered. Administrative costs are borne by the Council for Intersocietal Studies. According to Janda [46], this system is well used, but the usefulness of SDI systems has not yet been demonstrated in full generality.

3. More facilitation and encouragement, more immediate and rapid communication between authors and referees about the paper is very likely to improve its quality. Such communication samples the final one-way communication from author to readers in the published paper. It is the author's main chance to see if his intended audience understands and appreciates his message, in time for him to revise his work and writing if they do not.

4. Providing more definite and rewarding incentives to referees as well as assuring authors that their papers will be disseminated directly to readers who are most concerned is likely to increase their dedication to this important task of quality control in communication.

5. Much of each paper processed by this system is to be in machine-readable form for the system to be fast and efficient. This affords great opportunities for experimentation with content analysis, question answering and translation. Moreover, computer aids to the editing and publishing process, facilitated by having many manuscripts in machine-readable form,

may promise enough immediate cost–benefit ratio reduction to give editorial offices the needed incentive and confidence to venture into such innovations soon.

All these are benefits. They are difficult to quantify without gross over-simplifications. Very likely there is an enormous qualitative benefit from the more sensitive screening due to more refined referee selection, so that not only are fewer and more excellent papers filtered through, but the quality of all papers is improved as well. Though costs for the proposed system can be greater than for current systems, they can also be made lower. The benefits grow at a faster rate than the costs as more improvement features are added.

Quality control in publication has its dangers. The greatest stems from its resemblance to censorship. It could be argued that the penalty of rejecting a good paper is so high that it is far better to publish almost everything, and invest in expensive garbage-collection and post-publication screening, review-ing, and synthesis devices. Nonetheless, prepublication quality control seems to have a higher benefit–cost ratio. Since quality control must not be too restrictive or threatening, there is still ample opportunity for good postpublica-tion devices to screen and integrate.

Publishing only the best and then ascertaining that they reach readers to whom such publications make a difference, increases the number of significant new problems likely to be raised and solved. Future manuscripts (and propo-sals) may thus be better. This could have a self-amplifying effect in that good-enough papers can breed even better ones. Overall quality can thus be at least maintained, if not improved, perhaps even without bound.

Appendix A

SAMPLE EXPERIMENTAL REFEREEING DATA SHEET

MEMO TO: _____   _____

Title   Potential Referee's Name   Date

_____

Affiliation

_____

Address

ABOUT: Refereeing the enclosed manuscript. It is:

_____

Title of Paper

By: _____

Author's Name

Of: _____

Affiliation and Address

It pertains to: _____

Indexing Expression; Degree of Concern

Was submitted for publication in_____

Name of Journal

FROM: _____ , _____

Name of Editor   Position with Journal

_____

Address

REQUEST: This paper is sent to you because its profile matches your interest profile according to data available to us. This questionnaire is part of a system aiming to match manuscripts with referees who are the most qualified and concerned critics existing. This form is intended to lighten the refereeing task while providing us with the most valid data on which to base a fair and useful publication decision. Your help is essential in maintaining the self-correcting nature of science, in providing quality control in the publishing process which is acceptable to authors and readers alike.

It is not only appreciated, but will be tangibly recompensated.

URGENT: Please tear off this top sheet immediately upon receipt, answer the following questions, and return it in the enclosed self-addressed envelope.

1. Do you agree to read this paper and deliver your

report by _____?_____ Yes　　No

　　　　　　　　　　　　　　　　　　　　Yes, on alternate

　　　　　Date　　　　　　　　　　　　date:_____.

2. If not, please state your reasons:_____.
Please return the manuscript and the entire questionnaire in the enclosed envelope right away; thank you.

3. May we direct other, more suitable papers, at more appropriate times?
Yes　　No

4. If yes, specify, if you like, what kind of papers_____.

5. Please list three colleagues likely to be good, and willing, referees for this paper:
Mr._____ , at:_____.
Mr._____ , at:_____.
Mr._____ , at:_____.

6. The following is your interest profile as shown in our records:

Topics, Methods, Problems of Special Concern	Degree of Concern	Degree of Critical Competence

Do you judge this profile to be accurate for purposes of directing to you all, and only, papers you are really interested in and feel comfortably qualified to evaluate?   No   Yes

7. If No, please make suitable correction in item 6. Not all items need be filled in.

REFEREE'S EVALUATION

Please return this with the manuscript after you have read it. Feel encouraged to mark your comments and questions to the author on the enclosed manuscript as extensively as you like. In addition to expressing your opinions of the paper, possibly including comments to be communicated to the author, please answer as many of the following questions as you wish to:

1. To what extent does the paper contribute to the journal's editorial objectives, which are:_____

   _____

   Indicate this in your own words or by placing a mark on the vertical scale shown:

   Perfectly; ideal for journal. Reasons: (optional)

   Like most articles in the journal.

   Definitely not.

2. If there are other journals for which this paper is more suitable, please list:

3. How significant do you find the key question this paper addresses or raises.

   Unequalled in implications or applications;   Your own rating
   in upper 1 % of all papers I have *ever* read   (optional)
   on this topic.

   Average; like most papers I have *recently*
   read on this topic.

   In lowest 20 % of all papers I have *recently*
   read on this topic.

4. How valid do you find the main claims, the arguments/evidence to support them.

> Flawless and compelling
> Average
> Poor
> Wholly false, objectionable, confused.

5. How original, novel, substantive do you find this paper?

> Contains very much of solid substance which is totally new to me.
>> (You might wish to point out that this is an important replication of an experiment, a justifiable redundancy.)
> Nothing new to me or little substantive content.

6. How clear, organized and well-written do you find this paper?

> Absorbing, pellucid; masterpiece of clear thought and composition.
> Interesting, clear; my attention didn't wander.
> Required effort to maintain attention.
> My attention wandered; I couldn't read it in one sitting.
> Too boring, irritating, hard to read through, except I promised to read it.

7. What type of reader (e.g., laymen, experienced researchers specialized in this topic, etc.) do you feel cannot afford to be ignorant of this paper for any purpose (e.g., for reference, to gain insight, pleasure, etc. . . .)?

8. If you would like to express your overall opinion about the publishability of this paper, circle your recommendation:
   A—Publish—a must.
   B—Publish—if there is space.
   C—Publish—after some editing.
   D—Reconsider again, if resubmitted after minor changes, as indicated.
   E—Reconsider if resubmitted after a complete rewrite.
   F—Reject or submit to another journal.

9. If you wish, express your evaluation of the paper possibly including comments that may be forwarded to the author to help him revise the paper.

ACKNOWLEDGMENTS

Valuable discussions with C. Drott, W. Everett, B. Segur, A. Tars, W. Lehmann, G. Salton and S. Amarel stimulated and helped refine many of the ideas in this paper. This paper was prepared with the partial support of grant NSF GN716, Office of Science Information Services.

REFERENCES

1. Austin, C. J., "Medlars 1963–1967." National Library of Medicine, Bethesda, Maryland, 1968.
2. Bivona, W. A., "Selective Dissemination of Information," Vol. I: Pilot test at U.S. Army Natick Lab., Final Rep. No. IDC-8074-2) (ATLIS-15) Contract DA-19-129-AMC-957 (N) (AD-654 997). Information Dynamics Corp, Reading, Massachusetts, 1967.
3. Lancaster, F. W., "Medlars: Report on the Evaluation of Its Operating Efficiency." *Amer. Doc.* **20,** 119–142 (1969).
4. Maron, M. E. and Kuhns, J. L., "On Relevance, Probabilistic Indexing and Information Retrieval." *J. Assoc. Comput. Mach.* **7,** No. 3, July, 1960.
5. Swets, J. A., "Effectiveness of Information Retrieval Methods." Contract No. AF19(629)-5065 Proj. No. 8668. Bolt Beranek and Newman, Inc., Cambridge, Massachusetts, 1967.
6. Pollack, S. M., "Evaluation and Comparison of Information Retrieval Systems." Nat. Meeting of ORSA, *31st, New York*, 1967. Naval Postgraduate School, Monterey, California, 1967.
7. Cleverdon, C., "ASLIB Cranfield Research Project on the Comparative Efficiency of Indexing Systems." *Assoc. Spec. Lib. Info. Bur. Proc.* **12,** 421–31 (1960).
8. Swanson, D. R., "The Evidence Underlying the Cranfield Results." *Library Quart.* **35,** 1–20 (1965).
9. Hillman, D. J., "The Notion of Relevance (I)." *Amer. Doc.* **15,** 26–34 (1964).
10. Goffman, W. and Newill, V. A., "Communication and Epidemic Processes." *Proc. Roy. Soc. A* **298,** 316–337 (1967).
11. Rees, A. M. and Saracevic, T., "The Measureability of Relevance." *Proc. ADI* **3,** 225–233 (1966).
12. Cuadra, C. A., Katter, R. V., Holmes, E. H., and Wallace, E. M., "Experimental Studies of Relevance Judgments," Final Rep. Nos. TM-3520/001, TM-3520/003. Systems Develop. Corp., Santa Monica, California, 1967.
13. Herring, C., "Distill or Drown: The Need for Reviews." *Phys. Today* **21,** 27–33 (1968).
14. Branscomb, L. M., "Is the Literature Worth Reviewing?" *Sci. Res.* **3,** No. 11, 49 (1968).
14a. Kochen, M. ed., "The Growth of Knowledge." Wiley, New York, 1967.
15. Chomsky, N., "Cartesian Linguistics." Harper, New York, 1966.
16. Kochen, M., "Automatic Question-Answering of English-Like Questions About Simple Diagrams." *J. Assoc. Comput. Mach.* **16,** 26–48 (1969).
17. Harrah, D., "Communication: A Logical Model." M.I.T. Press, Cambridge, Massachusetts, 1963.
18. Kuhn, T., "The Structure of the Scientific Revolution." Univ. of Chicago Press, Chicago, Illinois, 1962.
19. Silverman, C., and Halbert, M., "Relevancy Revisited." *Proc. Amer. Doc. Inst. Ann. Meeting* **4,** 53–58 (1967).

20. Mooers, C., "A Mathematical Theory of Language Symbols in Retrieval." *Internat. Conf. Sci. Information* 11, 1327–1364 (1958).

21. Taube, M., "A Note on the Pseudo-Mathematics of Relevance." *Amer. Doc.* 16, 69–72 (1965).

22. Baxendale, P., "An Empirical Model for Computer Indexing." "Machine Indexing: Progress and Problems," p. 267. Amer. Univ., Washington, D.C., 1961.

23. Luhn, H. P., "Keyword-in-Context Index for Technical Literature." IBM ASDD Rep. RC-127, p. 16 (1959). IBM, Yorktown Heights, New York. Also in *Amer. Doc.* 11, 288–295 (1960).

24. Williams, T. M., "Topic Charting and Paraphrase Collecting Through Use of a Multi-dimensional Grammar." "Automatic and Scientific Communication Short Paper," Pt. I, pp. 47–50. *Amer. Doc. Inst.*, Washington, D.C., 1963.

25. Amer. Math. Soc., Math. Offprint Serv., Providence, Rhode Island.

26. Phelps, R. H., "Alternatives to the Scientific Periodical." *UNESCO Bull. Library* 14, 61–75 (1960).

27. Luhn, H. P., "Auto-Encoding of Documents for Information Retrieval Systems." *In* "Modern Trends in Documentation" (M. Boaz, ed.), pp. 45–58. Pergamon Press, New York, 1959.

28. Rath, G. J., A. Resnick, and Savage, T. R., "The Formation of Abstracts by the Selection of Sentences." *Amer. Doc.* 12, 139–143 (1961).

29. Tagliacozzo, R., Rosenberg, L., and Kochen, M., "Access and Recognition: From Users' Data to Catalog Entries." In Final Rep., Jan. 1970. NSF GN716.

30. Bohnert, H., "An English-like Extension of an Applied Predicate Calculus," *In* "High Speed Document Perusal" by M. Kochen, ed., pp. 83–96, Final Tech. Rep., AFSOR-2817, 1962.

31. Robinson, J. A., "The Generalized Resolution Principle." *In* "Machine Intelligence," Vol. 3. Amer. Elsevier, New York, 1968.

32. Darlington, T. L., "Translating Ordinary Language into Symbolic Logic," MAC-M-149. M.I.T., Cambridge, Massachusetts, 1964.

33. Elsdon-Dew, R., "The Library from the Point of View of the Research Worker." *South African Libraries* 23, 51–54 (1955).

34. Flood, M. M., "The Travelling Salesman Problem." *Operations Res.* 4, 61–75 (1956).

35. Crane, D., "The Gatekeepers of Science: Some Factors Affecting the Selection of Articles for Scientific Journals." *Amer. Sociologist* 32, 195–201 (1967).

36. Goudsmit, S. A., "What Happened to My Paper." *Phys. Today* 22, 23–25 (1969).

37. IBM "DATATEXT, Information to DATATEXT." IBM Tech. Publ. Dep., White Plains, New York, 1967.

38. IBM "IBM Magnetic Tape Selectric Typewriter," Training Manual. IBM, Office Products Div., White Plains, New York, 1969.

39. ASTROTYPE. Information Control Systems, Inc., Automatic Office Div., Ann Arbor, Michigan, 1969.

40. Reisner, P., "Semantic Diversity and a Growing Man-Machine Thesaurus." *In* "Some Problems in Information Science," M. Kochen, Ed., pp. 117–130. Scarecrow Press, Metuchen, New Jersey, 1965.

41. Montgomery, C., and Swanson, D., "Machinelike Indexing by People." *Amer. Doc.* 13, 369–366 (1962).

42. Salton, G., "Automatic Information Organization and Retrieval." McGraw-Hill, New York, 1968.

43. Magnino, J. J., "Computer Searching of Normal Text for Information Retrieval." *Patent Eng. Managers. Conf.*, June 1962. IBM, Thomas J. Watson Res. Center, Yorktown Heights, New York.

44. Damerau, F. J., "An Experiment in Automatic Indexing," IBM Res. Paper RC894. IBM, Yorktown Heights, New York, 1963.
45. *Science*, "Instructions to Reviewers." Amer. Associ. for the Advancement of Sci., 1515 Massachusetts Ave., NW, Washington, D. C. 20005.
46. Janda, K., "Information Retrieval: Applications to Political Science." Bobbs-Merrill, New York, 1968.

ISL—A New Programming Language for Information Retrieval

R. T. Chien, S. R. Ray, and F. A. Stahl

COORDINATED SCIENCE LABORATORY
UNIVERSITY OF ILLINOIS
URBANA, ILLINOIS

I. Introduction

Information retrieval systems have been an important research area for many years. Its broad impact on a variety of applications such as library automation and management information systems is well recognized. Recent developments in hardware, particularly in the area of large fast-access files have provided the basis for the development of large scale on-line information systems.

The efficiency of an information retrieval system is, however, highly dependent on the software it is implemented in. For on-line systems particular attention must be given to those features that would facilitate man–machine communication. After some careful consideration, it is felt that although languages like SNOBOL [1] and COMIT [2] have some very attractive features, none of the existing languages has been specifically designed for information retrieval. In particular, it is reasonable to expect that a language designed for information retrieval should have at least the following features:

1. The language must have interactive instructions for controlling display terminals.
2. There must be instructions to contol all I/O devices.
3. There must be instructions to do string manipulation.
4. There must be no software imposed data structuring.
5. The ability to construct efficient search strategies.
6. The ability to do numerical computations, logical operations, and transfers.
7. The availability of a utility sort routine.

55

The Information Search Language (ISL) [3, 4] is an attempt to put the important features needed for the design of information retrieval systems all in one package. The details of the design are given in the following two sections. In order to best illustrate the capability of ISL as an information retrieval language, two application programs REQUEST and RECALL will then be described.

The REQUEST Interactive Document Retrieval System [5] interprets queries in the form of a multiple-level Boolean hierarchy. It receives, displays, and then translates the query into a format which can be used to interrogate a bibliographic collection accessible through the computer's bulk storage, and then disseminate the results of the interrogation for display, printing, or storage on magnetic tape.

RECALL [6] is a set of programs that receives questions and a data base in natural language and attempts to *recall* those statements in the data base that could best be used in answering the question. A variety of strategy techniques are available.

II. The Information Search Language

ISL consists of a basic language, a sophisticated assembler, ILLAR [7, 8], and a large and expanding set of subprograms to handle special functions of the system, and an interactive program that allows programmers to initiate commands from a display console.

The ISL language has been designed in such a fashion as to allow sophisticated programming (as, for instance, the application programs described) and yet be very easily used by persons who have had very little programming experience. At first the user need only become familiar with a very modest number of easy to use instructions to input, manipulate, and output the data. In addition, if the manipulation is such that it requires decisions on the part of the user, then the interactive mode instructions may be used to alter the program. Knowledge of machine language is not necessary at all in order to use the basic language.

Since the ISL language is embedded in the ILLAR system, any of the features of ILLAR are available to the ISL programmer who wishes to take advantage of them. Of course, all of the machine language operations basic to the CDC 1604 computer are available for use.

The ILLAR system offers the following additional features: recursive subroutine capability, recursive MACRO capability, system MACRO capability, FORTRAN-like CALL with arguments, FORTRAN-like compile arithmetic operations, subroutine communication through arguments, automatic compilation of index save–restore conversions, symbolic address arithmetic, literal element and literal string capability, utility sort–merge routine, seventy-five pseudo-instructions. It should be stressed that the system macro capability proved invaluable for the implementation of ISL.

Furthermore, any FORTRAN statement can be used in an ISL program. Thus, all the powerful features of FORTRAN-like DO loops, arrays, COMMON, etc. are available.

III. The Basic ISL Language

The basic ISL language consists of the following five groups of instructions:

(1) *Word-oriented instructions:* LOAD, STORE, PLUS, MINUS, CON-VERT. LOAD, STORE, PLUS, and MINUS are concerned with arithmetic operations on the ISL "accumulator." The CONVERT instruction converts numbers to BCD character strings.

(2) *Character-oriented instructions:* STRING, MOVE, SEARCH, VSEARCH, SEEK, PUSH, POP. The STRING instruction is used to define strings of characters. The MOVE instruction allows the moving of a string from one area to another.

The SEARCH and VSEARCH instructions specify what string of characters is to be searched for, and what string is to be scanned. These instructions return a success–fail flag. Upon success they return location of the " matched " string of characters. Included in the search specification string may be any number of " don't care " characters. The " don't care " character is used in the string of characters to be searched for, to indicate that we " don't care " what characters come between the previous string and the following string. A detailed description of the SEARCH instruction can be found in the appendix.

The SEEK instruction is used to look for the occurrence of a single given character in a string. Although its function could be performed by the SEARCH instruction, the SEEK is much faster and has the added feature that it will seek in either direction on a character string. The PUSH and POP instructions are used to examine and replace characters of a string.

(3) *Transfer instructions:* IF, GOTO, TJUMP, LJUMP. The IF instruction is a conditional transfer and the GOTO instruction is an unconditional transfer. The TJUMP instruction is a multiple-branch transfer, based on typewriter control. The LJUMP instruction is the same as the TJUMP except that it is based on light-pen control.

(4) *I/O instructions:* TSTRING, READ, WRITE, PRINT, ISLTV, TVOFF/STOPTV, STRTTV. These instructions allow extremely easy use of the peripheral equipment. In interactive programs the execution of the

TSTRING instruction allows the user to enter a character string from the console typewriter. The PRINT instruction allows the programmer to specify the string to be printed, the column number in which to start, and how many lines to skip.

There are two instructions used to display character strings. The first of these is ISLTV which simply displays string with no checking of number of characters on a line, total number of characters, or total number of lines. The other routine STRTTV checks all of these items and ensures that what is put out to the scope does not wrap around the end of a line or the bottom of the screen. In the event that the characters will not fit on the screen, this routine provides light-pen pointers which allow a scroll-like roll of lines of characters up and down on the screen. An example of this is given in Figure 2 (in Section IV). The routine also has provision for taking photographs of the material displayed or printing what is displayed on the screen.

Because of the nature of ISL, the tape READ and WRITE routines are also oriented toward strings of characters rather than "card-images." ISL tape records are in variable length format and bookkeeping is done exclusively by the READ and WRITE routines.

(5) *Entry and exit:* BEGIN, RETURN. The BEGIN and RETURN statements in ISL take care of entry to and exit from ISL programs or subprograms. These instructions communicate the necessary arguments and facilitate the modularization of the system.

IV. Description of the REQUEST System

The REQUEST system is a series of interdependent interactive programs written in the ISL system. It *receives*, *displays*, and *translates* a user's query into a format that can interrogate a bibliographic collection accessible through the computer's bulk storage and then disseminate the results of the interrogation for *display*, *printing*, or *storage on magnetic tape* for later use. The form and content of the bibliographic collection is described elsewhere [5, 9].

In order to best illustrate the use of this system, we give a number of annotated examples. In the figures that follow, the underlined portions are the responses of the REQUEST system, the " ∧ " represents a carriage return typed by the user, and the " . " is typed by the user to terminate a subdivisional response. All parts not underlined are typed by the user.

EXAMPLE 1. Find all documents in the collection that cite articles by Borko. Figure 1 represents the various stages through which a user passes in stating this query.

Initially REQUEST asks the user for a query and the user states that the desired information is located in the citation part of the document. REQUEST

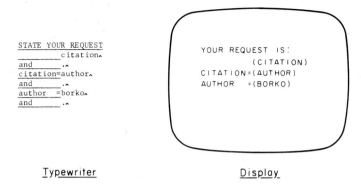

STATE YOUR REQUEST
_____citation.^
and _____.^
citation=author.^
and _____.^
author _=borko.^
and _____.^

YOUR REQUEST IS:
                    (CITATION)
CITATION=(AUTHOR)
AUTHOR   =(BORKO)

Typewriter   Display

FIGURE 1. Example of a simple query to the REQUEST system.

responds by asking what to look for regarding the citation part. The user replies, "look for the author." Finally, REQUEST asks what to look for regarding the author. The user replies the author's name. At this point REQUEST recognizes that the query has been completely stated and awaits a command from the user regarding the next phase of operation. The user may now: (1) reformulate the query, (2) get a printed copy of the query as

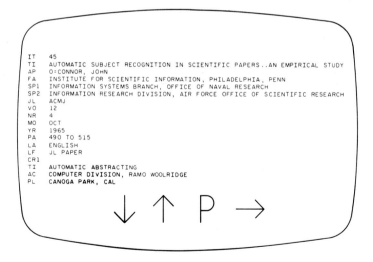

```
IT   45
TI   AUTOMATIC SUBJECT RECOGNITION IN SCIENTIFIC PAPERS..AN EMPIRICAL STUDY
AP   O:CONNOR, JOHN
FA   INSTITUTE FOR SCIENTIFIC INFORMATION, PHILADELPHIA, PENN
SP1  INFORMATION SYSTEMS BRANCH, OFFICE OF NAVAL RESEARCH
SP2  INFORMATION RESEARCH DIVISION, AIR FORCE OFFICE OF SCIENTIFIC RESEARCH
JL   ACMJ
VO   12
NR   4
MO   OCT
YR   1965
PA   490 TO 515
LA   ENGLISH
LF   JL PAPER
CR1
TI   AUTOMATIC ABSTRACTING
AC   COMPUTER DIVISION, RAMO WOOLRIDGE
PL   CANOGA PARK, CAL
```

↓ ↑ P →

FIGURE 2. Document data on the display scope.

it appears on the scope, (3) get a Polaroid photo of the query as it appears on the scope, or (4) initiate the interrogation. The user may choose (2) or (3) as many times as desired by typing PRINT or PHOTO for each copy, and then initiate either (1) or (4) by typing ERROR or SEARCH.

The command SEARCH initiates the interrogation of the bibliographic collection. Upon finding a document which satisfies the query, the REQUEST system displays the document data on the scope as in Figure 2.

The text represents the bibliographic material regarding the document that satisfied the query. Many times the entire text cannot be displayed on the scope, so the first two arrows at the bottom of the scope are used to "roll" the text in scroll fashion in front of the user. The P takes a photo of only the textual material appearing on the scope. After sufficient examination of the bibliographic material the user may press the light-pen against the right-most arrow to display a list of further options as in Figure 3. These options are:

1. RESTART—tells REQUEST that the user wants to formulate another query.
2. CONTINUE—tells REQUEST to look for another document that satisfies the current query.
3. EXIT—tells REQUEST to return the ILLAR monitor.
4. HOLD—tells REQUEST to restore current document as illustrated in Figure 2.
5. PRINT—tells REQUEST to print the entire current document.
6. TAPE7—tells REQUEST to store the current document on magnetic tape 7.

Thus, the user may build up a collection of desirable bibliographic references using the above-mentioned techniques. The user may choose to build up his collection on photos, printed copy, or magnetic tape. If he chooses the magnetic tape collection scheme, he may, by use of other available system

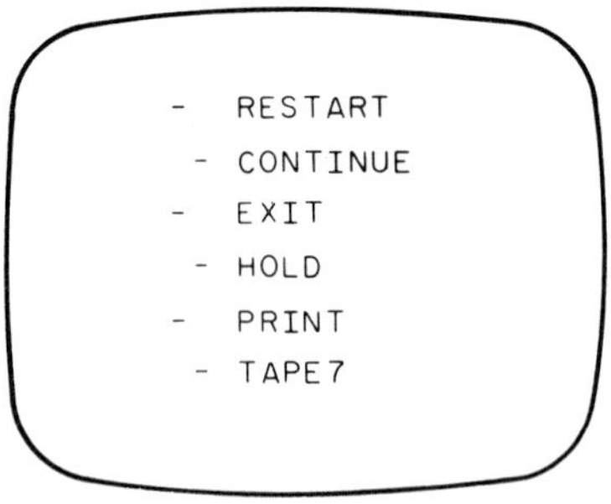

- RESTART
- CONTINUE
- EXIT
- HOLD
- PRINT
- TAPE 7

FIGURE 3 Options available to the REQUEST user.

routines, display, print, photograph, or duplicate onto another magnetic tape any part of the contents of his collection.

EXAMPLE 2. Find all articles in the collection that cite either Borko or Jacobson. The transmission of this query to REQUEST proceeds as in Figure 4. Here the logical *or* " + " indicates that the descriptor AUTHOR can be satisfied by either of the authors. In the same manner the user may at any point use the " + " feature. Some examples are given in Table I.

EXAMPLE 3. Find all documents in the collection that cite articles by Borko and Jacobson. Again we proceed as in the previous examples, but this time we respond as in Figure 5. Here, the logical *and* "*" indicates that the descriptor AUTHOR must be satisfied by the occurrence of *both* authors' names. Again, the "*" feature may be used at any point. Some examples are given in Table II. Of course, we may combine the use of the " + " and "*" features, as for example in Figure 6 and, in general, we may express any "product of sums" of terms by this technique.

EXAMPLE 4. Find all documents in the collection that are either written by or reference Borko. Notice in Figure 7 that both SOURCE and CITATION are satisfied by a variable called AUTHOR which has the value BORKO in *both* cases. Also, note that the REQUEST system only asks for the value of AUTHOR once. REQUEST assumes that if multiple occurrences of a variable term appear, then this variable term has only one interpretation, where a variable term is any term that can appear to the left of an equal sign, e.g., SOURCE, CITATION, AUTHOR in Figure 7.

EXAMPLE 5. In contrast, suppose that the user wants to find all documents in the collection that are written by Borko or reference Jacobson. This is realized in Figure 8. Notice that if the user replies

$$\text{author2} = \text{borko}$$

the resultant query is equivalent to that in Example 4.

The rules that govern the choosing of the variable term names, e.g., AUTHOR, AUTHOR1, AUTHOR2, etc., are as follows:

1. No variable term may exceed eight characters.
2. The first character of the variable term must be chosen in accordance with Table III.
3. All subsequent characters are chosen at the users' discretion, except for the use of the blank and + characters.

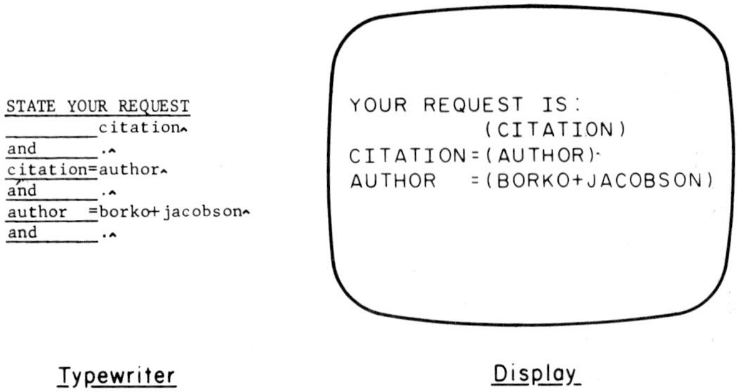

```
STATE YOUR REQUEST
                citation˄
_____ and         .˄
citation=author˄
  and           .˄
author  =borko+jacobson˄
  and           .˄
```

```
YOUR REQUEST IS:
            (CITATION)
CITATION=(AUTHOR)·
AUTHOR  =(BORKO+JACOBSON)
```

Typewriter   Display

FIGURE 4. Example of the use of the OR feature.

TABLE I

Typewriter	Display
source+citation˄ _and ___ .˄	(SOURCE+CITATION)
source = journal+publish+year˄ and ___ .˄	SOURCE = (JOURNAL+PUBLISH+YEAR)
citation=title+author˄ and ___ .˄	CITATION=(TITLE+AUTHOR)
year = 1966+1967+1968+1969˄ and ___ .˄	YEAR = (1966+1967+1968+1969)

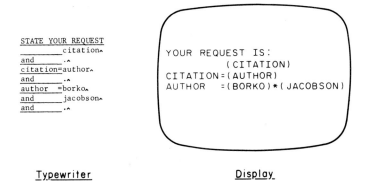

STATE YOUR REQUEST
_____citation.^
and_____.^
citation=author.^
and_____.^
author =borko.^
and_____jacobson.^
and_____.^

YOUR REQUEST IS:
          (CITATION)
CITATION = (AUTHOR)
AUTHOR   = (BORKO) * (JACOBSON)

Typewriter   Display

FIGURE 5. Example of the use of the AND feature.

TABLE II

Typewriter	Display
_____source.^ _____citation.^ and_____.^	(SOURCE) * (CITATION)
source =journal.^ and_____month.^ and_____year.^ and_____.^	SOURCE = (JOURNAL) * (MONTH) * (YEAR)
citation=title.^ and_____author.^ and_____.^	CITATION = (TITLE) * (AUTHOR)
title =information.^ and_____retrieval.^ and_____.^	TITLE = (INFORMATION) * (RETRIEVAL)

TABLE III

FIRST CHARACTER BY CATEGORY

Character	Category
A	Author
C	Citation
D	Descriptor
E	Edition
F	Affiliation
G	Page
I	Item
J	Journal
K	Acknowledged person
L	Language or Literary form
M	Month
N	Number
P	Place, publisher, part
R	Referring string
S	Source
T	Title
U	Universal (no restriction)
W	Sponsor
X	Chapter
Y	Year

A *literal* is any term that is not a variable term, e.g., BORKO, JACOBSON, INFORMATION RETRIEVAL, and, in general, any string of characters with the following restrictions:

1. No literal term may contain a " + ." The " + " is reserved for the " + " feature that "or's" two or more terms.
2. The last literal term used with the " + " feature (including the vacuous case) may not terminate in a blank character. If terminal blanks are desired, the user must indicate so by use of a " % " immediately following the last blank. Otherwise, a terminal blank character causes the entire working line to be erased. Thus, if the user wants to type " INFORMATION RETRIEVAL + AUTOMATIC INDEXING " and types " INFORNA ... " by mistake, he may type a blank and a carriage return causing the line to be erased and permitting the line to be typed again.

As a final example we demonstrate a more sophisticated query using most of the features available.

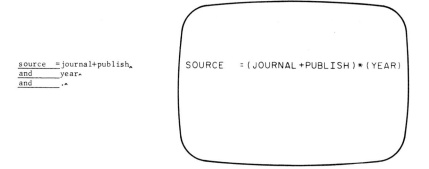

Typewriter   Display

FIGURE 6. Example of the use of both the AND and OR features.

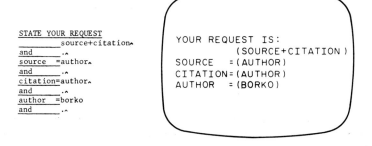

Typewriter   Display

FIGURE 7. Example of the use of a variable term.

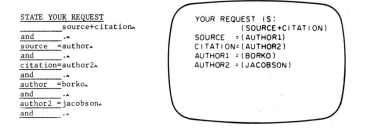

Typewriter   Display

FIGURE 8. Statement of the query in Example 5.

EXAMPLE 6. Journal papers written since 1967 dealing with information retrieval that reference journal or technical papers written by Borko on information retrieval. A statement of this query appears in Figure 9 and a sample retrieval appears in Figure 2.

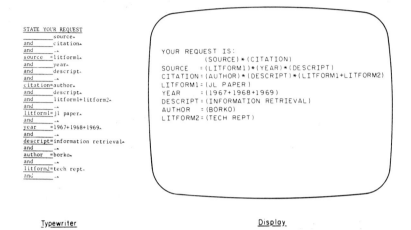

Typewriter   Display

FIGURE 9. Statement of the query in Example 6.

V. Description of the RECALL System

The RECALL system is a series of interdependent programs written in ISL designed to *recall* those statements in a natural language data base that could best be used in answering a given question, also in natural language.

There are two basic sets of programs: the phrase dictionary construction programs and the programs to try different strategies of recall on the data base.

Each entry in the phrase dictionary construction contains a maximal phrase and a set of pointers that refer to statements.

Maximal phrases are arrived at in the following manner:

1. Sentences of the data base are numbered consecutively.

2. A WIS index is processed on the sentences from (1). WIS means words in sentence, its name is derived from KWIC where we consider all words not just key words and the context is a sentence.

3. Consecutive entries of the index are compared to find the longest string of words that match. Thus, if

STOP AT A STOP SIGN ... 239
STOP AT A RED LIGHT ... 646

were consecutive entries, then

STOP AT A 239, 646

would be recorded.

4. Remove the prefixes from the output of (3). If one entry is the beginning part of another entry, and if these two entries have any numbers in common, then the numbers that are common to both are removed from the former. If an entry results with no numbers, it is deleted, i.e.,

STOP   239, 362, 424, 749
STOP AT   239, 646
STOP AT A 239, 646, 932

would result as

STOP   362, 424, 749
STOP AT A 932

5. The output from (4) is reverse sorted. That is, if an entry were

STOP AT A

it would be sorted as if it were spelled

A TA POTS

This results in a list of entries that have similar endings like

GO TO A
STOP AT A
HALT AT A

6. The suffixes from the output of (5) are removed. This is an analogous operation to removing the prefixes in (4). Thus if:

THE BOOK   269, 348
OF THE BOOK   269, 348, 729

were entries then

OF THE BOOK   269, 348, 729

would be recorded.

7. The output of (6) is re-sorted into normal alphabetical order.

The remaining phrases are called maximal phrases because they represent the longest strings of continuous text that are common to more than one sentence. Once the maximal phrases are determined they are listed along with the statement numbers in which they occur.

The phrase dictionary is used to recall relevant statements from the data base with respect to a given question. A variety of strategies are used to determine which statements should be considered. Some of the strategy techniques are described below.

1. Find all the maximal phrases of a given question and retrieve each of the corresponding statement numbers.
2. Find the maximal phrases of the question and retrieve only those statements that have two occurrences, three occurrences, etc.
3. Find the maximal phrases of the question and for each statement number also consider statement numbers $n - 1$ and $n + 1$.
4. Find the maximal phrases of the question and delete those that occur inside some other maximal phrase.
5. Find the maximal phrases of the question and choose only those statement numbers corresponding to the longest maximal phrase.

The following are sample recalls of these techniques:

EXAMPLE 7
Question:
How close can I park to a fire hydrant?

Relevant statement:
Parking is prohibited within 15 feet of a fire hydrant.

EXAMPLE 8
Question:
What does an octagonal sign mean?

Relevant statement:
An octagonal sign means stop.

VI. Conclusion

In this paper we have listed the necessary features of a language for information retrieval purposes. A new language ISL has been designed to incorporate these features in one package. In order to best illustrate the capabilities of ISL as a powerful tool in information retrieval research, two application programs, REQUEST and RECALL have been described in detail.

Both REQUEST and RECALL are components of information retrieval systems currently being developed, the discussion of which is beyond the scope of this paper. Therefore, we have limited our attention to those aspects of REQUEST and RECALL that are relevant to use of ISL.

Appendix

SPECIFICATION OF THE SEARCH INSTRUCTION

SEARCH—Search for a specified string of characters.

Form (a)   search $(x_1 x_2 x_3 \cdots x_n;) a1, a2, f, b1, b2$
      (b)   search   alpha, $a1, a2, f, b1, b2$

A continuous character string, the data string, is assumed to start at the value of $a1$ and end at the value of $a2$. The search specification string is given by the characters $x_1 x_2 x_3 \cdots x_n$ in form (a) or is defined by alpha in form (b) where alpha is the address of a string of characters elsewhere in the program. An attempt is made to match the specification string on the data string. If the attempt is successful, the value of f is set positive and the beginning and end addresses of the matched portion of the data string are placed in $b1$ and $b2$, respectively. If the match is not successful, f is set negative and $b1$ and $b2$ are left undefined.

Any one or more of the x_i (except for x_i and x_n or two adjacent x_i's) may be the "don't care" character ":" (colon). The presence of this character as x_i indicates we don't care how many or what characters occur in the data string between the match to x_{i-1} and the match to x_{i+1}.

ACKNOWLEDGMENTS

The authors wish to express their thanks to Messrs. Karl Kelley and Donald Lee of the Computer Group of the Coordinated Science Laboratory for their help in implementing the work described in this paper. This work was supported by the Office of Education under Contract No. OE C-1-7-071213-4557 and by the Joint Services Electronics Program (U.S. Army, U.S. Navy, and U.S. Air Force) under contract DAAB-07-67-C-0199.

REFERENCES

1. Farber, D. J., Griswold, R. E., and Polonsky, I. P., "The SNOBOL3 Programming Language." *Bell System Tech. J.* **45**, 895–944 (1966).
2. Yngve, V. H., "COMIT Programmer's Reference Manual." M.I.T. Press, Cambridge, Massachusetts, 1961.
3. Kelley, K. C., Ray, S. R., and Stahl, F. A., "Information Search Language," File No. 735. Dept. of Computer Science, Univ. of Illinois, Urbana, Illinois, 1967.
4. Kelley, K. C., Ray, S. R., and Stahl, F. A., "ISL—A String Manipulating Language," R-407. Coordinated Sci. Lab., Univ. of Illinois, Urbana, Illinois, 1969.
5. Carroll, D. E., Chien, R. T., Kelley, K. C., Preparata, F. P., Ray, S. R., Reynolds, P. R., and Stahl, F. A., "An Interactive Document Retrieval System," R-398. Coordinated Sci. Lab., Univ. of Illinois, Urbana, Illinois, 1968.

6. Jansen, J. M. Jr., "Phrase Dictionary Construction Methods for the R2 Information Retrieval System," R–449 Coordinated Sci. Lab., Univ. of Illinois, Urbana, Illinois, 1969.
7. ILLAR Assembly Program, Coordinated Sci. Lab., Univ. of Illinois, Urbana, Illinois, 1969.
8. ILLSYS Bulletin, Coordinated Sci. Lab., Univ. of Illinois, Urbana, Illinois, 1968.
9. Carroll, D. E., "Guidelines for an Information Retrieval Data Base." Coordinated Sci. Lab., Univ. of Illinois, Urbana, Illinois, to be published.

An Error Analysis for Functions of Qualitative Attributes with Application to Information Retrieval

D. M. Jackson†
CORNELL UNIVERSITY
ITHACA, NEW YORK

I. Preliminary Considerations

The types of classification which will be considered are unusual in that classes are intentionally allowed to overlap. The role of overlap between classes of terms as a possible precision device in information retrieval is clear, since the different senses or contextual uses of a term or keyword may be identified by determining the term's affiliations to different classes. In many applications, however, it is a requirement that the objects to be classified should be assigned to disjoint classes, and the clustering and hierarchical methods for achieving this comprise the main bulk of classification techniques. In plant taxonomy, for example, where the objectives are somewhat different, since categorical differences between the objects to be classified are of primary importance, Williams and Dale [1] are skeptical about the use of overlapping classifications. Techniques appropriate to these applications are given by Sokal and Sneath [2]. Nevertheless techniques for constructing overlapping classifications have been applied by Parker-Rhodes [3] and by Parker-Rhodes and myself [4] to mycological data containing ecological and meteorological descriptors, with some measure of success.

In information retrieval we are interested in forming classes of terms in such a way that they may be used to achieve an increase in retrieval performance. There is, however, no a priori reason for claiming that a particular classification, in which the members of the classes are related in some specific way, is better than any other classification of the terms. The value of a classification is determined empirically by evaluating the effect on retrieval performance when the classification is incorporated into the system. Thus, in constructing classifications for information retrieval, the Platonic concept of error in the assignment of terms to classes is entirely absent. That is, there is

† *Present affiliation:* The Ohio State University, Columbus, Ohio.

no prior classification which automatic techniques are intended to reconstruct in detail; and there is therefore no basis for the probabilistic assignment of terms to classes to give the extent that properties of particular terms in the vocabulary are inferable from a knowledge of the classes to which each belongs. Sutcliffe [5, 6] has attempted to replace the Platonic concept of error by comparing statistically a large number of classifications of the same population to determine the typical and atypical allocation of objects to classes. The stringent conditions under which observations on the objects must be made so that atypical class allocation may be adopted as an indication of error make this approach inapplicable in information retrieval.

Certain classifications suggest themselves as devices for improving retrieval performance, and it is quite consistent to assert that these improve retrieval performance provided that such an assertion is phrased in terms of an hypothesis which is susceptible to testing. It may be supposed, for example, that a classification of the term vocabulary into groups of synonyms can be used to improve the performance of a retrieval system beyond that obtained with other classifications. Gotlieb and Kumar [7] have proposed another classification based on the a priori (preassigned) semantic relationships between terms rather than on the relative frequency with which terms occur together in documents. The assertion that a particular classification improves performance for a particular collection may be tested directly by evaluating the effect of the classification on retrieval performance, and the validity of the assertion for document collections in general may be determined provided sufficiently many document collections are examined. However, the success with which terms have been arranged into groups of synonyms must be determined by inspection of the classes and an intuitive assessment of the constitution of each class. As a relation between terms, synonymy is quite strong and, indeed, methods have been proposed for isolating synonyms automatically by Sparck Jones [8] and by Lewis *et al.* [9]. Topical relatedness is, however, less definite and the answer to the question whether two terms are topically related (that is, the two terms may relate to the same topic area), as opposed to synonymously related, is less obvious. In probabilistic classifications, the probability of the assignment of terms to a class gives the reliability of the information conveyed by asserting that the term belongs to the class. Topical relatedness is not sufficiently definite a relationship in the first place to permit the calculation of probabilities with any degree of accuracy. Accordingly a classification in which the assignment of terms to classes is nonprobabilistic is more appropriate for dealing with topical relatedness.

The classifications which will be considered consist of nonhierarchically arranged classes of terms which show a marked tendency to occur together in the documents of the collection. The classes formed by this criterion will hopefully specify topic areas within the field covered by the collection, and accordingly terms which appear together in the same class will be said to be topically related. The criterion on which classes are formed is a weak one in that classes are to be composed of terms which *tend* to occur together in the documents of the collection. The criterion is therefore less restrictive than that for cliques† in which the classificatory criterion must be exhibited between every pair of objects belonging to a clique. A further requirement of the classification is that the classes be self-generated‡ in the following sense. Classes are defined as sets of terms which satisfy the classificatory criterion, and the complete term vocabulary must be explored to find such classes. It is inadmissible to specify a set of possible topic classes *ab initio*, and subsequently to distribute the terms to the most appropriate of these since, first, these classes must be treated as unknown; second, significant yet intuitively obscure classes would not be located; and third, the number of classes required is unknown. Such procedures, for example Sebestyen's [10], might however be adopted as an economical means of updating an existing classification to avoid complete reclassification of the term vocabulary as the document collection expands.

II. The Measurement of Similarity

Automatic classification is concerned with assigning objects to classes according to the information about each of the objects. The objects to be classified are described or defined in terms of measurements or observations made upon them, and the information is characteristically conveyed by specifying the qualitative or quantitative attributes which the objects possess. Qualitative attributes are sometimes called "qualities," and may be two state, indicating the presence or absence of the quality, or may be multistate. The attribute "leaf-shape," for example, in which linear, obovoid, and pandurate must be distinguished, is three-state. The attribute "leaf-length," possibly averaged over a suitable sample, is quantitative. A great deal of discussion in taxonomic literature has been devoted to the problems arising from the interdependence of attributes. Suppose, for example, that the binary attributes "black" and "white" were used in describing the objects of a population. Then, provided that these attributes were relevant to the population, the value of one of the attributes would determine the value of the other. A less obvious example is given by the use of "carnivorous" and "ungual." Here the dependence is not a logical one. Sokal and Sneath ([2], p. 66) are of the opinion that dependencies between attributes, which are known without recourse to

† A *clique* is a maximal complete subgraph of a graph in which the presence of an arc between a pair of nodes indicates that the nodes are related. The degree of relatedness may be specified by the length of the arc.

‡ Williams and Dale ([1], p. 38) use the term "self-structuring."

analysis, must be eliminated before the objects are classified. Williams and Dale ([1], p. 42) while admitting that such dependencies may dominate the analysis, consider that their use in classification is a matter of taste—the sole criterion is the interest or otherwise of the user. Thus, since the dependence between "carnivorous" and "ungual" has been established, subsequent users can afford to be more sophisticated in their choice of initial attributes. The problem corresponds in information retrieval to the presence of terms which co-occur frequently compared with the frequency of co-occurrence of either term. The acceptability of the dependencies must be determined by their effect on retrieval performance. There is evidence that they have a deleterious effect. The dependence, however, is not a logical one.

Suppose that x and y are two objects of a population U and suppose that $d(x, y)$ is the similarity between x and y. Then the following conditions are imposed:

a. $d(x, y) = d(y, x)$ for all x, y in U (symmetry),
b. $d(x, y) \geq 0$ for all x, y in U,
c. $d(x, y) = 0$ if $x = y$ for x, y in U (indistinguishability of identical objects),
d. $d(x, y) = 0$ only if $x = y$ for x, y in U (distinguishability of nonidentical objects),
e. $d(x, z) \leq d(x, y) + d(y, z)$ for all x, y, z in U (triangle inequality).

A distance function which satisfies (a)–(e) is called Euclidean. A function in which (e) is not everywhere true is called a quasimetric. A function in which (d) is not everywhere true is called pseudometric (or semimetric). Functions have been examined for which (e) is replaced by the more restrictive condition:

e'. $d(x, z) \leq \max(d(x, y), d(y, z))$ for all x, y, z in U.

Functions which satisfy (e') are called ultrametric, and their use in constructing taxonomic hierarchies has been discussed by Johnson [11] and by Jardine et al. [12]. A number of functions satisfying some or all of (a)–(e) have been proposed for information retrieval and for wider applications. Typical among the functions used in ecology and anthropology, for example, are those of Pearson [13], Mahalanobis [14], and Rao [15]. These functions are intended for use when the descriptions of the objects to be classified themselves result from the statistical determination of the mean and variance of a character or attribute over a sample of all instances of the object in the population. The counterpart in information retrieval is the determination of the "distance" or similarity between index terms, taking account of the variability in the assignment of terms to documents by a sufficiently large number of indexers independently indexing the collection. The virtue of the uniterm indexing scheme rests in its simplicity and cheapness to apply in practice. The possibility of repeated indexing of the same document collection would grossly add to the cost of obtaining the initial index descriptions, and therefore cannot be considered.

Observations on the terms of the vocabulary consist of the names (call numbers) of those documents to which the terms have been assigned. Since the documents of the collection are indexed using uniterms, each document may be characterized by a vector whose components, one or zero, indicate whether or not a particular term has been used in indexing the document. The complete collection may therefore be represented by a rectangular array, D, the ith row of which gives the index description of the ith document. $D_{ij} = 0$ indicates that document i has not been indexed by term j, while $D_{ij} = 1$ indicates that it has. Since, in associative retrieval, it is the terms which are to be classified by their co-occurrence in documents, the terms are the objects of the universe (the term vocabulary) while the documents are two-state or binary attributes. D is called the document array or the document matrix. Co-occurrence of terms within documents may be determined from the matrix D quite simply. Consider two terms t_j and t_k. Then the frequency of co-occurrence of the terms is given by $|D_{\cdot j} \wedge D_{\cdot k}|$ where $D_{\cdot j}$ denotes the jth column of the document array D. The relative frequency of co-occurrence of terms within documents may now be defined as:

$$s_1(t_j, t_k) = |D_{\cdot j} \wedge D_{\cdot k}| / |D_{\cdot j} \vee D_{\cdot k}|. \tag{1}$$

This is a quasimetric and varies between 0, when t_j and t_k never occur together, and 1, when t_j and t_k always occur together. The function, which arises naturally in information retrieval, is ascribed to Tanimoto [16]. It is biased in favor of positive occurrence of terms in documents. The common nonoccurrence of terms in a document does not contribute toward the similarity of the two terms. It has already been seen in Section I that the similarity between pairs of terms is based on actual occurrence of terms in documents. A symmetrical form of the function may, however, be defined. A function with similar properties is the correlation coefficient, defined by

$$s_2(t_j, t_k) = \left(\frac{|D_{\cdot j} \wedge D_{\cdot k}|^2}{|D_{\cdot j}| \cdot |D_{\cdot k}|} \right)^{1/2}. \tag{2}$$

It is clear that other functions may be defined for calculating the similarity between pairs of terms based on their frequency of co-occurrence within documents. Account may be taken, for example, of the variation in the numbers of terms assigned to documents. The functions defined above, however, have the substantial practical advantage of making the manual inspection of classes, member by member, a relatively straightforward matter.

III. Constraints on Classification Algorithms

The following are constraints generally placed on classification algorithms:

a. The classification must be *well defined*. That is, application of the algorithm must supply a single result.

b. The algorithm must be unaffected by a permutation of the names of the terms. That is, the algorithm must be independent of the *labeling* of the terms.

c. The algorithm must be independent of *scale*. That is, the algorithm must be unaffected by multiplication of the similarity matrix by a positive, nonzero constant.

Independence of scale is an obvious requirement since the scale of the similarity function is essentially arbitrary. The stronger condition of invariance under a monotonic transformation of the similarity function has also been suggested, and this leads to methods in which distances or similarities between objects are largely irrelevant. The methods rely on the inequalities between the similarities of pairs of objects. Similarity functions induce a partial ordering on the set of objects to be classified, and a classification is constructed such that a partial ordering derived from it agrees as closely as possible with the partial ordering induced on the data. The measurement of the agreement between the partial orderings is given by Benzécri [17]. The methods are accordingly insensitive to monotonic transformations of the similarity function, with the result that a number of similarity functions given by Sokal and Sneath may be regarded as equivalent. A review of these methods is given by de la Véga [18]. Independence of labeling requires that a classification should not be dependent on the order in which the terms are treated, and is demonstrable only in a classification in which all classes which satisfy the classificatory criterion have been enumerated. For the majority of classification algorithms, however, computational limitations prevent the discovery of all of the classes. A permutation of the names of the terms would result in a classification which, although sharing a substantial number of classes, would differ in a number of classes. The failure of (a) and (b) are related. Relabeling enables more classes to be found, and examination of all permutations corresponds to inspecting all subsets of the terms to determine which satisfy the classificatory criterion. It is clearly impracticable to examine all subsets since there are too many of them. Provided a large enough number of classes is found, the failure of (a) and (b) is unimportant.

IV. Errors in the Assignment of Attributes to Objects

In any practical application of classification techniques, errors are liable to occur during the collection or compilation of the information about the objects to be classified, and it is therefore appropriate to examine the effect of such errors on classifications subsequently produced. We shall be concerned only with sets of objects which have been described by the set of qualities which they possess. The possession of a quality is not quantified; its presence or absence only is recorded. The attributes and the objects are given numerical codes, typically integers running from 1 to m for the attributes, where m is the number of attributes used for describing the data collection, and running from 1 to n for the objects, where n is the number of objects in the population. The occurrence of the number j in the list of attributes belonging to object i indicates that object i possesses attribute j, while the absence of j indicates that object i does not possess attribute j. The following remarks describe the types of error which may occur.

a. In the large collections of information to which automatic classification procedures must be applicable, there is a certain probability of finding " transcription " errors. These errors are purely clerical in origin and arise, for example, when information is transcribed into a form suitable for processing by computer. Some of the errors may be detectable if conventions are imposed on the presentation of the data. If the attributes are required to be presented in increasing order of their code numbers, then an attribute which is out of order in the sequence of attribute code numbers relating to a given object signals an error somewhere in the sequence. Stronger conventions may be imposed on object codes if it is assumed, as a precaution, that objects which do not have a description in terms of the available attributes, have been removed. Accordingly, object codes must appear as a sequence of successive integers in increasing order of magnitude, and their failure to do so is indicative of an error. The codes themselves may be tested to ensure that they are well formed and are in the appropriate ranges, namely 1 to m for the attributes, and 1 to n for the objects.

b. The description of an object may be incomplete. There may be no way of arriving at a set of attributes adequate to describe the population of objects until some crude form of classification has been done. For example, information consisting of the " significant " and " relevant " symptoms exhibited by a set of patients may have been collected by a number of doctors. Observations made by one doctor on his patients may not have been made by another doctor on his patients, although the conditions of the patients may have been clinically similar. If information of this type, collected over a period of time, is to be classified, retrospective judgments may enable some, but probably not all, of the original information to be retrieved with some degree of accuracy.

c. The data may be heterogeneous, in the sense that a number of attributes may not be relevant to a number of the objects. Since, however, the attributes considered are binary, " not relevant " must be compounded with " absent." The situation is clarified if three-valued attributes are used, the additional value corresponding to "not relevant." Alternatively, if the number of attributes affected is small, they may be removed completely from the descriptions. unavoidably incurring, however, the removal of all their useful references to a proportion of the objects. The loss of these useful references may be a greater disadvantage than the confusion incurred by compounding "not relevant" with "absent."

d. An object may be mistakenly described by an attribute which it does not possess.

Each of these types of error may clearly occur in documentary data. (a) may occur whenever a set of documents is prepared for machine use. (b) may occur when the collection expands to include material not envisaged at the time the original documents were indexed. For example, in computer literature, the distinction now drawn between "parallel" and "series" computation may not have been made originally, although in retrospect, the distinction would have been a relevant one. Errors of type (c) obtrude, but their effect on classification may be eliminated by a suitable choice of similarity function. Provided that only the positive assignment of a pair of terms to a document contributes toward the similarity between the terms, the distinction between "not-relevant" and "absent" is immaterial. The fact that a document was not indexed by a particular pair of terms does not contribute to the similarity between the terms. The similarity function must therefore not be symmetrical in "1" and "0." Neither of the similarity functions defined in Section II are symmetrical in "1" or "0." Uniterm indexing is susceptible to errors of type (d) since no control is exercised over the term vocabulary. Techniques which reduce the effects of this type of error on subsequent classification are of particular interest.

It will be assumed throughout that errors occur independently, in that an error does not necessarily imply the existence of another. Consider, for example, the transcription errors which may arise in a binary sequence of n digits in which information is carried by the position of a digit in the sequence as well as by its value. The complete omission of a digit from the sequence implies that the subsequent digits are all shifted up by one place. Thus errors will be propagated in each subsequent digit position, after and including the omitted digit, whose value differs from the immediate neighbor to the right. Although an indexed document may be represented as a sequence of binary digits, this representation is used only when the document is processed within the computer. It will be assumed that the documents are coded initially in a form in which positional information of a term code is not utilized so that propagated or systematic errors may be reduced.

In each of these cases, it is hoped that a classification of the material may be achieved in spite of the errors the material contains. Obviously, the original information is not recoverable and the best which can be done is to ensure that the erroneous parts of the data do not exert a significant effect on the classification as a whole. Accordingly, a condition, in addition to those of Section III, must be imposed on the classification algorithm as follows. Classifications must be *stable* with respect to small changes in the material to be classified. That is, small changes in the material to be classified lead only to small changes in the classification.† For this condition to be appropriate, it must be demonstrated that small changes both in the data and in the classification are measurable quantities.

Small changes in a document array may be measured quite simply. Suppose that two document arrays are given, representing differing index descriptions of the same document collection. It is known that document i of one array may be identified with document i of the other array. The difference between the document descriptions may be discovered by inspecting row i in each array. Over the whole collection, a measure of the difference between the two arrays may be obtained by regarding the arrays as preference tables and computing Kendall's [19] coefficient of agreement.

Changes in the classifications are less easily measurable, although a classification of the type described in Section I, like the document collection, may be represented by means of a binary array. In a classification array C, the element C_{ij} of the ith row indicates the presence or absence of term j in class i. Suppose that classification arrays C and C' are produced from two document arrays D and D' which represent differing index descriptions of the same document collection. The classes of C and C' are defined extensionally and the names which are given to each class are entirely arbitrary. It is therefore not appropriate, although it was for the document arrays, to identify the ith row of C (that is, class C_i) with the ith row of C' (that is, class C_i') in the sense that the differences between D and D' cause C_i to devolve into the class C_i'. Nor is it possible to show that C and C' are conformable by determining a permutation p of the integers, such that C_i may be identified, in its extension, approximately with $C_{p(i)}$, since it cannot be assumed that C or C' exhaust the classes which may be found in D or D'. The problem of measuring small differences between pairs of classifications has been treated elsewhere by myself [20], and further details will not be given here.

V. Error Analysis

Suppose that there are M terms in the vocabulary and N documents in the collection D. The ith row of the binary array D gives the terms j which appear in the index description of document D_i. If $D_{ij} = 1$, then term j appears in

---

† A connection may be seen between *stability* and *continuity*. Suppose that a classification is produced by a transformation of the data. Small changes in the data necessarily lead to small changes in the classification, provided that the transformation is continuous. The classification is therefore stable. It is assumed here, however, that the classification algorithm cannot be regarded as a continuous transformation.

document i, while if $D_{ij} = 0$, term j does not appear in document i. The array D accordingly consists of NM bits. Errors of the type listed in Section IV (a)–(d) all have the effect of changing a "0" into a "1" or a "1" into a "0" for a number of the D_{ij}'s. The errors are assumed independent and equiprobable, as stated in Section IV. The effect of the errors is to change the array D into the array D'. Let r be the probability of finding an error in a particular D_{ij}. Thus rMN is the number of errors in the array. The number of errors which will be tolerated may be decided in advance, and from this a value of r may be obtained. Consider now two arbitrary terms t_j and t_k represented by the binary vectors A and B, both of length N, and suppose that these vectors are scrambled by errors into the vectors A' and B', the vectorial representations of the same terms in D'. In terms of the document array D, A and B are given by $D_{\cdot j}$ and $D_{\cdot k}$ respectively, where $D_{\cdot j}$ is the jth column of D. Thus (A, B) is transformed into (A', B') by a *scrambling* S. Let f and f_S be the values of similarity between A and B before and after A and B have been transformed into A' and B'. Suppose that ϕ is the function of f and f_S which is to be investigated and that ϕ^* is the statistical estimate for ϕ. For example, ϕ may be the mean square deviation. Let S^* be the set of all possible scramblings for the pairs of vectors of length N. Then

$$\phi^* = \sum_{S \text{ in } S^*} P(S)\phi(f_S, f),\qquad (3)$$

where S denotes a particular scrambling in S^*, and $P(S)$ is the probability of the particular scrambling S. Consider now a particular document i. Let A_i and B_i be the ith component of A and B. The following combinations may occur for (A_i, B_i): $(0, 0)$, $(1, 0)$, $(0, 1)$, and $(1, 1)$. For simplicity, denote $(0, 0)$ by a, $(1, 0)$ by b, $(0, 1)$ by c, and $(1, 1)$ by d. When A and B change into A' and B', any one of a, b, c, and d, may be changed into any other. a, b, c, and d will be called *categories*, and changes from any one of the categories in (A, B) to any other in (A', B') will be called *transitions*. Let S_{lm} be the number of l's which are converted from m's. Then the following relations hold among the S_{lm}:

$$\sum_l S_{lm} = n_m,\qquad (4a)$$

where n_m is the number of m's in (A, B);

$$\sum_m S_{lm} = m_l,\qquad (4b)$$

where m_l is the number of l's in (A', B');

$$\sum_m n_m = \sum_l m_l = N,\qquad (4c)$$

where N is the number of documents in the collection.

A distinction must be drawn between the problem treated here and the large class of problems called *matching problems*. Barton [21] gives a statement of the problem, for simplicity with reference to packs of cards although the theory is applicable to any set of objects, as follows: "To fix ideas we consider a 'target pack' of N cards laid out in a row and a 'matching pack' of the same number of cards laid out one by one beside the target forming N *pairs* of which r are pairs of like cards (or matches)." The problem is to find the distribution of r. There are a number of conditions which may complicate the simplest case in which there are N distinct cards. For example, there may be k sorts of cards with a_i cards of the ith sort; or there may be K packs of cards between which simultaneous matches are to be found. These problems differ from the one treated here because, continuing the card playing terminology, they are concerned with matches between two packs of cards where one of the packs has been laid out in random order. Instead, the problem treated here deals with the number of matches for two given arrangements under the condition that there is a probability that the cards will be misread, thereby affecting the counting of matches. Levene [22] encounters a matching problem in studies of Mendelian inheritance, and considers the effect of misclassifying the objects, between which matches are to be made, on the distribution of the number of matches. Although Levene's problem, with its treatment of misclassification, is closer to the problem treated here, it is still remote from it for the reason given above.

Let $P(l, m)$ be the probability of the transition $m \to l$. There are n_a a's which must be distributed among the categories a, b, c, d in such a way that there are S_{aa} in a, S_{ba} in b, S_{ca} in c, and S_{da} in d. Let T_a be the probability of a particular one of these. Then

$$T_a = \frac{n_a!}{S_{aa}!\,S_{ba}!\,S_{ca}!\,S_{da}!}\, P(a, a)^{S_{aa}} P(b, a)^{S_{ba}} P(c, a)^{S_{ca}} P(d, a)^{S_{da}}$$

$$= \frac{n_a!}{\prod_l S_{la}!} \prod_l P(l, a)^{S_{la}}.$$

Now $P(S) = \prod_m T_m$, so substituting the above expression for T_a, we obtain

$$P(S) = \frac{\prod_m n_m!}{\prod_{l,m} S_{lm}!} \prod_{l,m} P(l, m)^{S_{lm}}. \tag{5}$$

Now, from Eq. (3)

$$\phi^* = \sum_{S\,\text{in}\,S^*} P(S)\phi(f_S, f)$$

$$= \sum_{\substack{m_i \\ \Sigma_i\, m_i = N}} \sum_{\substack{S \\ \Sigma_i\, S_{ij} = n_j \\ \Sigma_j\, S_{ij} = m_i}} P(S)\phi(f_S, f)$$

by splitting the sum into first a sum over all scramblings which reach a particular m_a, m_b, m_c, m_d and then a sum over all permitted values of these. Therefore we may write

$$\phi^* = \prod_m n_m! \sum_m \phi(f_s, f)R,\tag{6}$$

where

$$R = \sum_{\substack{S \\ \Sigma_i S_{ij}=n_j \\ \Sigma_j S_{ij}=m_i}} \left(\frac{\prod_{l,m} P(l, m)^{S_{lm}}}{\prod_{l,m} S_{lm}!} \right).$$

Consider now the polynomial $R^* = [\sum_{l,m} p_m q_l P(l, m)]^N$ This is a polynomial of degree N in $p_l q_m$. Then by the multinomial expansion

$$R = \frac{1}{N!} \text{ coefficient of } \prod_l p_l^{n_l} \cdot \prod_m q_m^{m_m} \quad \text{in} \quad R^*$$

$$= \frac{1}{N!} \text{ coefficient of } \prod_m q_m^{m_m} \text{ in coefficient of } \prod_l p_l^{n_l} \quad \text{in} \quad \left[\sum_l p_l \sum_l q_l P(l, m) \right]^N$$

$$= \text{ coefficient of } \prod_m q_m^{m_m} \text{ in } \frac{1}{\prod_l n_l!} \prod_m \left(\sum_l q_l P(l, m) \right)^{n_m}$$

$$= h(\mathbf{m}, \mathbf{n}), \text{ say.}$$

Therefore, from Eq. (6)

$$\phi^* = \prod_m n_m! \sum_m \phi(f_s, f)h(\mathbf{m}, \mathbf{n}),\tag{7}$$

where

$$h(\mathbf{m}, \mathbf{n}) = \text{coefficient of } \prod_m q_m^{m_m} \quad \text{in} \quad \frac{1}{\prod_l n_l!} \prod_m \left(\sum_l q_l P(l,m) \right)^{n_m}$$

The formula will now be applied to the similarity function $s_1(t_j, t_k)$, defined in Eq. (1), to obtain an expression for ϕ^* in terms of the error probability r. Let a, b, c, d denote, as before, the categories $(0, 0)$, $(1, 0)$, $(0, 1)$ and $(1, 1)$. Since $s_1(t_j, t_k)$ is symmetrical in t_j and t_k, there is no distinction between $(0, 1)$ and $(1, 0)$ and accordingly these will be replaced by the category $x = b \vee c$. The determination of ϕ^* may, therefore, proceed using only the three categories a, x, and d. Suppose that, before scrambling, the number of occurrences of each category is n_a, n_x, and n_d respectively, and that, after scrambling, the number of occurrences of the same categories is m_a, m_x, and m_d. Then the values of the similarity between t_j and t_k before and after scrambling are given respectively by

$$f = n_d/(N - n_a) \quad \text{and} \quad f_s = m_d/(N - m_a).\tag{8}$$

Now r is the probability that there is an error in a particular digit of the document array D. Then the transition probabilities are given, for each pair of categories, by

$$P(l, m) = \begin{pmatrix} s^2 & rs & r^2 \\ 2rs & r^2 + s^2 & 2rs \\ r^2 & rs & s^2 \end{pmatrix}, \tag{9}$$

where $s = 1 - r$. Thus, from the expression for $h(\mathbf{m}, \mathbf{n})$ given in Eq. (7) and substituting the expressions for $P(l, m)$ given in Eq. (9), we have

$$h(\mathbf{m}, \mathbf{n}) = s^{2N} \prod_m n_m! \sum_I C_I t^{N - (I(a, a) + I(x, x) + I(d, d)) + I(a, d) + I(d, a)} (1 + t^2)^{I(x, x)}, \tag{10}$$

where the sum is taken over all $I(l, m)$ such that $\sum_m I(l, m) = m_l$ and $\sum_l I(l, m) = n_m$. Also, in the above,

$$C_I = 2^{m_x - I(x, x)} / \prod_{l, m} I(l, m)! \quad \text{and} \quad t = r/s. \tag{11}$$

Thus ϕ^* may be expressed as a polynomial in t, which may be truncated once a sufficient number of terms has been collected, depending upon the magnitude of t. The expression for ϕ^*, for the particular similarity function chosen, however is unmanageable and no further reduction of ϕ^* to simpler terms has been achieved.

The analysis may, however, be carried further for functions ϕ which are expressible as polynomials in m_a, m_b, m_c, and m_d. Suppose that ϕ is expressible in this form. Then

$$\phi(f_S, f) = \sum_i a_i \mathbf{m^i}, \tag{12}$$

where

$$a_i \mathbf{m^i} = a_{i_x, i_y} \cdots m_x^{i_x} \cdot m_y^{i_y} \cdots .$$

Now from Eq. (3)

$$\phi^* = \sum_{S \, \mathrm{in} \, S^*} P(S)\phi(f_S, f),$$

where S^* is the set of all possible scramblings. Therefore,

$$\phi^* = \sum_i a_i B_i, \quad \text{where} \quad B_i = \sum_S \mathbf{m^i} P(S). \tag{13}$$

Now

$$\mathbf{m^i} = \prod_l m_l^{i_l} = \prod_l \left(\sum_m S_{lm} \right)^{i_l}$$

so that

$$B_i = \sum_S \prod_l \left(\sum_m S_{lm} \right)^{i_l} P(S).$$

$P(S)$ is given in terms of the $P(l, m)$ by Eq. (5). We define the operator D_{pq} by

$$D_{pq} \equiv P(p, q) \frac{d}{dP(p, q)}. \tag{14}$$

Then differentiating $P(S)$ formally with respect to $P(p, q)$, we have $D_{pq} P(S) = S_{pq} P(S)$. Therefore,

$$B_i = \prod_l \left(\sum_m D_{lm} \right)^{i_l} \sum_S P(S)$$

$$= \prod_l \left(\sum_m D_{lm} \right)^{i_l} \sum_S \prod_m \left(\frac{n_m!}{\prod_l S_{lm}!} \prod_l P(l, m)^{S_{lm}} \right),$$

so

$$B_i = \prod_l \left(\sum_m D_{lm} \right)^{i_l} \prod_m \left(\sum_l P(l, m) \right)^{n_m}. \tag{15}$$

Consider now, in the notation of Section II, the similarity function $s_3(t_j, t_k)$, defined by

$$s_3(t_j, t_k) = (|D_{\cdot j} \wedge D_{\cdot k}| + |\bar{D}_{\cdot j} \wedge \bar{D}_{\cdot k}|)/N, \tag{16}$$

where t_j and t_k are two arbitrary terms. The similarity function is symmetrical in t_j and t_k and is also symmetrical in 0 and 1. There is, therefore, no distinction between the categories $(1, 0)$ and $(0, 1)$ and these may accordingly be replaced by the category $x = b \vee c$. In addition, there is no distinction between a and d so these may be replaced by the single category $y = a \vee d$. Suppose that f and f_S are the values of $s_3(t_j, t_k)$ before and after scrambling. Then $f = n_y/N$ and $f_S = m_y/N$, where N is the number of documents in the collection. Suppose that ϕ is the mean square deviation of f due to the presence of errors. Therefore, $\phi = (f_S - f)^2$, whence

$$\phi = (n_y/N)^2 + (-2n_y/N^2)m_y + (1/N^2)m_y^2.$$

Thus ϕ is expressible as a polynomial of degree two in m_y. Now, from Eq. (12), $\phi = \sum_i a^i \mathbf{m}_i$, whence, identifying coefficients in $s_3(t_j, t_k)$:

$$a_{00} = (n_y/N)^2, \qquad a_{01} = -2n_y/N^2,$$

and

$$a_{02} = 1/N^2.$$

All other a_i are zero. Thus since from Eq. (13), $\phi^* = \sum_i a_i B_i$, then

$$\phi = a_{00} B_{00} + a_{01} B_{01} + a_{02} B_{02},$$

where the B's are given from Eq. (14) and Eq. (15) by

$$B_{i_x, i_y} = \prod_l \left(\sum_m D_{lm}\right)^{i_l} \prod_m \left(\sum_l P(l, m)\right)^{n_m}$$

$$= (D_{xx} + D_{xy})^{i_x}(D_{yx} + D_{yy})^{i_y}(P(x, x) + P(y, x))^{n_x}(P(x, y) + P(y, y))^{n_y}.$$

The transition probabilities $P(l, m)$ are given by

$$P(x, x) = P(y, y) = r^2 + s^2, \qquad P(x, y) = P(y, x) = 2rs.$$

Now B_{00} corresponds to $i_x = 0$ and $i_y = 0$. Therefore,

$$B_{00} = (P(x, x) + P(y, x))^{n_x}(P(x, y) + P(y, y))^{n_y} = (r + s)^{2N} = 1.$$

B_{01} corresponds to $i_x = 0$ and $i_y = 1$, so

$$B_{01} = (D_{yx} + D_{yy})(P(x, x) + P(y, x))^{n_x}(P(x, y) + P(y, y))^{n_y}$$

$$= 2rsn_x + (r^2 + s^2)n_y.$$

Finally, B_{02} corresponds to $i_x = 0$ and $i_y = 2$, so

$$B_{02} = (D_{yx} D_{yx} + 2D_{yx} D_{yy} + D_{yy} D_{yy})(P(x, x) + P(y, x))^{n_x}(P(x, y) + P(y, y))^{n_y}$$

$$= 2Nrs(r^2 + s^2) + (n_y + 2(n_x - n_y)rs)^2.$$

Therefore,

$$\phi^* = 4r^2s^2(n_x - n_y)^2/N^2 - 4r^2s^2/N^2 + 2rs/N$$

for a given pair of terms t_j, t_k. Thus for any pair of terms in the vocabulary, ϕ^* must lie between K and $K + 4r^2s^2$ where $K = (2rs/N)(1 - 2rs/N)$. ϕ^* is zero for this similarity function, as expected, when $r = 0$ or $r = 1$, corresponding respectively to the cases where there are no errors at all, and where there are errors in every term assignment.

The error analysis of the similarity function $s_1(t_j, r_k)$, that is, the Tanimoto function, will now be reconsidered. Suppose that f and f_s are the values of $s_1(t_j, t_k)$ before and after scrambling. Then, as before, f and f_s are given by $f = n_d/(N - n_a)$ and $f_s = m_d/(N - m_a)$. Again, the mean square deviation will be considered. Thus

$$\phi = (f - f_s)^2 = \left(\frac{n_d}{N - n_a} - \frac{m_d}{N}\left(1 - \frac{m_a}{N}\right)^{-1}\right)^2.$$

Providing m_a/N is sufficiently small, the binomial series expansion of ϕ may be truncated and expressed as a polynomial in m_a and m_d. With this provision, the value of ϕ^* may be obtained using the second of the two general expressions for ϕ^* given above. However, if m_a is to be small compared with N then, assuming r to be small as well, the proportion of documents of the collection to which any term is assigned must be large. This is unlikely to be true in practice. It is more likely that the number of documents to which a particular term has been assigned will vary considerably from term to term. It is therefore unfeasible to treat the Tanimoto function in this particular way, at least for the type of data which is considered here.

VI. Conclusion

The methods derived above for obtaining an estimate ϕ^* for a statistical function ϕ of the similarity between pairs of terms, when the assignment of terms to documents is susceptible to errors with probability r, have been shown to be applicable in certain circumstances. No estimate, however, has been obtained for the asymmetric Tanimoto function for the reasons already given. However, an estimate has been obtained for the symmetrical Tanimoto function, and therefore all similarity functions expressible as polynomials in m_x and m_y, since the coefficients B_i do not depend on the particular function under examination.

The analysis given is applicable outside the field of information retrieval which has been considered here. The analysis is applicable, in principle, to classification techniques, whether hierarchical or nonhierarchical, which utilize a similarity matrix giving the similarities between the objects of the population, provided that the objects are described in terms of mutually independent binary attributes and provided that these attributes are susceptible to errors independently and equiprobably, with an assignable probability r.

ACKNOWLEDGMENTS

I am indebted to Dr. R. M. Needham of the University Mathematical Laboratory, Cambridge, England, for his encouragement in the planning of this work. This work was supported, in part, by Grant No. GN-543.1 from the Office of Scientific Information Service of the National Science Foundation and, in part, by the Office of Scientific and Technical Information of the United Kingdom.

REFERENCES

1. Williams, W. T., and Dale, M. B., Fundamental Problems in numerical taxonomy. *Advances in Botanical Res.* **2**, 35–68 (1965).
2. Sokal, R. R., and Sheath, P. H. A., "Principles of Numerical Taxonomy." Freeman, San Francisco, California, 1963.
3. Parker-Rhodes, A. F., Statistical aspects of fungus forays. *Trans. British Mycological Soc.* **38**, 283–290 (1955).

4. Parker-Rhodes, A. F., and Jackson, D. M., Automatic classification in the ecology of the higher fungi. *In* "Numerical Taxonomy" (A. J. Cole, ed.) pp. 181–215. Academic Press, New York, 1969.
5. Sutcliffe, J. P., A probability model for errors of classification. I. General considerations. *Psychometrika* **30**, 73–96 (1965).
6. Sutcliffe, J. P., A probability model for errors of classification. II. Particular cases. *Psychometrika* **30**, 129–155 (1965).
7. Gotlieb, C. C., and Kumar, S., Semantic clustering of index terms. *J. Assoc. Comput. Mach.* **15**, 493–513 (1968).
8. Sparck Jones, K., Synonymy and semantic classification. Ph.D. Thesis, Cambridge Univ., Cambridge, England, 1964.
9. Lewis, P. A. W., Baxendale, P. B., and Bennett, J. L., Statistical discrimination of the synonymy/antonymy relationship between words. *J. Assoc. Comput. Mach.* **14**, 20–44 (1967).
10. Sebestyen, G. S., Recognition of membership in classes. *IRE Trans. Information Theory* **7**, 44–50 (1961).
11. Johnson, S. C., Hierarchical clustering schemes. *Psychometrika* **12**, 241–254 (1967).
12. Jardine, C. J., Jardine, N., and Sibson, R., The structure and construction of taxonomic hierarchies. *Math. Biosci.* **1**, 172–179 (1967).
13. Pearson, K., On coefficients of racial likeness. *Biometrika* **18**, 105–117 (1926).
14. Mahalanobis, P. C., On the generalised distance in statistics. *Proc. Nat. Inst. Sci. India* **12**, 49–55 (1936).
15. Rao, C. R., "Advanced Statistical Methods in Biometric Research." Wiley, New York, 1952.
16. Tanimoto, T. T., An elementary theory of classification and prediction, IBM Rep. IBM, Yorktown Heights, New York, 1958.
17. Benzécri, J. P., Sur les algorithmes de classification. Texte multigraphié, 1965.
18. de la Véga, W. F., Techniques de classification automatique utilisant un indice de ressemblance. *Revue Française Sociologie* **8**, 506–520 (1967).
19. Kendall, M. G., "The Advanced Theory of Statistics," Vol. 1. Griffin, London, 1943.
20. Jackson, D. M., Comparison of classifications. *In* "Numerical Taxonomy" (A. J. Cole, ed.), pp. 91–111. Academic Press, New York, 1969.
21. Barton, D. E., The matching distributions: Poisson limiting forms and derived methods of approximation. *J. Roy. Statist. Soc. Ser. B* **20**, 73–92 (1958).
22. Levene, H., On a matching problem arising in genetics. *Ann. Math. Statist.* **20**, 91–94 (1949).

Logical Aspects of Question-Answering by Computer

J. L. Kuhns

THE RAND CORPORATION
SANTA MONICA, CALIFORNIA

I. Introductory Remarks

In this chapter, we will consider the problem of computerized question-answering from the point of view of certain technical, although elementary, notions of logic. While the work reported here has general application to the design of information systems, it is specifically motivated by the RAND Relational Data File, a data-retrieval system whose design features were proposed by Levien and Maron [(1965, 1966), see also Levien (1966), Maron (1966)]. This system, for which a prototype has been implemented (Levien, 1969), deals with the retrieval and processing of information from a large file of *relational* sentences. (In the present version, there are about 70,000 sentences.) These file items concern factual information on research in the field of cybernetics—what Levien and Maron call *context* data. By that is meant such information as who wrote what paper, with what organization is someone affiliated, what conferences were held—and where—and who attended them, etc.

We will not discuss specific details of the system but rather an abstract version of it. Our purpose is to demonstrate how notions in logic can be used to influence the design of components of an information system. A secondary purpose is to show how logic can be applied to the analysis of natural language. We also hope the reader will benefit from an elementary exposition of some notions in the *theory of relations*.

II. Overview of an Information System

In Figure 1, we show a simplified diagram of an information system. There are two inputs: data of some sort and queries—information requirements of users. The problem, in its broadest outline, is to match an input query to the batched input data. But this match must be done on a common ground; that is, both data and query must be cast into comparable strings of symbols. Thus,

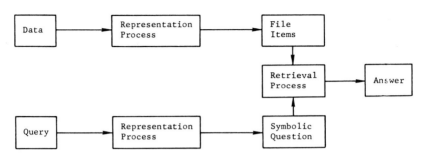

FIGURE 1. Schematic diagram of an information system.

the two inputs are accompanied by two representation processes which result in what we shall call *file items* and *symbolic questions*. At this stage, we leave open the question of the mode of these auxiliary processes—they may be either manual or automatic. Neither will we specify the exact form of the input data. Let us however consider the given expression of the user's information problem to be a natural-language query. Now, the design of the system should be guided by the *logical analysis* of such queries rather than an analysis restricted to traditional grammar. A specific example will illustrate this idea.

III. Analysis of a Natural-Language Question

Suppose our system is to store bibliographic and related data on logic, and suppose that an inquirer, wishing to interrogate the system, poses the question

$$\text{What books has Reichenbach written?} \tag{1}$$

How can a computerized system answer this?

First, let us examine the relationship between the question and its answer; i.e., as a relationship between expressions. A member of the set of answering expressions would be the title "*Elements of Symbolic Logic*" because

$$\text{Reichenbach wrote } Elements\ of\ Symbolic\ Logic \tag{2}$$

and

$$Elements\ of\ Symbolic\ Logic \text{ is a book.} \tag{3}$$

Let us symbolize these two elementary sentences. The first is analyzed as expressing a *relation* holding between two individuals—a person and a written work. In logical notation, this relation can be designated by "W" associated with two argument positions. Introducing "a" and "b" as symbolic translations of "Reichenbach" and "*Elements of Symbolic Logic*", respectively, then (2) receives the symbolic translation

$$aWb. \tag{4}$$

" *W* " (together with its associated argument positions) is called a *two-place predicate* and designates a relation; "*a*" and "*b*" are *argument expressions*, in this case, individual constants, designating individuals. Similarly, the sentence (3) can be symbolized

$$Bb, \tag{5}$$

where " *B* " (with its associated argument position) is a translation of " book " and, as a *one-place predicate*, designates a property, namely, the property of being a book. [The concept of one-place predicate is closely related to the concept of *class*; thus, (5) can also be read

$$b \quad \text{belongs to the class} \quad B. \tag{5'}$$

This second, *extensional* interpretation is especially appropriate for noun phrases such as " a book " occurring in (3).]

The method of *propositional data storage* as used in the Relational Data File (Levien and Maron, 1965, 1966) provides a method for storing sentences which is analogous to the symbolic translations given above. Thus, to store the sentence (2), the English words are first translated into computer words (analogous to " *W* ", " *a* ", " *b* "). Next, the three computer words are stored in the file (in our case, a disk file). Finally, a fourth computer word is used to identify the sentence so stored. Thus, we have a data line of the design

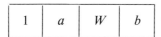

Similarly, the sentence (3) [or (5)] leads to a data line having the design

| 2 | — | B | b |

with no entry in the second place.†

A *data base* then consists of two parts: (1) a dictionary of individual constants and predicates (together called *descriptive names*); (2) a collection of elementary, i.e., atomic sentences, which are certain strings of descriptive names.

An example dictionary is shown in Table I. We can regard it as an inventory of our universe of discourse.

An example file is shown in Table II. This describes a possible state of the universe of discourse.

Returning to the input question (1), let us give it a similar symbolic translation. We have three major classes of logical " parts of speech " to work with:

† In the actual file, this data line is also stored in relational form, i.e., as a logical relation between a thing and a property (class). Thus, the stored data line would be similar to (5').

argument expressions, predicates, and logical signs (to be explained). The result of the analysis of the question will be to identify the lexical units that correspond to these classes.

The argument expressions are "What" and "Reichenbach". "What" has the status of a variable; we call it an *interrogative descriptive variable*.†
Everything else in (1) is a complicated relation-expression; we will refer to it as "R_3" because it turns out to have three levels of complexity. Thus, the symbolization must reduce somehow to

$$xR_3 a. \tag{6}$$

Since a principal concern is the possibility of the automatic creation of symbolic questions, we must be careful not to overlook any machine-recognizable clues. Thus, it will be helpful to have a symbolism that mirrors the English word order as much as possible. The relational notation used in (6) already seems to be a good choice.

TABLE I

AN EXAMPLE DICTIONARY

a	Reichenbach
b	*Elements of Symbolic Logic*
c	*On Meaning*
d	Russell
e	Whitehead
f	*Principia Mathematica*
B	(the property of being a) book
P	(the property of being a) paper
W	wrote (the relation of authorship in the broad sense)

TABLE II

AN EXAMPLE FILE

1	a	W	b
2	—	B	b
3	a	W	c
4	—	P	c
5	d	W	f
6	e	W	f
7	—	B	f

† The meaning of "What" depends on the kind of question in which it occurs. Thus, in question (1), "What" has an *extensional* connotation—it asks for an inventory. However, in a question such as "What is an apple?", it asks for an *intension* (see Section IV).

Returning to the example question (1), we note that the candidates for answers are restricted to the class of books. Thus, R_3 is a *relation with a restricted domain.* The operation for forming this [in a slightly modified notation of Whitehead and Russell (1950)] is indicated by writing the predicate that defines the restriction (in this case, "B") as a left subscript to the relation-expression. Thus, we have

$$R_3 = {}_B R_2, \tag{7}$$

where R_2 is to be further analyzed. (The formal definition of a relation with restricted domain is

$$x {}_F Ry = {}_{Df} Fx.xRy, \tag{8}$$

where "." is the sign of conjunction.)

Now, R_2 is close to the relation W of the example file. It is not the same, however, because of the reversal of the argument expressions. Apparently this is due to the splitting of the relation expression in (1) by the individual constant. The effect is that a proper symbolization requires the use of the *converse* of a relation. The converse relation is indicated in English sometimes by the passive voice. Thus, *has been written by* is the converse of *has written.* Sometimes, it is indicated by another expression; for example, *child of* is the converse of *parent of.* In questions, the splitting of the relation expression flags its appearance. The formal definition of the converse $\check{R}$ of R is

$$x\check{R}y = {}_{Df} yRx. \tag{9}$$

Thus, we have

$$R_2 = \check{R}_1, \tag{10}$$

and, finally,

$$R_1 = \text{has written.} \tag{11}$$

If we identify R_1 with W of the file, then, by using (6), (7), (10), and (11), the symbolization of (1) becomes

$$x {}_B[\check{W}]a. \tag{12}$$

But let us replace the abbreviations by the English expressions and compare the result with the original question. We have

$$\text{What}_{\text{books}}[(\text{has written})^{\check{}}]\ \text{Reichenbach.} \tag{13}$$

Note how the analysis closely matches the English word order; only the second argument expression has been shifted to another position.

By studying a small collection of natural-language questions, we have derived some general principles of symbolization and then assimilated these principles into a computer program. The program analyzes an input string—a question—by applying a series of *rewrite rules* (explained in the example to follow). The analysis terminates when either the entire string has been reduced to the symbol " Q " (for " question ") or if no more rules apply. The present program is written in the IBM 7040/7044 FORTRAN IV language and has 30 rules. The root of the program consists principally of a large *computed GO TO statement* which directs control to numbered FORTRAN statements, each heading a body of code representing a single analysis rule. Each rule is in four parts: (1) an identification number; (2) a rewrite instruction; (3) a symbol definition (in case a rewrite involves an abbreviation); (4) a transfer condition (giving the next rule).

The output is in two parts: a *symbol definition table*, which constitutes the analysis of the question; and a *rewrite table*, which is for research purposes and gives the sequence of string modifications.

The printouts for the analysis of question (1) are shown in Figures 2 and 3. (In this experimental program, the English words are truncated after six characters.) Figure 2 gives the symbol definition table. The printout is read

	SYMBOL		DEFINITION					
1	V(1)	=	WHAT					
2	A(1)	=	HAS					
3	C(1)	=	REICHE					
4	P(1)	=	BOOKS					
5	R(1)	=	A(1)	WRITTE				
6	R(2)	=	CNV	(	R(1)	)		
7		=						
8	R(3)	=	RD	(	R(2)	,	P(1)	)
9	Q(1)	=	V(1)	R(3)	C(1)			

FIGURE 2. Symbol definition table for the computer analysis of the natural-language question, " What books has Reichenbach written?"

RULE NUMBER	STRING NUMBER	WORD	STRING						
	1	WHAT	BOOKS	HAS	*	REICHE	*	WRITTE	.
1									
	2	V(1)	BOOKS	HAS	*	REICHE	*	WRITTE	.
3									
	3	V(1)	BOOKS	A(1)	*	REICHE	*	WRITTE	.
4									
	4	V(1)	BOOKS	A(1)	C(1)	WRITTE	.		
6									
	5	V(1)	P(1)	A(1)	C(1)	WRITTE	.		
15									
	6	V(1)	P(1)	CNV	(	R(1)	)	C(1)	.
16									
	7	V(1)	P(1)	R(2)	C(1)	.			
17									
	8	V(1)	RD	(	R(2)	,	P(1)	)	C(1) .
18									
	9	V(1)	R(3)	C(1)	.				
27									
	10	Q(1)							

FIGURE 3. Rewrite table for the computer analysis of the natural-language question, "What books has Reichenbach written?"

from the bottom up. Thus, in line 9, the question is analyzed as having the form of a variable "$V(1)$" followed by a relational expression "$R(3)$" followed by an individual constant "$C(1)$". [Compare with (6).] $R(3)$ is identified in line 8 as being a *relation with restricted domain* (RD); namely, the *converse* (CNV) of *has written* (lines 6, 5, 2) with domain restricted to the class of *books* (line 4).

In Figure 3 we show the rewrite table. String 1 is the input question. The only input markings we use are asterisks to set off individual constants. Rule 1 was first applied—it determined "what" as an interrogative descriptive variable by a dictionary look-up.

Rule 3 determined the auxiliary "has"—also by a dictionary look-up. The individual constant "Reichenbach" was next recognized (Rule 4) by the input markings. In the next rule application (Rule 6), we determine the one-place predicate "books" not by a dictionary look-up but by its position between a variable and an auxiliary (this seems to be a common structure in questions). By Rule 15, which is next to be applied, we determine the relational expression by the occurrence of an argument between an auxiliary and a string without arguments; this yields the symbol definition in line 5 of Figure 2; at this point, " $C(1)$ " is transferred to the end, and as a part of this transformation the converse is introduced. Rule 16 executes an abbreviation, as does Rule 18. Rule 17 restricts the domain because of the adjacency of " $P(1)$ " with " $R(2)$ ". Finally, Rule 27 recognizes string 9 as a permissible form of a question.

IV. Answering the Question

In the transformation of (1) into (13), we have given a *gross semantic analysis* of the natural-language question. This is meant in the following sense: we have stipulated that "has written" corresponds to a relation, "book" to a property, "Reichenbach" to an individual, and "what" to an unknown. But to answer the question requires us to have a trick for representing the finer meanings to a computer.

Philosophy tells us there are two aspects of meaning to be considered;

	SYMBOL		DEFINITION		
1	A(1)	=	DID		
2	C(1)	=	RUSSEL		
3	C(2)	=	WHITEH		
4	R(1)	=	A(1)	COAUTH	WITH
5	R(2)	=	CNV	(R(1)	)
6		=			
7	S(1)	=	C(2)	R(2)	C(1)
8	Q(1)	=	S(1)		

FIGURE 4. Symbol definition table for the computer analysis of the natural-language question, "Did Russell co-author with Whitehead?".

RULE NUMBER	STRING NUMBER	WORD STRING								
3	1	DID	*	RUSSEL	*	COAUTH	WITH	WHITEH	*	·
4	2	A(1)	*	RUSSEL	*	COAUTH	WITH	WHITEH	*	·
4	3	A(1)	C(1)	COAUTH	WITH	*	WHITEH	*	·	
15	4	A(1)	C(1)	COAUTH	WITH	C(2)	·			
16	5	CNV	(	R(1)	)	C(1)	C(2)	·		
23	6	R(2)	C(1)	C(2)	·					
25	7	C(2)	R(2)	C(1)	·					
28	8	S(1)	·							
	9	Q(1)								

FIGURE 5. Rewrite table for the computer analysis of the natural-language question, "Did Russell co-author with Whitehead?".

extension and *intension* (see Carnap, 1956). The intension of a one-place predicate is the property designated by the predicate, and the extension is the class of things having that property. Similarly, the intension of a two-place predicate is the relation designated by the predicate and the extension is the class of ordered pairs of individuals which stand in that relation.

Now, the example file of Table II gives, relative to our universe of discourse, the extensions of certain "primitive" predicates. Thus, the extension of " W " is given in lines 1, 3, 5, and 6 as $\{(a, b), (a, c), (d, f), (e, f)\}$; the extension of " B " in lines 2 and 7 as $\{b, f\}$; and the extension of " P " in line 4 as $\{c\}$. For this reason, the file is called the *extensional file*.

In order to answer the input question (1), the meanings of the English phrases must be traced back to these stored lists. That is, the answer is to be found in the extension list of " $_B[\breve{W}]$ " (a list of pairs) among the entries in the first members corresponding to " a " in the second. This "calculation" can be done by working with *arrays*; each logical operator of the symbolic question corresponds to a certain *array manipulation*. For example, the array for the converse $\breve{W}$ is obtained from the array for W by interchanging the columns; the array for a restriction of domain, say of R to B, is obtained by deleting those rows in the array for R whose first-place members are not in the array for B.†

In the foregoing, we have assumed that "has written" can be identified with "wrote" (and hence with " W "). This is the *intensional aspect* of the problem. We must have a relational sentence stored stating the synonymity of the two expressions. Similarly, we must have a store of logical definitions such as (8) (for restriction of domain), and (9) (for the converse). This second file is called the *intensional file*. The dictionary itself can be regarded as part of the intensional file.

Synonyms are the simplest example of a more general class of representations of intensions called *meaning postulates* (Carnap, 1956). These define certain relations in the terms of more primitive predicates, or express in some way relations between relations, or between relations and properties, or between properties and properties. Consider, for example,

$$\text{Did Russell co-author with Whitehead?} \qquad (14)$$

The computer analysis of this is given in Figures 4 and 5. The input question is analyzed as a sentence (line 8 of Figure 4) which is to be affirmed. The analysis reduces to the meaning of the predicate "*did co-author with*" (line 4 of Figure 4). Now, it is clear that the example file contains all the information necessary to answer this. The problem is to relate "did co-author with" with

---

† A more efficient procedure for evaluation is to process the symbolic question after first transforming away the domain restriction and converse; i.e., to process $Bx.aWx$ and hence to "intersect" two columnar arrays.

"wrote". This is done by forming the *relative product* of W with its converse. The relative product of two relations R and S, in symbols "$R \mid S$", is defined formally by

$$x(R \mid S)y =_{Df} (\exists z)(xRz.zSy), \tag{15}$$

where "$(\exists z)$" is the existential quantifier. Thus, we have

$$\text{did co-author with} = W \mid \breve{W}. \tag{16}$$

Perhaps we may wish to modify (16) so that no person is co-author with himself; i.e., we intersect $W \mid \breve{W}$ with the relation of *diversity* to complete the definition.† The *intensional definition* (16) thus relates the meaning back to the extensional file.

V. Symbolic Questions and Value Sets‡

We have seen that the problem of answering a question by computer involves processing a formula of the predicate calculus. This formula may either stem from the conversion of a natural-language question to a symbolic question or it may be input directly as a formulation of the user's information requirement. [For example, in the current version of the Relational Data File, an information requirement is expressed by means of a special programming language called INFEREX (see Levien, 1969, pp. 17–23); INFEREX instructions involve relational sentences which are essentially equivalent to formulas of the predicate calculus.] We have outlined the logical relationship between the query and the "answer" as embedded in the data base. Let us now take a closer look at the actual mechanism of the answering process.

The formulas§ to be considered are first classed according to the presence of *free variables*. For example, there are sentence-like expressions such as

$$Bx.aWx, \tag{17}$$

in which a free variable occurs; and there are formulas such as

$$(\exists x)(dWx.eWx) \tag{18}$$

---

† Note that the co-authorship relation is *symmetrical*. The introduction of the converse in the computer analysis (line 5 of Fig. 4) is therefore redundant; it is necessary, however, from the linguistic structure of the question and the generality of Rule 15. To see this, replace "co-author with" by "study under". Line 7 of Fig. 4 could then be interpreted as "Whitehead taught Russell".

‡ For a more detailed discussion of the ideas in this section, see Kuhns (1967).

§ From this point on, we will consider formulas to be without special operators; that is, we suppose that restrictions of domain, converses, relative products, etc., have been eliminated through definitions [e.g., (8)–(10)].

with no free variables (the variable " x " is *bound*). The first is an *open sentential formula*; the second a *closed sentential formula* or simply a *sentence*. The number of free variables in a formula is called its *degree*. Thus, (17) is a formula of degree one, while (18) is of degree zero.

The "answers" to a question leading to an open formula such as (17) are those descriptive names that, when substituted for the free variable, yield a true formula relative to the data base. These names comprise what we call the *value set* of the sentential formula.†

(The value set is analogous to the extension, but the value set consists of names, while the extension consists of things. We introduce this new notion for a further reason. We want the members of a value set to have a certain form; e.g., in general, we would not want a description, as, for example, "Reichenbach's 10th book", to be a member of a value set, for this would be counter to our intuitions regarding the character of an answer. The issue is further complicated by the fact that, although in some cases the value set coincides with an extension-list for *some* predicate,‡ we may want to have a predicate itself in a value set; e.g., as in "answers" to questions such as "What relation holds between a and b?"§ For these reasons, the concept of value set of a sentential formula seems justified.)

For a formula of degree zero, i.e., a sentence, we take its value set (or simply the value) to be an expression denoting its truth value—say a numeral, "1" for true, "0" for false. Thus, we assume a system consisting of a data base and a sentential formula to be processed. The problem is to calculate its value set.

Let us now look at a source of difficulty. Suppose an inquirer asked

$$\text{Who did not write } \textit{Elements of Symbolic Logic?} \qquad (19)$$

i.e., the symbolic question is

$$\sim(xWb), \qquad (20)$$

where " $\sim$ " is the negation sign. A human would reject this question as unreasonable, but what should a machine do with it? Should it print every name in the dictionary except "Reichenbach" or should it somehow prohibit the question? With directly input sentential formulas, the problem is

---

† If a formula is of a degree greater than one, each member of the value set will be a *sequence* of descriptive names, the length of the sequence corresponding to the degree.

‡ Thus, for (17), the predicate would be formed by applying the λ-operator (see Carnap, 1956, p. 3) or be given directly by " $_B[\check{W}]$ ".

§ Remarks on the subject of questions which are of particular interest for our purposes are given by Carnap (1937, p. 296), Reichenbach (1947, pp. 339–342), Jespersen (1965, p. 303). Remarks on the notion of "giving an extension" are given by Carnap (1956, p. 82).

even worse—there could be mistakes which cause logical combinations leading to nonsense. For example, consider the disjunctive formula of degree
two:

$$(xWb) \vee (yWb) \tag{21}$$

(where " $\vee$ " is the sign of logical disjunction). Now, any substitution instance
which makes either component of (21) true will make the entire formula true.
Consequently, (21) leads to a value set of ordered pairs corresponding to the
free-variable sequence " x, y " in which a pair has either the form " $(a, \ldots)$ "
or the form " $(\ldots, a)$ " with any descriptive name replacing " $\ldots$ ".

We will attack this problem of "unreasonable" questions by first defining
a precise concept called *definite formula*. This will then be used to explicate†
the vague notion of "reasonable" question. The basic consideration in our
definition is this: the difficulty with (20), or (21), is that its value set will
change if, without changing the file, a new descriptive name is added to the
dictionary. A formula that does not have this objectionable property for any
data base is called *definite*.

The formal definition is as follows. We first develop the notion for a given
data base D.

Definition. Given a data base D and a formula **s** on D, we define **s** to be
semidefinite with respect to D by means of the following *logical test procedure:*
Calculate the value set of **s**, call it $\omega(\mathbf{s})$. Form a "pseudo" data base D_* by
adding a new descriptive name, say " $*$ ", to the dictionary of D (this, of course,
leaves the file unchanged). Calculate $\omega_*(\mathbf{s})$, i.e., the value set of **s** on D_*. If

$$\omega_*(\mathbf{s}) = \omega(\mathbf{s}),$$

then we say **s** is *semidefinite* on D.

Finally, so that definitude is a logical property, i.e., independent of any
particular data base, we define:

Definition. **s** is definite if and only if **s** is semidefinite on every data base.

For example, let **s** be the formula

$$Bc \; . \sim (xWc). \tag{22}$$

This is semidefinite on our example data base because $\omega(\text{"}Bc\text{"}) = 0$, and hence

$$\omega_*(\mathbf{s}) = \omega(\mathbf{s}) = \text{the null set.}$$

On the other hand, (22) is not definite because, in a world where Bc was the
case, " $*$ " would belong to $\omega_*(\mathbf{s})$; i.e.,

$$\omega_*(\mathbf{s}) = \omega(\mathbf{s}) \cup \{\text{"} * \text{"}\}.$$

† We use "explicate" in the technical sense of Carnap (1956, p. 8).

Let us next turn to the problem of characterizing the definite formulas. The first result is that atomic formulas, i.e., those without operators, are definite. (Note that the atomic formulas include both the sentences in the file and those sentential formulas with variables whose value sets can be determined by a direct match with file items—the value set given by the sequence of variable replacements that produce the match.)

Consider then formulas with operators—the molecular formulas. An inventory of the operators is as follows: the *singulary* operators are the signs for negation ($\sim$), existential quantification [$(\exists x)$], and universal quantification [$(\forall x)$]; the *binary* operators are the signs for conjunction (.), disjunction ($\vee$), implication ($\supset$), equivalence ($\equiv$), and, for reasons to be given later, we also include a special operator for the negation of implication ($-$). (This last operator can be read "but not"; it is equivalent to the combination ".$\sim$".) A sentential formula then has either one or two *components* depending on whether the major operator is singulary or binary.

Let us now characterize the definitude of formulas with *definite components*. The first step is to calculate the *free variable set* of the components. The free variable set of an atomic formula is simply the set of distinct variables occurring in it (without regard for their order); that of a binary formula is the set union of the free variable sets of the components, that of a negation is the same as that of the component; and finally, the free variable set of a quantification is the free variable set of the component less the quantified variable. A formula is of degree zero if and only if its free variable set is null.

Let $\bar{\phi}(\mathbf{r})$, $\bar{\phi}(\mathbf{s})$ be the free variable sets of the sentential formulas $\mathbf{r}$ and $\mathbf{s}$, respectively. We have the following:

Characterization Theorem. If $\mathbf{r}$ and $\mathbf{s}$ are definite, then:

(a) $(\exists x)(\mathbf{r})$ and $(\mathbf{r}).(\mathbf{s})$ are definite.
(b)   If $\bar{\phi}(\mathbf{s}) \subseteq \bar{\phi}(\mathbf{r})$, then $(\mathbf{r}) - (\mathbf{s})$ is definite.
(c)   If $\bar{\phi}(\mathbf{r}) = \bar{\phi}(\mathbf{s})$, then $(\mathbf{r}) \vee (\mathbf{s})$ is definite.
(d)   If $\bar{\phi}(\mathbf{r}) = \bar{\phi}(\mathbf{s}) = $ the null set, then $\sim(\mathbf{r})$, $(\mathbf{r}) \supset (\mathbf{s})$, and $(\mathbf{r}) \equiv (\mathbf{s})$ are definite.

Thus, the free variable sets lead to certain *sufficient* conditions for definitude. We next have a companion theorem on *necessary* conditions.

Theorem. The conditions listed in the characterization theorem are necessary for definitude with the following additional provisions†:

(a)   For $(\mathbf{r}) - (\mathbf{s})$, providing $\mathbf{r}$ is not contradictory.

† By "contradictory" in (a), we mean a formula which is either false on every data base (if of degree zero) or has a null value set on every data base (if of degree greater than zero). By "tautology" in (c) we mean a *sentence* which is true on every data base.

(b) For $(\mathbf{r}) \vee (\mathbf{s})$, providing neither $\mathbf{r}$ nor $\mathbf{s}$ is contradictory.

(c) For $(\mathbf{r}) \supset (\mathbf{s})$, providing $\mathbf{r}$ is not a tautology.

(d) For $(\mathbf{r}) \equiv (\mathbf{s})$, providing neither $\mathbf{r}$ nor $\mathbf{s}$ is a tautology.

[It turns out that the additional provisions are logically interesting, for it has been shown by Di Paola (1968) that the class of definite formulas is not recursive.]

How do we apply the characterization theorem? If the free variable conditions are met, then the value sets can be calculated in terms of the value sets of the components. The specific rules for doing this are given by Kuhns (1967, pp. 67–80).† From a standpoint of machine processing, therefore, the most desirable type of formula is one that is definite in every part of its structure. This class of formulas we will call *proper*. More precisely, a formula is proper if (1) it is atomic (and hence definite), or (2) it is definite and its components are proper. The characterization theorem and its companion theorem can therefore be read with " proper" replacing " definite."

But what of formulas that are definite but improper? Consider, for example, the natural-language question:

Are all of the publications of Reichenbach books? (23)

We can symbolize this as

$$(\forall x)(aWx \supset Bx). \qquad (24)$$

Now, the component of this formula is indefinite because any substitution for " x " that makes the antecedent " aWx " false makes the implication true. On the other hand, the entire formula is definite. This can be seen by eliminating the universal quantifier; i.e., (24) is equivalent to

$$\sim(\exists x)(aWx - Bx) \qquad (25)$$

and this is definite by parts (b), (a), and (d) of the characterization theorem.

The problem now arises: Is it possible to transform a definite but improper formula into proper form? If it can be so transformed, we say it is *admissible*.‡ We have proved (Kuhns, 1967, pp. 92–95) that every definite formula without quantifiers is indeed admissible. We have also shown the admissibility of certain special, but nevertheless important, universal formulas. However, the *general* admissibility of definite formulas is an open question.

---

† The characterization theorem identifies four classes of situations regarding free variable sets. In the computation rules for binary formulas, these situations, corresponding to parts (a), (b), (c), and (d) of the theorem, lead to four kinds of procedures. We term these *Cartesian* (only for "."), *restrictive* (for "." and "$-$"), *set* (for ".", "$-$", and " $\vee$ "); corresponding to set intersection, difference, and union, respectively), and *Boolean arithmetic* (for all binary operators and negation).

‡ The example (25) uses the operator "$-$"; this is why it was introduced—to widen the class of proper formulas.

VI. A Concluding Remark

We believe that automatic question-answering provides a fertile field for applied logic. We have seen how notions in logic can be applied to the analysis of natural-language questions and to the design of data bases. We have also seen how the information systems themselves involve new and interesting concepts which lead to problems of both theoretic and practical importance.

ACKNOWLEDGMENTS

I wish to thank my colleagues at RAND for their help in this work. In particular, my thanks go to N. D. Cohen, J. Economos, R. E. Levien (Project Leader for the Relational Data File Project), G. Levitt, M. E. Maron (formerly of RAND and former project co-leader), and G. R. Martins, who reviewed the manuscript of this chapter.

REFERENCES

Carnap, R. (1937). "The Logical Syntax of Language" (English ed.). Routledge and Kegan Paul, London.

Carnap, R. (1956). "Meaning and Necessity" (Enlarged ed.). Univ. of Chicago Press, Chicago, Illinois.

Di Paola, R. A. (1968). The Recursive Unsolvability of the Decision Problem for the Class of Definite Formulas, RM-5639-PR. The RAND Corp. Santa Monica, California [also published in *J. Assoc. Comput. Mach.* **16**, 324–327 (1969)].

Jespersen, O. (1965). "The Philosophy of Grammar." Norton, New York.

Kuhns, J. L. (1967). Answering Questions by Computer: A Logical Study, RM-5428-PR. The RAND Corp., Santa Monica, California.

Levien, R. E. (1966). Relational Data File II. Implementation, P-3411. The RAND Corp., Santa Monica, California [also published in G. Schecter (ed.), Information Retrieval: A Critical View. *Proc. 3rd Annual Nat. Colloq. on Information Retrieval, May 1966*, pp. 225–241. Thompson, Washington, D. C., 1967].

Levien, R. E. (1969). Relational Data File: Experience with a System for Propositional Data Storage and Inference Execution, RM-5947-PR. The RAND Corp., Santa Monica, California.

Levien, R., and Maron, M. E. (1965). Relational Data File: A Tool for Mechanized Inference Execution and Data Retrieval, RM-4793-PR. The RAND Corp., Santa Monica, California.

Levien, R., and Maron, M. E. (1966). A Computer System for Inference Execution and Data Retrieval, RM-5085-PR. The RAND Corp., Santa Monica, California [also published in *Comm. ACM* **10**, 715–721 (1967)].

Maron, M. E. (1966). Relational Data File I: Design Philosophy, P-3408. The RAND Corp., Santa Monica, California [also published in G. Schecter (ed.), Information Retrieval: A Critical View. *Proc. 3rd Annual Nat. Colloq. on Information Retrieval, May 1966*, pp. 211–223. Thompson, Washington, D. C., 1967].

Reichenbach, H. (1947). "Elements of Symbolic Logic." Macmillan, New York,

Whitehead, A. N., and Russell, B. (1950). "Principia Mathematica," 2nd ed. Cambridge Univ. Press, London and New York.

Intermediate Languages for Automatic Language Processing

Michael Otten†
INTERNATIONAL BUSINESS MACHINES, INC.
BETHESDA, MARYLAND

and Milos G. Pacak
NATIONAL INSTITUTES OF HEALTH
BETHESDA, MARYLAND

I. Introduction

An intermediate (or intermediary) language is any language which serves as a means of communication between any permutation of humans and machines not able to communicate together in their own native languages. There are four basic types of intermediate languages which are treated in the literature: pure natural languages, formalized natural languages, artificial international languages, and pure artificial languages. We shall examine each of these categories in terms of its potential for automatic information processing, and then discuss two particular instances of information processing: machine translation and information retrieval. This tutorial review and commentary will focus on the functional aspects of intermediate languages, within a general historical perspective. More general surveys of approaches to machine translation and information retrieval are available in the literature [1–4].

II. Intermediate Languages

The evolution of the 5000 to 6000 "natural languages"‡ is comparable to the evolution of biological life forms by natural selection. This analogy is strengthened by the fact that from 1000 to 2000 mutant species of languages have become extinct during the past 200 years [5]. An artificial language may

† *Present affiliation:* Corporate Headquarters. International Business Machines, Inc., Armonk, New York.

‡ Separate natural languages imply, in this context, "groups that cannot intercommunicate."

then be defined as any language which has not evolved by the process of natural selection. Akhmanova [6] takes the position that, "All that is available to knowledge can be expressed in any existing language." Whorf [7] disagrees with such a statement, believing that certain types of abstract thinking are not possible in some languages. If languages evolve by natural selection, then we would expect that some languages should be better suited than others for particular functions or in special environments. Machine translation and information retrieval are two functional areas where the problems of automatic natural language data processing are clearly of great importance, and have yet to be solved.

Historically, because of language differences between locales, certain natural languages were used as aids to communication of thought among distant groups with common interests. For example, Latin was the language of science and religion in Europe, while French was the language of eighteenth century diplomacy. It would be difficult to pinpoint the times when these relatively formal intermediate languages ceased to be the norm. The cause is perhaps easier to identify: As science, religion, and politics have become increasingly the domain of the general public, it has become impossible to impose an irrelevant discipline on the development of these human pursuits. Contributions were not language dependent, and were therefore made and recorded in the natural language of the contributor. To the extent that a limited formal notational language has been essential to certain fields (especially chemistry and mathematics), communication has remained more or less feasible without the need of professional translation between natural languages. Subjects with a strong foundation from an earlier era (e.g., medical anatomy) have maintained a relatively standardized international language. On the other hand, young and dynamic fields (e.g., computer science) have been unable to establish a strong standard terminology, even within single language cultures such as the United States, in spite of compelling reasons to do so.

The need for communication among different natural language groups is justification for treatment of the translation problem; but, there is another problem area where intermediate languages might be of use. Computer aided information retrieval systems require storage of information in machine processable form. While it is possible to store and retrieve natural language data without knowledge about the meaning of the text, to collate or abstract information relevant to users of varying interests requires automatic analysis of natural language. The so-called information explosion has made it even more difficult than in previous times for any individual human to gain access to all potentially useful information without recourse to external aid. Such access is sufficiently difficult and costly to cause many scientists to believe that if a project costs less than several thousand dollars, it is easier to repeat work already done rather than to search for it in the literature.

A. Natural Language

Natural languages are the only type of intermediate languages which have historically received acceptance. One of the strongest justifications for using a natural language to represent information, especially for machine storage and retrieval, is that only natural languages have the inherent complexity and ambiguity which is in fact a part of much information data. This concept is relevant if the meaning of an individual word is extended to cover new situations or knowledge. It is for this reason that natural languages are frequently rejected as intermediate languages, "since the interlingua must ensure a monovalent, explicit, and maximally economical notation for meaning extracted from the input text, and no natural language satisfies these requirements" [8]. We believe that this problem of ambiguity can be resolved in theory by a precise (therefore unnatural) language with no vocabulary bounds. Rather than resort to lexical ambiguity, there could be a means by which new words would be introduced into the lexicon to represent new ideas. Thus, an unambiguous language must have the capacity for the creation of new semantic categories, to be flexible and expandable with the real world domain of knowledge. Further, shadings of meaning might be expressed by specifying a locus between two precise concepts, with quantifiable weighting establishing position on a spectrum. Jespersen is reported to have said that language serves three functions: one is to communicate ideas, another is to conceal ideas, and the third is to conceal the absence of ideas. If ambiguity, or polysemantic values, are a part of an idea, this ambiguity can presumably be precisely specified in terms of statistical uncertainty.

Idioms, abbreviations, acronyms, and homographs are some of the most common problem elements of natural languages [9]. An interesting example of an idiom is the reported Russian to English translation of the phrase, "out of sight, out of mind," which became "invisible idiot." The expression, "time flies," is often used as an example of a homograph, where either word could be noun or verb. To demonstrate the magnitude of these problems, Harper [10] analyzed a sample page of Russian scientific text, finding 151 different words in 266 running words. Twenty-four words were used idiomatically, while an additional 46 words (30% of the total) had multiple semantic values, whose ambiguity could not be resolved by structural analysis. Harper recommended contextual analysis as the solution to the problems of syntactic and semantic ambiguity, but later research in this area has indicated that knowledge of an entire cultural context is necessary to resolve difficult ambiguities. From a practical point of view, emphasis on context has been an important and fruitful direction for linguistics research. Idioglossaries (described further in the section on artificial languages) and immediate constituent, predictive, and dependency grammars are examples of linguistic techniques based on contextual analysis [11]. Alternative approaches, such as represented by context free transformational grammars, are more often used for general linguistic description [12].

The ambiguity and acceptable syntactic variability of natural languages do not facilitate automatic information processing. While it does not seem possible to require humans to communicate with machinelike exactitude, neither is it necessary or efficient to expect machines to process internally or synthesize ambiguous natural language. As humans input information for machine storage, interaction with natural language must be processed at the initial input analysis stage. Beyond this point, pure natural language should be avoided, as there is no reason for further introduction of ambiguity to the information.

B. Formal Natural Language

The primary improvements of a formal natural language over a purely natural language are the removal of ambiguity, systemization of irregular forms, and the streamlining of the language. A formal natural language retains the fundamental lexical and syntactic content of a natural language, so that users who know the related natural language may learn the rules and limitations with minimum difficulty. Unfortunately, if a formal language is too similar to a natural language, users may easily revert to natural language constructions which might be misinterpreted under the formal rules.

Examples of formal natural languages include Dodd's Model English [13], Basic English [14], and FASE (Fundamentally Analyzable Simplified English) [15]. Basic English, for example, has an elemental vocabulary of 850 words, including 400 "things," 200 "picturables," 100 "general qualities," 50 "opposites," 100 "operations," and a dozen or so "rules" (e.g., "plurals in 's'.") More complex concepts (e.g., "automobile") are expressed in terms of the basic vocabulary (e.g., "a carriage machine moved by an engine"). Such an approach, well designed for rapid mastery of the components of a foreign language essential for basic communications, permits a fairly compact vocabulary for information processing or storage, and may be quite acceptable for output. However, the translation of a natural language expression into such a form is not likely to be easy. Complex abstractions are extremely difficult to define with any inflexible finite lexicon. Norton's *The General Basic English Dictionary* defines over 20,000 words in the 850 words of Basic English, but the problem of accommodating the expansion of knowledge is still present. Further, a finite lexicon does not guarantee simple and unambiguous syntax.

FASE is closer to natural English, focusing its attention on formal syntax. It would seem possible to teach well-motivated people its positional rules without too much trouble, but its lack of semantic orientation makes it more suitable for computer synthesized output than input or internal processing. A human writer of FASE might make a mistake which would result in misinterpretation by the computer. As Kuno [16] points out, "the user of FASE must know, for each sentence he writes, what is the first analysis assigned to the sentence by the computer." Yet, humans have this same problem when interpreting natural language text, just as computers have with programming languages.

C. INTERNATIONAL LANGUAGES

The goals of artificial international languages are largely the same as for formal natural languages. However, rather than creating such a language from the base of one natural language, an attempt is made to incorporate in the new language the optimum features of several natural languages. The advantages and disadvantages are similar to those of a formal natural language, although it might be hoped that a compromise language among several language groups might lead to greater acceptance by speakers of more than one natural language. Historically, the orientation of this sort of language has been towards the translation problem, while the formal natural language has been proposed more often as a step toward the solution of the information retrieval problem. International languages represent the earliest attempts to create intermediate languages.

Esperanto is probably the best known of the international languages, although other attempts to construct such languages include Esperanto II, Ido, Interlingua, Occidental, and Novial [17]. The strongest argument against the general usefulness of these languages is their lack of widespread acceptance. Further, as none of them appears to have been designed for machine translation or information retrieval, it is not likely that they should prove useful in these fields. Yet many of the ideas which have come from their development may prove to be indicators of important design considerations for future intermediate languages. For example, the segmentation of word forms into their productive components (stems, prefixes, suffixes) is a way to reduce substantially the size of a dictionary.

The primary objection to international or formal natural languages for information processing is the possible human confusion with purely natural languages, resulting in misapplication of the rules of usage. Such languages are indeed necessary for output of information in a form to be understood by humans. However, this output need not have the flexibility of pure natural languages, as there is no need for the generation of information in all the various (infinite) ways possible with a natural language.

D. ARTIFICIAL LANGUAGES

Kellogg [18] defines an artificial language as "a system of signs deliberately constructed by a person or a small group of people, over a comparatively short interval of time, for a particular purpose." We would submit that the "short interval of time" is not necessary, as long as standardization can be maintained, with syntactic and semantic compatability with previous versions. Otherwise, obsolescence is inherent in any proposed language. The use "for a particular purpose" is more a pragmatic warning to language designers than a definitional constraint on the concept of artificial languages. Insofar as any artificial language is at least based on the concepts and things expressed symbolically by natural languages, both formal natural languages and international languages are artificial languages. This section will concentrate on some concepts of artificial languages which are based on general linguistic principles, not tied to any particular natural languages, except as a matter of notational convenience.

A language may be treated in lexical terms, such as is done in a dictionary, as well as from the point of view of syntax, which treats the structural organization of sentences and phrases. Basic English is an example of an attempt to formalize language on the lexical level alone. FASE is a similar example of concentration on the syntactic elements of language. We shall attempt to show in our discussion of a few techniques that effective semantic analysis requires both lexical and syntactic processing.

Open-stack libraries are probably the oldest and most common examples of language-independent information retrieval systems. Books are filed according to a limited dictionary of categories represented by words, noun phrases, or numerical indices. A researcher will usually depend on a few key bibliographic references to find his way into the appropriate area of the library stacks. From here, browsing becomes an efficient search strategy. The Dewey decimal and Library of Congress classification schemes are examples of organizational techniques that file information into general and more specific subject categories, utilizing a type of tree structure to facilitate information retrieval. From a practical point of view, two major weaknesses of this approach are the lack of sufficient differentiation, and the difficulty of cross-referencing on the book shelves.

Idioglossaries (sometimes called microglossaries) are also based on differentiation of specialized areas of knowledge. This technique involves the establishment of separate lexicons for various fields of knowledge. Thus, different subjects have different dictionaries for an intermediate language, although the syntax might well be shared. The SNOP (Systemized Nomenclature of Pathology) dictionary is being used in this way at the National Institutes of Health to permit computerized medical language processing [19].

Identical words or noun phrases may be found in different idioglossaries, corresponding to the overlap of concepts among different subject areas. Lexical homographs may frequently be assigned a single meaning on the basis of which idioglossary contains the word and is also relevant to the known subject matter of the text. More difficult ambiguities cannot be resolved without syntactic or further contextual analysis. Programming languages, such as FORTRAN and COBOL, are examples of specialized languages with syntax and a small vocabulary defined with unique semantic values, in terms most efficient for their particular use.

The thesaurus is one of the most powerful techniques in the quest for semantic comprehension for an intermediate language. *Roget's International Thesaurus of English Words and Phrases* is a classic example of this approach, although not oriented toward automatic data processing. Here the library approach to separate subject categories is adopted, with the ability to point to multiple semantic values, as in the cross-references of a card catalog. The intermediate language is coded according to semantic categories, and it is feasible to apply these codes to any natural or artificial languages. A refinement of thesaurus techniques has been developed at the University of Milan, and is based on the assignment of correlational indices to word combinations in terms of semantic and syntactic functions [20]. The techniques used are based on a hypothetical model of human linguistic thought processes. Von Glaserfeld is attempting to extrapolate from this approach a practical semantic-oriented language, employing some of the forms of a formal natural language as a vehicle for his research [21]. Salton [22], in his book on automatic information organization and retrieval, provides a lucid description of specific automatic and manual techniques used for thesauri generation.

There is an increasing interest in the complex area of semantics, but the implementation of theories has yet to distinguish the superiority of any particular approach. To date, the best-explored approaches to semantics have utilized lexical and syntactic "cross-classification" schemes to represent semantic values [23, 24]. More complex conceptualizations, such as Blum's work with a three-dimensional model [25], have received less attention thus far, perhaps because they are more complicated to implement with conventional binary computers.

III. Machine Translation

There are two fundamental approaches to machine translation. The classic approach is analogous to the human technique of translating directly from one language to another. The idea is to apply a unique set of transformation algorithms to analyze each source natural language, and synthesize directly a translation into a particular target natural language. The second approach is to translate the source language into a target intermediate language. This intermediate language representation then serves as the source for translation into several target languages.

Even the direct one-to-one natural language to natural language "binary" approach always uses an intermediate machine language representation, usually in the form of a coded analysis of the source language text. But this intermediate batch of coded information is organized only with the object of permitting the generation of a valid synthesis in the target language with a minimum of human intervention. Any procedure which might facilitate the transformation of text from one language to another may be valid, with or without regard for the true syntax or semantic content of the steps in the transformation. There is no requirement that the intermediate machine language representation of the text have any similarity to the intermediate representation between any other two languages, for equivalent information content.

The main argument in favor of an intermediate auxiliary language for machine translation is based on the principle of economy. If an intermediate language is employed, for each language there must be an analysis and a synthesis into the intermediate language, as well as an analysis and synthesis from the intermediate language. Assuming similar levels of complexity of all analyses and syntheses for n natural languages, $4n$ algorithms become necessary for the intermediate language approach. But, working directly from one language to another, an analysis and a synthesis program are required for each permutation of languages. Thus, "binary" translation requires $2n(n-1)$ algorithms, as opposed to $4n$ algorithms for translations employing an intermediate language. The break-even point is at three languages. Therefore, for four or more languages, it would appear that an intermediate approach to translation is more efficient. For example, Figure 1 shows the algorithms required for translation among four languages, where the intermediate language technique uses only 16 separate complex operations, rather than the 24 required for binary translation.

A counter-argument to this line of reasoning is that analysis and synthesis may be easier operations, in terms of any two languages, than establishing an appropriate intermediate language as a go-between for all language pairs. It this is so, our assumption of equal complexity for all analysis and synthesis algorithms breaks down. However, Harris [26] reports that, "the types of base transformations of various languages are very similar one to the other." Also, Pacak [27] has found, for several Slavic languages, that absolute and partial morphological similarities are common. But, even if a binary analysis and synthesis could be shown to be less complex than the intermediate language routines, this would only raise the break-even point at which the number of languages would justify the intermediate language approach. The

Binary Approach

A—(analysis)—(synthesis)—B—(analysis)—(synthesis)—A
A—(analysis)—(synthesis)—C—(analysis)—(synthesis)—A
A—(analysis)—(synthesis)—D—(analysis)—(synthesis)—A
B—(analysis)—(synthesis)—C—(analysis)—(synthesis)—B
B—(analysis)—(synthesis)—D—(analysis)—(synthesis)—B
C—(analysis)—(synthesis)—D—(analysis)—(synthesis)—C

Intermediate Language Approach

A—(analysis)—(synthesis)—I—(analysis)—(synthesis)—A
B—(analysis)—(synthesis)—I—(analysis)—(synthesis)—B
C—(analysis)—(synthesis)—I—(analysis)—(synthesis)—C
D—(analysis)—(synthesis)—I—(analysis)—(synthesis)—D

FIGURE 1. Translation algorithms among four languages.

number of algorithms still only increases linearly with n, while being proportional to n^2 for the binary approach.

An intermediate language should contain by itself all the information from the source language which is to be put into the target language. This means that if style is a part of the desired information, indicators of style must be in the intermediate language, as well as indicators of content. However, the problem of content translation is sufficiently difficult, so that we shall ignore refinements in such areas as style. For most nonliterary applications, translation of content is all that is required. Proponents of binary translation might assert that the extra level between languages in the intermediate language approach permits an extra leakage of information. Acknowledging that information, or at least innuendoes and subtleties, may be lost in binary translation, certainly the extra step of an intermediate language would seem to increase the loss of such data. This problem is evident within a single language when abstracting or even paraphrasing is attempted. Except in the case of full synonyms, any change in wording is likely to result in at least a change of emphasis. The issue here is whether or not the additional information loss is significant, and this must depend on the quality of the various algorithms for any approach, including human translation.

One of the reasons that binary translation has been favored in the United States might be the belief that translations from Russian to English are more important than translations of other languages. This could be based on a preoccupation with the scientific progress of our primary competitors. Many also feel that most significant scientific work is reported either in English or Russian. Further, Russian is considered a language which is largely unknown to Americans, unlike French or German, for example. This line of reasoning, unfortunately for other language groups in the world, would seem to have been sufficiently valid to distract linguistics research in the United States, resulting in concentration on Russian to English translation as a primary goal of American machine translation work. In spite of early expectations to find a quick method for automatic Russian to English translation, most computational linguists would agree with Oettinger's remark [28] that it is only "a dwindling lunatic fringe who still believe automatic mechanical translation to be just around the corner." Bar-Hillel [29] has taken an even stronger position against the practicality of automatic machine translation. Failure to find an easy solution to the machine translation problem has perhaps redirected machine translation research to careful scientific study rather than brute force techniques. Interestingly, Russian scientists have shown greater interest in intermediate languages than American workers in the field of automatic natural language processing [30].

If the Tower of Babel condition is accepted as irremediable, another argument for an intermediate language is the easier access for smaller language groups (especially in underdeveloped countries) to the mainstream of scientific thought. From an idealistic point of view, it would seem desirable that the smaller cultural groups should have access to scientific information without being forced to learn Russian or English. Each language group, to gain access to published world thought, would have to develop only one algorithm for synthesis into their language, and, later, one algorithm for translation of their language into the intermediate language. The alternative is to learn either Russian or English in addition to their native tongues, which might prove more economical than the development of automatic translation techniques. In a sense this would be accepting the major natural languages as de facto intermediate languages; but the marginal value of using such nonartificial languages for any automatic information processing has been discussed in previous sections of this paper.

IV. Information Retrieval

Information retrieval and machine translation are conceptually analogous problems in terms of automatic information processing. Many machine translation experts have abandoned their work, having discovered that language translation is not a straightforward "mechanical" task; and, although information retrieval workers have frequently recognized the potential value of linguistics research to their field [31], specific collaboration seems to be lacking. The concepts of intermediate languages appear to provide a foundation for concurrent treatment of these two areas of interest. The manipulation of information within a single language is really only a special case of language data processing.

In simple systems, information may be stored as strings of characters accessed by highly formalized commands. As greater processing complexity is required for the stored information, it becomes necessary for the machine to "understand" storage contents, as well as input commands, in order to output the requested information. According to Ivanov [32]:

In the projected information machine, all the aggregates of information, pertaining to a definite field of knowledge, should be written in abstract machine language. The linguistic problems of creating such a language for an information machine are closely related with the problem of translation into this abstract language from separate specific languages.

Many scientists feel that humans may even find it useful to use the resulting abstract machine languages for aiding normal thought processes. This is consistent with the belief that language shapes thoughts as well as giving expression to them. ALGOL (the "Algorithmic Language") is an example of such a formal language, particularly in its use as a standard of communications (e.g., in *The Journal of the Association for Computing Machinery*).

Computer-oriented information retrieval may be directed toward direct access to information elements or access to pointers to information elements. On the one hand, a user might want to retrieve all available documents on a particular subject. This sort of retrieval problem may be best met with indexed subject heading systems such as MEDLARS (Medical Literature Analysis and Retrieval System) at the United States National Library of Medicine. More complex is the retrieval of factual data from a massive data base, where the answer to a question might not be specifically organized and filed in the form of the desired output. To perform such a task, information should be organized so that the machine can process the semantic content of its store. This is a problem of considerable difficulty, probably of the same order of magnitude as the problem of automatic machine translation between natural languages. A brute force approach to this problem might be to store the content of encyclopedias, with indexed access to the data as in a standard encyclopedia. To appreciate the magnitude of this job, we must realize that an encyclopedia (e.g., *The Encyclopaedia Britannica*) may have more than 200 million characters in it. Yet, storage of such a large data base is now technologically feasible; it is more a question of economics. An interesting collection of essays on the desirability of encyclopedic information machines has been compiled by Kochen [33]. However, exhaustive morphological, syntactic, and semantic analysis is not necessary for the development of restrictive information retrieval or question answering systems, which can still satisfy the requirements of many users. For example, Simmons *et al.* [34] developed a system based on coordination of stored index terms and limited structure matching, which stored original natural language text as its data base, answering queries which might match some statement in the data base. Black [35] introduced a significant degree of deductive reasoning to his question answering system, but still required a significant amount of unguided searching.

Semantic considerations have become increasingly important in question answering programs. Raphael's Semantic Information Retrieval (SIR) system translated a restricted subset of English into a data base organized in terms of a limited number of fundamental relations. Using the known properties of these relations, elementary deductions permitted the program to answer queries to which no input statement corresponded directly [36]. A promising approach to development of a machine resident semantic data base is reported by Quillian [37] who proposed a semantic network memory which would interpret natural language input with the aid of weighted associations in the memory, translate the new information into its internal artificial language representation, and then assimilate the new information into its semantic data base structure (memory), thereby usefully increasing the knowledge (intelligence) of the system. Other interesting examples of implementations of question-answering languages include Easy English [38] and DEACON [39].

V. Conclusions

The linguistic problems in machine translation and information retrieval suggest that an artificial language, based on the construction of well-defined semantic categories, might be a potentially effective approach for future work. A standard but expandable lexicon, coupled with rigid syntactic rules, should facilitate efficient automatic information handling. Further, the psychological barrier to acceptance of an artificial intermediate language, as was encountered by proponents of international intermediate languages, is not as serious when finite automata become the repository for the language. Once a computer is taught (programmed) a language, in theory, other finite-state machines can be taught exactly the same language. As yet, there has been relatively little work done in the United States from this point of view, largely because of an understandable reluctance to face the complexity of semantics. Unfortunately, the problems of machine translation and information retrieval no longer permit avoidance of semantic issues. Artificial intermediate languages offer a theoretically viable framework for treatment of the problems of automatic information processing.

REFERENCES

1. Borko, H., ed., "Automated Language Processing." Wiley, New York, 1967.
2. Simmons, R. F., "Automated Language Processing." *Annual Rev. Information Sci. Tech.* **1**, 137–169 (1966).
3. Kent, A., ed., "Information Retrieval and Machine Translation," Pts. 1 and 2. Wiley (Interscience), New York, 1960.

4. Bobrow, D. G., Fraser, J. B., and Quillian, M. R., "Automated Language Processing." *Annual Rev. Information Sci. Tech.* **2**, 161–186 (1967).
5. Lotz, J., "Speech—Man's Natural Communication."*IEEE Spectrum* **4**, 82 (1967).
6. Akhmanova, O. S., "The Place of Semantics in Modern Linguistics." "Exact Methods in Linguistic Research," translated from the Russian by D. G. Hays and D. V. Mohr (eds.), p. 20. Univ. of California Press, Berkeley, California, 1963.
7. Whorf, B. L., "A Linguistic Consideration of Thinking in Primitive Communities." "Language, Thought and Reality," pp. 65–86. M.I.T. Press, Cambridge, Massachusetts, 1966.
8. Mel'Chuk, I. A., "Machine Translation and Linguistics." "Exact Methods in Linguistic Research," translation from the Russian by D. G. Hays and C. V. Mohr (eds.), pp. 64–65. Univ. of California Press, Berkeley, California, 1963.
9. Pacak, M., "Homographs: Classification and Identification." "*Etudes de Linguistique Appliquée*," Vol. 5, pp. 89–105. Didier, Paris, 1967.
10. Harper, K. E., "Semantic Ambiguity." *Mech. Translation* **4**, 68 (1957).
11. Robinson, J., Endocentric Constructions and the Cocke Parsing Logic, AD-614896. U.S. Clearinghouse for Federal Scientific and Technical Information, Springfield, Virginia, 1965.
12. Chomsky, N., "Aspects of the Theory of Syntax." M.I.T. Press, Cambridge, Massachusetts, 1965.
13. Reifler, E., "The First Conference on Mechanical Translation." *Mech. Translation* **1**, 27 (1954).
14. Richards, I. S., "Basic English and Its Uses." Norton, New York, 1943.
15. McMahon, L. E., "Fundamentally Analyzable Simplified English." Bell Telephone Laboratories News, New York, June 20, 1966.
16. Kuno, S., "Automatic Syntactic Analysis," *Seminar on Comput. Linguistics, Bethesda, Maryland, 1966* (A. W. Pratt, A. H. Roberts, and K. Lewis, eds.), Public Health Service Pub. No. 1716, p. 35. U.S. Govt. Printing Office, Washington, D. C., 1966.
17. Martinet, A., "La Linguistique et les Langues Artificielles" (in French), p. 43. Word, New York, 1946.
18. Kellogg, C. H., "Designing Artificial Languages for Information Storage and Retrieval." *In* "Automated Language Processing" (H. Borko, ed.), p. 325. Wiley, New York, 1967.
19. Pratt, A. W., and Pacak, M. G., "Automated Processing of Medical English." *Internat. Conf. Computational Linguistics, Stockholm, 1969.*
20. Ceccato, S., *et al.*, "Mechanical Translation: The Correlational Solution." AD-409607. U.S. Clearinghouse for Federal Scientific and Technical Information, Springfield Virginia, 1963.
21. von Glaserfeld, E., "Automatic English Sentence Analysis." AD-657043. U.S. Clearinghouse for Federal Scientific and Technical Information, Springfield, Virginia, 1967.
22. Salton, G., "Automatic Information Organization and Retrieval," pp. 23–65. McGraw-Hill, New York ,1968.
23. Fodor, J. A., and Katz, J. J., "The Structure of a Semantic Theory." *In* "The Structure of Language: Readings in the Philosophy of Language," pp. 479–518. Prentice-Hall, Englewood Cliffs, New Jersey, 1964.
24. Bolinger, D., "The Atomization of Meaning." *Language* **41**, 555–573 (1965). This is one of several critical replies to the Katz and Fodor Approach.
25. Blum, H., "A New Model of Global Brain Function." *Perspect. Biol. Med.* **10,** 381–408 (1967).

26. Harris, Z. S., "Mathematical Structures of Language," p. 156. Wiley (Interscience), New York, 1968.
27. Pacak, M., "Slavic Languages: Comparative Morphosyntactic Analysis." *Mech. Translation* **8**, 11–14 (1964).
28. Oettinger, A. G., "Automatic Processing of Natural and Formal Languages." *Proc. IFIP Congr. New York, 1965*, pp. 9–16. Spartan Books, Baltimore, Maryland, 1965.
29. Bar-Hillel, Y., "Language and Information," p. 217. Addison-Wesley, Reading, Massachusetts, 1964.
30. Andreyev, N. D., "The Intermediary Language as the Focal Point of Machine Translation." *In* "Machine Translation" (A. D. Booth, ed.), pp. 1–27. Wiley, New York, 1967.
31. Zull, C. G., "On the Possible Relevance of Linguistics to Information Retrieval." *Proc. Amer. Soc. Information Sci.* **5**, 285–287 (1968).
32. Ivanov, V. V., "Linguistic Problems in the Creation of a Machine Language for an Information Machine," translated from the Russian in JPRS-2150. U. S. Clearinghouse for Federal Scientific and Technical Information, Springfield, Virginia, February, 1960.
33. Kochen, M., "The Growth of Knowledge: Readings on Organization and Retrieval of Information." Wiley, New York, 1967.
34. Simmons, R. F., Klein, S., and McConlogue, K., "Indexing and Dependency Logic for Answering English Questions." *Amer. Doc.* **15**, 196–204 (1964).
35. Black, F., "A Deductive Question-Answering System." *In* "Semantic Information Processing" (M. Minsky, ed.), pp. 354–402. M.I.T. Press, Cambridge, Massachusetts, 1968.
36. Raphael, B., "A Computer Program Which 'Understands'." *Proc. Fall Joint Comput. Conf., San Francisco, 1964*, **26**, 577–589. Spartan Books, Baltimore, Maryland, 1964.
37. Quillian, M. R., "The Teachable Language Comprehender: A Simulation Program and Theory of Language." *Comm. ACM* **12**, 459–476 (1969).
38. Rubinoff, M., Bergman, S., Caulin, H., and Rapp, F., "Easy English, a Language for Information Retrieval through a Remote Typewriter Console." *Comm. ACM* **11**, 693–696 (1968).
39. Craig, J. A., Berezner, S. C., Carney, H. C., and Longyear, C. R., "DEACON: Direct English Access and CONtrol." *Proc. Fall Joint Comput. Conf. San Francisco, 1966*, **29**, 365–380. Spartan Books, Baltimore, Maryland, 1966.

GIRL—Graph Information Retrieval Language— Design of Syntax

S. Berkowitz

NAVAL SHIP RESEARCH AND DEVELOPMENT CENTER
WASHINGTON, D.C.

I. Introduction

A graph is a set of nodes and links. For the purpose of the paper, one can think of the graph as being built of node–link–node triplets. For example, Figure 1 shows a triplet in which one can think of node A as the *argument*, link B the *function*, and node C the *value*.

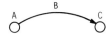

FIGURE 1. Node–link–node triplet.

GIRL (Graph Information Retrieval Language) is a programming language which permits the insertion, retrieval, and deletion of information mapped onto graph structures. The ease with which GIRL traces or dynamically transforms flowchart-like organizations makes the language especially suitable for the symbol manipulation involved in syntactic and semantic network generation and recognition, data and program management systems, and scheduling system simulation. For example, in GIRL one can write a compiler-compiler, a personnel background inventory, or a job shop simulator.

The language is introduced from the designer's viewpoint by reviewing some of the decisions and compromises necessary to meet the design goals. A more formal presentation of the language, in the form of a Backus Naur Form (BNF) syntax, is presented in Appendix A. Finally, some possible extensions to the language are discussed.

A recent paper by Feldman and Rovner (1969) presents a language (LEAP) which, like GIRL, is designed to manipulate information in graph structures, but which is organized along ALGOL lines and has a quite different design strategy. The paper contains a discussion and comprehensive bibliography of

119

the languages and programming systems which lie in the background of current thinking on associative languages. This background includes techniques not only from such standard symbolic processors as LISP (McCarthy et al., 1962), IPL-V (Newell, 1961), and AMBIT/G (Christensen, 1967), but also from algebraic processors such as ALGOL (Van Wijngaarden, 1968) and FORTRAN (IBM, 1968).

II. Design Considerations

The designing of GIRL has, at times, been an exciting experience. In the final analysis, GIRL does not turn out to be the answer to everybody's symbol manipulation problems, but it does permit graph tracing and transformation with a pleasing conciseness. The following sections present some aspects of the design philosophy of GIRL. The categories selected as section headings are by no means independent, but suffice to emphasize the critical design areas. One should be aware that the following discussion is not a user's manual, but a critique of the why and wherefore of GIRL. The semantics required to understand the syntax in Appendix A will appear shortly in a user's manual. As will be apparent from Section III on "Extensions and Applications," the design of the language is not complete. However, the subset of the language presented here has a wide range of applications, and it was felt that even the incomplete language was worthy of presentation if for nothing else than to draw criticism.

A. The Numeric–Symbolic Dichotomy

Programming languages operate on one of two types of objects:

1. *Numerals* (which represent numbers). For example, all so-called algebraic languages, such as FORTRAN, whose sentences represent arithmetic manipulation of numbers are in the class of number-oriented languages.
2. *Literals* (which represent their abstract selves). For example, all *string-transforming* languages, such as SNOBOL whose sentences represent sequence manipulation of literals, are in the class of symbol-oriented languages.

In a sense, of course, the above distinction is not as clear as it may seem. A numeral is a type of literal, and a number is a type of symbol. Moreover, a number-oriented language may deal with nonnumeric literals, and a symbol-oriented language may deal with arithmetic operations. For example, FORTRAN has Hollerith expressions, and SNOBOL has arithmetic operations. Nevertheless, in most programming languages there is a clear distinction in the emphasis on numeric or nonnumeric operations. Such a bifurcated emphasis is a direct result of the physical design of computers whose nonassociative memories and arithmetic units are disposed favorably toward numeric data processing. The software simulation of associative memories frequently required for nonnumeric data processing places a computation time penalty on symbol manipulation. Consequently, the few brave souls who do try to combine the two forms of processing, as in PL/I, find themselves in the dilemma of having a somewhat less than general symbolic processor, and a somewhat slowly running numeric processor.

With the above difficulties in mind, it was decided to design GIRL principally for nonnumeric processing. At the same time, it was decided to embed the language in an algebraic language such as FORTRAN or ALGOL by writing a preprocessor to the algebraic compiler. The preprocessor would distinguish the GIRL statements from the algebraic language (largely as a set of subroutine calls) before turning to the algebraic compiler to translate the entire program. This approach has some advantages:

1. One can interleave graph-processing operations with algebraic operations so that it is possible to transform and numerically interpret or take statistics on the graph in one program.

2. Since the algebraic portion of the program runs under its original compiler, there is no loss in computation time.

3. By separating algebraic and graph operations, one achieves a certain elegance and ease of programming. The resulting programs are at once concise and at the same time self-explanatory.

On the other hand, there are some disadvantages:

1. A preprocessor is a clumsy means of compiling and the resultant two-phase compiler is time consuming.

2. The passing of variable and data structures from the graph processor to the numeric processor is a delicate operation, from the point of view of the user. The alternative would be to mesh algebraic and graph operations, a difficult task for the compiler.

Aside from difficulties in compilation, the preservation of the elegance and clarity of the language was a strong factor in deciding to keep algebraic and graph operations distinct. On the other hand, GIRL does provide internally for an indirect mesh of operations by means of a GIRL FUNCTION. The FUNCTION, as in FORTRAN, is single-valued and has the form: $*I_0(I_1, \ldots, I_n)$, where the I_i are identifiers or numbers. The value of the FUNCTION is either a node or link sequence of the graph, depending on the location of the FUNCTION in the GIRL statement. The FUNCTION itself is a set of GIRL and algebraic statements, as in the calling program.

As a symbol processor, GIRL is a primitive language, designed to be, for example, the assembly language for a computer with an associative memory. Thus, it is powerful in the sense that one can compile other symbol processors in terms of GIRL, but is weak in the sense that it does not have, internally, the pattern-matching capabilities of some higher-level languages. Section III contains some suggestions to extend GIRL in the direction of pattern-matching.

B. IDENTIFIERS

The basic and immediate requirement for creating GIRL identifiers is that each identifier must be associated with the address of some arbitrary node of the graph under consideration. One creates an identifier simply by having the compiler or preprocessor regard a character string as an algebraic variable whose value is an internal address. An identifier may refer then to both a node corresponding to the address, and/or to some *type* of link (or function, so to speak). Remember that, for an underlying associative memory scheme, all nodes refer to an internal numeric address, are linked to all other nodes, and are available at the inception of processing. Inserting a node–link–node element of a graph (the formalism of which is explained in Section II,C) is merely the action of activating (by identification) a link between nodes. Even though it is precise to speak of identifying a link, we shall indulge, without ambiguity, in the terminology of "inserting a link" or "linking."

One of the problems in describing identifiers arises either in the compilation or preprocessing phase when an identifier such as 2F must be converted to a character string which is acceptable to the algebraic compiler as a variable. In such a conversion, a convenient, albeit naïve way to store the association between an identifier and a node is to string the identifier on a vocabulary tree, thus taking advantage of the speed of the underlying associative memory for retrieval purposes. For example, consider placing the word R3V on a vocabulary tree, as shown in Figure 2.

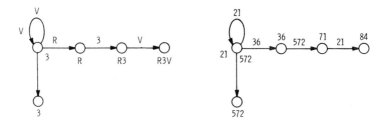

FIGURE 2. Left: Insertion of R3V on vocabulary tree.

FIGURE 3. Right: Internal representation of vocabulary insertion of Figure 2.

Of course, one does not insert the letters themselves; rather, one inserts random numbers associated in a precomputed table with single characters, so that the graph of Figure 2 might actually have the internal interpretation shown in Figure 3.

In preparing the vocabulary tree, one first assigns a random internal address (i.e., a node) to each character, and then arbitrarily picks one character (say V with address 21) to head the tree. Each character (say 3 with address 572) is placed on the tree by linking the head node to the character node via the character address as link. Words of length greater than one are inserted on the vocabulary tree by continuing the first-level character insertions, and assigning a random node to the whole word. For example, in Figure 2, 3 is the link to a new random node from the random node linked by R and V. Similarly, one continues the chain by using V as a link to a new random node (84) associated now with R3V.

A difficulty with the above representation for a vocabulary tree is that if the nodes of the tree also form part of a graph being used for other purposes, then it will not always be possible to discriminate between links of the tree and other links of the graph. Besides the possible occurrence of such a situation during compilation of GIRL, a more likely occurrence might be during execution of a program which is processing the syntax of another language whose multi-character identifiers are stored on a vocabulary tree. For instance, in Figure 4, it is not clear which node is associated with the identifier LN, nor is it clear whether or not LN8 is an identifier. One might solve the problem by demanding that links in the graph to be processed be more than one character in length, or by insisting that the function performed by the link be distinguished as an identifier function. These demands, however, seem either too restricted or too complicated to implement. Rather, one can introduce an end-of-word marker, say (prime) as shown in Figure 5, which is a redrawing of Figure 2. Now the vocabulary nodes are separated from the graph by the primed links.

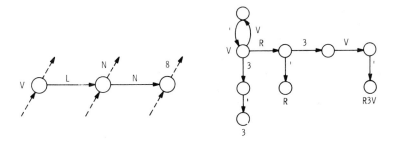

FIGURE 4. Left: Ambiguity in the vocabulary.

FIGURE 5. Right: Resolution of previous ambiguity.

The question now arises as to whether or not the prime (') may be part of an identifier, for if L0 and L0', as an example, were distinct identifiers, one has the ambiguity shown in Figure 6; namely, that one cannot tell the difference between the node L0 and the node X when seeking to retrieve the node associated with the word L0. If one were to identify L0 with X in an attempt to resolve the ambiguity, one would simply run into the difficulty presented in Figure 4. Therefore, the prime (') must be a distinguished element and not form part of any identifier. The discussion below will consider in detail further restrictions on the character set from which one may construct an identifier.

One can best understand the difficulties involved in allowing an arbitrary character string to be an identifier by investigating two applications concerning GIRL: (1) segmenting an input sentence of GIRL, and (2) constructing a context-free generative grammar in GIRL.

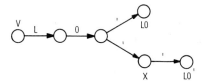

FIGURE 6. Ambiguity in vocabulary tree.

In order to segment an input string of GIRL, one must pose several restrictions on the form of identifiers. In the first place, one might demand that blanks separate each primitive segment (identifier, operator, delimiter, etc.). Thus the *blank* would become another distinguished element, and one could write an identifier otherwise arbitrarily. On the other hand, the insertion of blanks between every primitive segment is an unacceptable chore for the user. A second approach might be to have two vocabulary trees, one for identifiers and one for operators and delimiters. Elements of the latter tree, except for a juxtaposition operation which would require a blank as separator, presumably separate identifiers in a string. But the attempt to separate identifiers from operators and delimiters requires either two distinct character sets or special precedence restrictions. An example of the latter restriction might be that if juxtaposition is not permitted, operators may not form the first part of any identifier, and vice versa. But restrictive rules of formulation are difficult to characterize and even more difficult for the user to implement. Therefore, it seems that two distinct character sets are necessary for the solution to the segmentation problem. Moreover, with two distinct character sets, only one vocabulary tree is required unless the operator-delimiter set is expandable; for if the set is fixed, the operators may be drawn from a set of distinguished characters, and may be segmented by individual tests. Thus, in GIRL, identifiers are composed of a sequence of any length of alphabetic and/or numeric characters. All other characters are reserved for operators and delimiters (with the exception of $ which designates a random node or link). An identifier, say $X1$, is created by the symbolism $'X1$ following a node or link. If the node or link is to be generated randomly, one writes $\$'X1$, which means: ($) generate a random node and ($'X1$) call it $X1$. Internally, $X1$ is placed on the vocabulary tree and is associated with the random node generated by $.

Although the decision to separate character sets may suffice for purposes of segmentation, there are some objections to such a procedure when constructing a generative grammar. A first, naive approach to setting up the grammar is shown in Figure 7, where the proposition

LIST =: NUMBER | NUMBER, LIST

is entered. If such a structure were permissible, one would want the character ",'' to be an identifier in GIRL, a situation not allowed by the separate character set decision. However, the structure actually leads to errors when, for example, the proposition

LISTA =: LETTER | LETTER, LISTA

is also entered, as Figure 8 indicates. There are several ways out of the difficulty, but a discussion of these alternatives is not germane to this paper. What

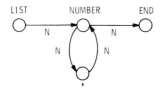

FIGURE 7. Generative grammar entry. N: next in sequence.

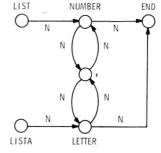

FIGURE 8. Ambiguous grammatical representation. N: next in sequence.

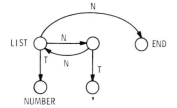

FIGURE 9. Unambiguous grammatical representation. N: next in sequence; T: type.

is relevant is that all of the alternatives require indirect means of relating the identifier node with its place in the proposition. For example, Figure 9 illustrates such an alternative. Although the indirection shown in Figure 9 does not obviate the need for an arbitrary identifier formation, the need is less pressing because the identifier will not occur in its expected place in a linear description of the graph. For example, the insertion in GIRL of the proposition shown in Figure 7 (as explained in more detail in Section II,C) is

$$\text{LIST N NUMBER N (, N NUMBER, END)} \tag{1}$$

which means

    a. link LIST to NUMBER by N,
    b. link NUMBER to , (comma) *and* to END by N,
    c. link , (comma) to NUMBER by N.

On the other hand, the insertion of Figure 9 is

$$\text{LIST (T NUMBER, N($ (T , , N LIST) , END)),} \tag{2}$$

which means

    a. link LIST to NUMBER by T,
    b. link LIST to a random node *and* to END by N,
    c. link the random node to , (comma) by T, and to LIST by N.

Clearly, the second description is not as readable as the first, and the necessity for " , " to be an identifier is not so clear. Hence, the decision for character set separation remains unchanged. There are other considerations as to the form of an identifier, but the above factors were most significant.

Aside from the internal consistency of the language, as discussed above, there is one last factor that one must take into consideration before settling on the form of an identifier: viz, implementation of the embedding of GIRL in some algebraic language. Optimally, one would like to write a compiler that would translate or interpret both GIRL and the algebraic language at once. However, due to the usual time, manpower, and systems software administrative problems it has proven more feasible to write a preprocessor in, for example, FORTRAN, PL/I, or SNOBOL from GIRL to the algebraic language. The preprocessor, on the other hand, entails the further difficulty that, since no scan of algebraic sentences will take place, there is room for confusion between created identifiers of GIRL and the variables of the algebraic language. As a consequence, one may submit to expediency and require that the identifiers of GIRL be restricted to the form allowed by the algebraic language, thus forcing the programmer to keep track of the variables and identifiers. Alternatively, one may create distinguished identifiers for the preprocessor of GIRL which would not be permitted in the GIRL algebraic expressions. As a matter of fact, we have chosen the latter path both to reserve temporary storage in the pre-processed compilation, and avoid a difficulty in the insertion operation to be explained below. The implementation of this decision takes the form of reserving identifiers which begin with LVV. The use of the preprocessor rather than an interpreter does offer one advantage; namely, that one can use the identifier tree (or a similar device) in the preprocessing stage to produce algebriac variables rather than waste time looking up identifiers on the identi-fier tree during the execution stage.

C. Operators and Delimiters

As discussed above, operators and delimiters are drawn from the characters which are neither numeric, alphabetic, nor $. We shall presume these charac-ters to be $*$. , / ( ) $=$ $'$ $+$ $-$ and blank.

For operators, the primary design goal was to produce a linear string of actions which represented a trace of the actions on a graph in the plane. Aside from the action of identification, which was discussed in Section II,B, there are three basic actions related to the manipulation of a graph: (1) insertion, (2) retrieval, and (3) deletion.

The basic building block of a graph is the node–link–node triplet, as shown above in Figure 1, consisting of A the *argument* (or *subject*), B the *function* (or *predicate*), and C the *value* (or *associate*).

To a great extent, the formal representation of the basic actions applied to the node–link–node triplet is a matter of legibility, an aesthetic criterion. Thus, there does not seem to be any tightly logical basis by which one can choose the favored action. Nevertheless, there are some factors that lead one to concentrate the initial design on the action of *insertion*, namely:

1. The function of insertion is opposed both to retrieval (as *write* is to *read*) and to deletion (as *write* is to *erase*).

2. Insertion is an action which requires specification of three identifiers (the node–link–node triplet), whereas both retrieval and deletion require only two identifiers.

3. For some applications in which the graph is used purely as a storage medium, retrieval might be the action most often used. However, in many situations, whether the data base is fixed or not, insertion must be used not only to initially set up the graph, but also to structure traces and transforma-tion in the graph. As a result, the frequency of insertion is at least as great as that of retrieval, and certainly more than the frequency of deletion.

There are at least two varieties of notation for insertion that one might consider.

1. From a function–argument–value viewpoint, one might choose the notation B(A) = C to represent an insertion of the value C of the function B of argument A. Presumably, then, B(A) would represent a retrieval, and successive retrievals would have the form D(B(A)). In addition, if a function can have a set of values (as will be discussed later in Section II,E on data structures), one might choose to write B(A) = C1, C2, C3. The advantage of this notation is that it resembles, to some extent, the insertion of a BNF string, which might be a frequent input to the graph. On the other hand, the infix nature of the parenthesization does not allow for an easy scan of the graph. Moreover, it is the retrieval action that seems basic and most concisely expressed here than the action of insertion.

2. If, instead of using parentheses as argument delimiters and commas as value delimiters, one used them as delimiters for an operand sequence, one might input a value C as A B C, and a set as A B (C1, C2, C3). That is, A B distributes over the parentheses to mean: A B C1 and A B C2 and A B C3. The effect of this notation is to evaluate an expression in a left-to-right scan (as in prefix notation) rather than from lowest parenthetic level to highest (as in infix notation). Thus, the notation affords an immediate one-to-one scan of the graph, although it is somewhat removed from BNF notation. Moreover, if one chooses the plus sign (+) to represent a retrieval and the minus sign (−) to represent a deletion, the opposition of insertion to the operations retrieval and deletion is accomplished, as specified for insertion, as desired for the reasons previously given.

There are many representations for insertion, but, of the two just specified the latter is most desirable, although not entirely free of problems. For example, in the discussion above concerning the grammatical representation in Figure 9 and formulation (2), the ambiguity between place and function in Figure 8 is resolved at the cost of some considerable indirection; but there is still an ambiguity, at least for a one pass scan, in the succession of commas (one an identifier, one a delimiter), which must be resolved by yet more indirection in using an acceptable identifier for the first comma, as in the following:

$$\text{LIST (T NUMBER, N (\$ (T COMMA, N LIST), END))}. \qquad (3)$$

One could attempt to solve the problem of indirection by allowing a straightforward notation like formulation (1), namely,

$$\text{LIST NUMBER (, LIST , END)}$$

and by then replacing the surface structure automatically by the unambiguous representation (3). However, not only are there problems of ambiguity and implementation involved, but also, more important, one has tacitly fixed the links of the graph to mean either "next" or "type," a circumstance which defeats the whole purpose of designing a flexible graph processor.

Another problem with the operand sequence interpretation of the delimiters is indicated in the following example.

$$A(+S'A, -A) \tag{4}$$

The interpretation of (4) is: (a) find the node linked to A by the link S and call it A; (b) then delete the A link (the new A or the old A?) associated with the node A (again, the new or old?). It is convenient to resolve the ambiguity in (4) by replacing each identifier with its associated node in a left-to-right scan, so that the internal representation of (4) might be

$$432(+61 \ 'A, \ -51) \tag{5}$$

where the value of $432 + 61$ happens to be 51.

Effectively, each identifier in a GIRL statement is first replaced by its current corresponding node value in a left-to-right scan, and only then is the statement executed. As a consequence, the preprocessor, which outputs identifiers, not evaluations, must maintain some distinguished storage in order to prevent destruction of an evaluation by a subsequent shift of identifier interpretation. As above, identifiers beginning with LVV have been arbitrarily reserved for distinguished storage, and are not available to the programmer. This is one of several examples of a sacrifice of descriptive simplicity for operational efficiency. An alternative approach would have been to evaluate the identifier as its associated node whenever encountered, thus eliminating the need for distinguished storage. However, in order to perform the same series of actions as in (4), one would have to write

$$\begin{aligned} A \ 'B + S \ 'A, \\ B - A. \end{aligned} \tag{6}$$

Since (4) is a natural representation for updating a pointer, the cumbersome expression (6) is not desirable.

Finally, note that it is convenient to define insertion as a non-destructive action, in which case one can easily augment the value set, but one must delete the stored set of values before replacement by a new set. The alternative would have been to consider insertion as destructive, and to insert both the previously stored and the additional value set when set augmentation was desired. Since augmentation, in the latter instance, would require a means of identifying the sets, and since augmentation is at least as frequent as replacement, a nondestructive insert was selected. As a concession to the needs of replacement, however, a means of item deletion within a set will be introduced later.

The above notations do not exhaust the possibilities of mixtures of operators and delimiters, but give a fair notion of some of the issues involved.

D. LABELS AND TRANSFERS

In order to transfer from one executable GIRL statement to another, one requires statement addresses or *labels*. As a concession to the user and in order to enhance readability, the convenience of allowing numeric and alphabetic characters and $ (alone, as a random address) as labels was condoned, as opposed, for example, to FORTRAN in which only integers are permitted. The algebraic compiler suffers no hardships for allowing this convenience since the program requires translation by a preprocessor in any case. However, since the preprocessor must always generate its own labels, it is convenient to restrict the choice of labels in the algebraic statements so that a two-pass compiler for checking redundant labels will not be needed. For example, if FORTRAN were the algebraic language in question, one might decide to allow labels in algebraic statement to include only positive integers less than 20,000. The choice of labels in GIRL is not affected. In addition, it would be helpful for the preprocessor to treat the label of a GIRL statement simply as an identifier of length no greater than four and thus to disregard the segmentation problem involved in allowing characters reserved for operators and delimiters to be part of a label.

The necessity for labels arises from the need to transfer to one labeled program statement or another as a consequence of the success or failure of an operation. A feasible notation for such a conditional transfer is the following:

$$X + Y1 \ /R \ /35,$$

which means: if Y1 links X to any node, go to statement 35; if not, go to statement R. One can construct an unconditional transfer simply by insisting that the two labels be the same. Other meaningful variants of the notation are:

$$X + Y1 \ /R \qquad \text{(go to R if failure, otherwise continue)},$$
$$X + Y1 \ //R \qquad \text{(go to R if success, otherwise continue)}.$$

In a similar manner, the transfer notation holds for the insertion and deletion operations. That is, insertion would fail if the node–link–node triplet had already been inserted and deletion would fail if the node–link pair had not been inserted. One might also consider the necessity of employing another transfer mode to denote the undefined state of a node or link in order to realize macroscopic programming for garbage collection, but we felt, at this point, that retrieving useless working space is an action best relegated to the microscopic facility of the underlying memory simulator. However, one can undefine an identifier by writing, for example, $' - Y1$, so that it is possible for the garbage collector, at least by exhaustive search, to locate nodes which have no referand.

For the transfers described above, one could have resorted to the transfer capabilities of the algebraic language, but the conceptual unit expressed on one line of code would have to be separated into several lines. Similarly, one could resort to the transfer capabilities of the algebraic language for the fundamental graph tracing action of comparing the referenced nodes of two identifiers for identity, but it is conceptually convenient to treat comparison as a binary GIRL operation, exactly as one would treat retrieval or deletion. Thus,

$$X = Y /21 /R5$$

means: If X and Y refer to the same node, go to R5; otherwise, go to 21.

E. Data Structures

The modes of data that one might wish to associate with a given graph structure are represented by the following three types of nodes: (1) identifier-associated nodes, (2) number-associated nodes, and (3) character-associated nodes. Nodes which are associated with identifiers may be terminal or nonterminal, but nodes which are associated with numbers or members of the character set must be terminal. Moreover, each end node of a node–link–node triplet may in fact be a *set* of nodes arbitrarily and variously associated with identifiers, numbers, or characters. Although the node sets were designed merely to hold commonly associated values, the sets are in fact ordered *lists* and can be randomly accessed (i.e., randomly from the user's viewpoint, sequentially from the preprocessor's viewpoint). Since lists can be simulated by appropriate entries on the graph, one might ask why list structures are needed at all. Indeed, there is no clear answer to this question. It is simply another compromise between user convenience and operating efficiency, highly dependent on the nature of the programs being written. It seems reasonable to say, however, that, on the basis of some limited programming experience, data lists greatly facilitate the processing of the syntax of artificial languages.

There are several possible notations for indexing nodes on a list. For example, one might choose to write X G (1F, 2R), meaning that F and R have been made first and second items on the list linked by G to X. This insertion would require either that integers be barred as identifiers or that an insertion universally have four arguments. The first option is an undue restriction on the form of identifiers, and the second option effects a hardship on the preprocessor. Even more important, the suggested notation is too powerful in the sense that the design goal is not to create a general list processor, but to treat sets of values associated in common with a given argument node. Since the set has to be ordered in any event, one might be able to take some advantage of the sequencing, but not at the expense of programming efficiency.

Thus, for example, the design goal should stop short of making "insertion into a specified list location" a primitive to the instruction set.

One possible alternative notation is to allow the optional indexing of nodes or links. For example, X + G.5 might mean: Find the node linked to X by the fifth item on the list named G. But if one regards .5 as an index to G, there is some difficulty in deciding whether a transfer following the expression should refer to the existence of a list or to the existence of the fifth item on the list. One might redesign the transfer notation to be tri- or quadripartite in order to take into consideration all the existence and success conditions, but the most feasible way out of the difficulty is to regard the index mark "." as an operation on the resulting node of the action X + G. On the other hand, such a decision provokes a question which has fundamental design implications: What is the meaning of

$$X + G \; 'X1,$$
$$X1.5 + R.$$

That is, can one name a list and then index the list by means of the name? Up to now, the language has reserved identification for nodes. Indeed, X + G 'X1 means: give the name X1 to the first node on the list referenced by X + G. Such identification would not suffice for an external list name since a node may appear on several lists. Clearly, a separate list-naming operation is required. Thus, X + G '.X1 means: (a) $ 'X1 (b) internally associate the new node X1 with X and G (by graph or table lookup). The last condition is significant since the naming of a list or sublist (e.g., X1.5 '.X2) would require information as to either the formation of the list (i.e., X and G) or the address of the next node on the list or both. Such additional information would require precisely that redundant storage of internal links which would be necessary if the list were stored explicitly as a node chain in the external graph, thus voiding the necessity for lists. Similarly, consider the following case of iteration:

1	Let $I = 1$.
2	X + G.I.
.	
.	
.	
n	Let I be I + 1.
$n + 1$	Return to 1 unless I exceeds k, in which case continue.

Unless one counts down the list referred to by X + G each time one encounters statement 2, a condition requiring $k(k + 1)/2$ accesses, one must maintain an inventory of internal list names with precisely the same redundant information required for the external list names described above. Thus, there is a space–time uncertainty relation by which one can trade storage for execution time by either counting down a list or storing excess information for either external or internal list names or both.

As a side issue, one should note that the use of I in the case of iteration cited above brings up the problem as to whether one should regard an integer following a point as an identifier having an integral value or as an integer *per se*. For convenience of the user, it seems most reasonable to insist that integer indices be regarded literally whereas, for example, 143X is interpreted as an identifier.

As a final note to this section, we define by example the notation for number and character associated nodes. For insertion, one has

$$X \, G \, '/5/X1 *4$$
$$X \, G \, ''A + 2''$$

which means: insert the character string X1 *4 of length 5 and the value of the integer expression A + 2, respectively, as values of the function G of X. Number and character data may be interspersed with identifier nodes on lists. For retrieval, deletion, or comparison, the index operation gives the user access to items on a list without being able to specify the node type. For additional convenience to the user, it is a matter of no great difficulty to introduce type index operations as follows (for example):

$X + G .. 4$ (find the fourth identifier on list $X + G$),
$X + G .'4$ (find the fourth number on list $X + G$),
$X + G ./4$ (find the fourth character on list $X + G$).

Thus, the user can scan the list without knowing the precise location of data types.

From the foregoing discussion, one can see that the data structure available to the user is rich and potentially intricate. One can arrange data as single nodes or as lists of nodes, all interconnected in a graph of link associations which may include cycles. Moreover, the nodes may be named externally (by ') or internally (by $). The nodes may be identifier-, number-, or character-associated. The identifier-associated nodes may be item-referent or list-referent.

F. Output

The preceding sections have described the insertion, retrieval, and deletion of nodes, integers, and character strings. One must still communicate the retrieved information to the outside via the algebraic language program. For nodes and integers, the situation is clear. Simply name the information and treat the name as an algebraic variable. Thus, if one had inserted A B ''3, then

A + B 'X1 would imply that X1 had the value 3 when X1 was regarded as an algebraic variable. For character strings, however, one must take into account the fact that the string may be of arbitrary length. In order to characterize the computer-independent output of strings, it seems reasonable to stipulate that the retrieve operation will produce no more than one character at a time. If one inserts A B '/3/+6H, then A + B 'X1 will imply that X1 is a variable which contains a representation of the character + in a form suitable for output by the algebraic language program. If the remaining characters are desired, one need only ask for A + B .I 'X1, for I = 2, 3.

G. IMPLEMENTATION

A preprocessor for GIRL has been written in FORTRAN IV and imposed on an efficient hashed addressed memory scheme. GIRL statements are distinguished from the FORTRAN program in which they reside by locating a G in the first column of the card on which the statement has been punched.

III. Extensions and Applications

As described above, GIRL is a language in which the syntax provides considerable, albeit primitive, computational power in the manipulation of graph structures. Whether or not a more sophisticated operation set is desirable is a subject for debate. In any event, there are several extensions to the language, which, at the cost of operating efficiency, can significantly upgrade the usefulness of the language. The extensions fall, more or less into two classes: set transformability and representational flexibility.

1. *Set Transformability.* The language does allow for set formation and search, but higher-order operations are not available. Thus, if X1 and Y1 were the names of lists, it might be desirable to assign a meaning to Z X1 Y1. Briefly then, one needs an internal means of handling vectors of vectors of nodes and/or links, a traditionally complex, cumbersome task, Moreover, subset matching is extremely awkward with the current GIRL operation set and one needs some means of speaking freely of set union, intersection, complementation, and quantification. In short, one must impose a predicate calculus on the operation set. It may be feasible, however, to define the set operations in terms of GIRL subroutines.

2. *Representational Flexibility.* In the course of describing GIRL, we have tacitly employed representations of the language on several levels, namely:

    a.   syntax (which determines how the preprocessor translates the coded program),

b. code (which is translated by the preprocessor),

c. graph (which is the result of executing the translated code),

d. memory (which is an internal one-to-one mapping of the graph).

At each level there are features not currently available to the user which might be of interest if one could establish their economic feasibility. For example, one might welcome the opportunity to define new operators at the syntax level, or to alter or create new GIRL code during execution as Hollerith data in the graph, and then evaluate the code by a repass through the translation–execution cycle. Furthermore, one might require the capability of inputting or outputting graph structured information, perhaps on a graphics display. The output, for example, might take the form of displaying the answer to such a demand as: "Output the subgraph whose nodes are chained to node A by B links". Finally, one might want to access the internal memory structure from the GIRL program by requesting the contents of the node register associated with an identifier. The accessibility of memory would effectively permit algebraic, symbol, and machine language operations in one language.

Some of the above extensions are slated for the near future, but some are admittedly wishful thinking. The number of applications that GIRL will encompass is limited only by the number of ways one can interpret organizational structures. We envisage programs in areas such as:

1. information management systems for personnel, project, and logistics inventories, for ship design data banks, and for operations analysis as in gaming or job shop simulations;

2. linguistic analysis of compilers or even compiler-compilers; and

3. artificial intelligence, automata theory, and signal analysis problems in which combinatorial nets play an important role.

The appendixes which follow briefly describe the syntax of GIRL and illustrate how to code in GIRL.

Appendix A

SYNTAX OF GIRL

In the following abbreviated syntax of GIRL, the usual BNF notation suffices for the metasyntactic symbols =: (is defined to be), and | (inclusive "or"); a string of small roman characters represents a syntactic category; and FORTRAN Hollerith characters form the terminal alphabet. A brief functional description of the syntactic categories (in alphabetical order) of the mnemonics precedes the syntax.

Mnemonic	Category description	Mnemonic	Category description
a	alphabet	int	integer
ad	address	is	insertion or simple node
ae	algebraic expression	ix	algebraic or Hollerith
an	alphanumeral		index
b	blank (space) string	lab	label
bl	single blank	lea	list entry type a
bo	binary operator	leb	list entry type b
boi	binary operator and	ll	label list
	index	lta	list type a
d	data (numeric or	ltb	list type b
	Hollerith)	na	node type a
def	definition of identifier	nb	node type b
din	data insertion	nc	node type c
dt	define and transfer	op	operator
e	empty (null)	sen	sentence
fun	function	r	retrieval, deletion,
h	Hollerith		comparison, index
i	identification	t	transfer, identify
id	identifier	ta	transfer
idn	identifier-associated	un	unparenthesized node
	node	und	unparenthesized or
in	insertion		identifier-associated
ins	integer string		node

SYNTAX

1. Null and Blank

e	=:	(null category)
bl	=:	(blank character)
b	=:	bl | bl b

2. Identifier

int	=:	0 | 1 | 2 | 3 | 4 | 5 | 6 | 7 | 8 | 9
ins	=:	int | int ins
an	=:	A | B | C | D | E | F | G | H | I | J | K | L | M | N | O | P | Q | R | S | T | U | V | W | X | Y | Z | int
op	=:	+ | − | ' | . | * | / | (|) | = | , | $

```
a   =:    an | op
id  =:    an | an id
i   =:    'id | i 'id | i '.id
```

3. *Label and Transfer*†

```
lab =:    id | $
ll  =:    lab | lab, ll
ad  =:    i b lab i | i b lab | lab i | lab
t   =:    /ad | //ad | /ad/ad | e
ta  =:    /lab | //lab | /lab / lab
dt  =:    i t | t
```

4. *Node Structure*

```
h   =:    a | a h
ae  =:    (integer-valued algebraic expression as defined by the lan-
          guage in which GIRL is embedded)
d   =:    '/ins/h t | "ae"t
idn =:    lab | * id (ll)
in  =:    idn b idn b idn dt | in b idn b idn dt
din =:    idn b idn d | in b d
bo  =:    + | − | =
boi =:    bo | . | . −
r   =:    in | is boi is
is  =:    r | idn dt
un  =:    r | din | r boi din | r ix idn dt
ix  =:    .' | ./ | ..
und =:    un | idn dt
na  =:    is (lta) t
lta =:    lea | lea, lta
lea =:    boi und | boi na | boi nb | boi nc | is nc | is (ltb) | is b und
nb  =:    is boi (ltb) t
ltb =:    leb | leb, ltb
leb =:    und | na | nb | nc
nc  =:    is b is (ltb) t
```

5. GIRL *Statement*

```
def =:    lab dt
fun =:    FUNCTION (ll)
sen =:    un | na | nb | nc | def | fun | ta
```

† In the remainder of the syntax, from the preprocessor's viewpoint, blanks may be supplied or not at will, except where required explicitly. On the other hand, parenthesization may not be capricious, but must follow the syntax literally.

Appendix B

SAMPLE PROGRAMS

The following two sample programs are intended only to give the reader an idea of the use of the language. For a more detailed and comprehensive description, consult the user's manual.

Problem 1. Insert the graph structure of Figure 10. The coded solution is

$ 'R1 B $ 'R2 A (R2, $ 'R3 (A R2, B(R2, R1, $ 'R4 B(R4, R2))))

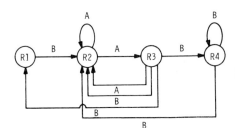

FIGURE 10. Graph structure of Problem 1.

Problem 2. In any connected graph with entry R1M and links 5A, B, determine if there is a node ZR4 retrievable by a link 5A.

Program. Search the graph from the entry. Place each node to be considered on a thread. Test only 5A linked nodes for equality with ZR4. Avoid duplication on thread (caused by cycles in graph) by linking each unique node to be considered to a random node. When ZR4 is found or thread is exhausted, delete thread from the graph and exit. (Assume FORTRAN as the algebraic language.)

Coded Solution

	1	FORMAT (5H0 YES)
	2	FORMAT (4H0 NO)
G		R1M 'X0
G		$ 'X1 'X2 'X3 1 X0 9 $
C	***	FIND X0 + 5A
G	A	X0 + 5A /B '.X4
		I = 1
C	***	SEARCH X0 + 5A LIST
G	A1	X4.I/B (= ZR4//YES, 'X5 (+9 //A2, 9 $))
G		X3 0 $ 'X3 1 X5
	A2	I = I + 1
G		/A1/A1

```
C      ***     FIND X0 + B
G       B      X0 + B/C '.X4
               I = 1
C      ***     SEARCH X0 + B LIST
G       B1     X4.I/C 'X5 (+9 //B2, 9 $)
G              X3 0 $ 'X3 1 X5
        B2     I = I + 1
G              /B1/B1
C      ***     FIND THE NEXT ELEMENT ON THE THREAD
G       C      X2 + 0 /NO 'X2 + 1 'X0 /A/A
       YES     WRITE (6, 1)
G              /D/D
        NO     WRITE (6, 2)
C      ***     REMOVE THREAD FROM THE GRAPH
G       D      R1M −9
G       E      X1 (+0 /EXIT 'X1 + 1 −9, −0, −1) /E/E
G      EXIT    X1 −1
               STOP
               END
```

ACKNOWLEDGMENT

I am indebted to Professor Allen Newell for his suggestions concerning a graph processing language.

REFERENCES

Christensen, C. (1967). An example of the manipulation of directed graphs in the AMBIT/G programming language, *Proc. ACM Symp. on Interactive Systems for Expt. Appl. Math., Washington, D. C., 1967* (Klerer and Reinfelds, eds.). Academic Press, New York, 1968.

Feldman, J. A., and Rovner, P. D. (1969). *Comm. ACM* **12**, 439–499.

IBM (1968). FORTRAN IV Programmer's Guide, File S360-25, Form C28-6817-0. IBM, New York.

McCarthy, J., Abrahams, P. W., Edwards, D. J., Hart, T. P., and Levin, M. I. (1962). "LISP 1.5 Programmer's Manual." M.I.T. Press, Cambridge, Massachusetts.

Newell, A., ed. (1961). "Information Processing Language-V Manual." Prentice-Hall, Englewood Cliffs, New Jersey.

Van Wijngaarde, A., ed. (1968). Draft Report on ALGOL 68, Mathematisch Centrum MR 93, Amsterdam, The Netherlands.

On the Role of Exact and Nonexact Associative Memories in Human and Machine Information Processing

Nicholas V. Findler
STATE UNIVERSITY OF NEW YORK
BUFFALO NEW YORK

I. Introduction

The research endeavor usually called simulation of cognitive processes has proved to be more than a transient fad, some playful activity of a few over-enthusiastic computerites. One must admit, however, that the initially high rate of achievements has slowed down. The problems to be solved next are real tough nuts; the available hardware and software do not seem to be adequate enough for the tasks at hand. One would like to make some kind of a global attack to integrate and advance the piecemeal results rather than pick another isolated, smallish, howsoever interesting, problem area.

Bearing this ultimate objective in mind, we embarked on a long-term research project to model the static and dynamic aspects of the human memory. We feel that if we could build a system that is teachable *ab initio* to an arbitrary extent of sophistication, that can structure and restructure singular and multiple experiences, recognize statistical and deterministic constraints in forming and searching domains of interest, and perform certain other basic and compound processes, then we would gain the upper hand in dealing with a large number of problems of cognition.

We have developed a tool for these investigations, an Associative Memory, Parallel Processing Language, AMPPL-II. We have recently reported on it [1]. We therefore describe here only some salient features of the language, which are necessary for the exposition. The basic purpose of this paper is to formulate certain problems and to discuss a few ideas.

II. On Living Systems

Let us first define some terminology. In living memories, structural elements of information are linked together by associations, which serve as storing and retrieving pathways as well. The efficiency and efficacy of storing, modifying, and retrieving information depend on the representation in and the topological structure of the *associative memory*. The whole system is very dynamic, much of our cognitive activity consists of reinforcing and/or restructuring the associative linkages as the consciously generated or "automatically" appearing hypotheses operate on previous experiences.

There is a vast number of intriguing questions one would like to obtain an answer to. Such questions include (a) how redundancy is formed and made use of; (b) how numerical and nonnumerical items of information are represented and how they interact with each other; (c) what is involved in pattern normalization, template matching, and noise reduction (the word "pattern" being used in the most general sense possible); (d) how abstraction takes place, what is the "optimum" level of abstraction when the amount of lost information is not too much but processing becomes significantly easier; (e) how feedback operates, not only in the sensory pathways but also in the process of restructuring cognitive maps; (f) what is the form, "calling sequence," I/O format, etc. of the subroutines that so obviously exist in the nervous system; and so on.

There is evidence that, although human information processing is to a large extent serial, a certain level of *parallelism* also exists. It is plausible also to assume several basic scanning mechanisms, such as the ones on guard for danger signals from the environment or the ones which perceive high intensity sensations.

It may be useful to separate, in operational terms, two kinds of associative memories. In the *exact associative memory*, the search processes are performed on the basis of finding the intersection of several sharply defined matching descriptors. Because of the non-uniqueness of many associations and because retrieval requests may be incomplete, there can be several respondent pieces of information. However, illformulated and imprecise tasks cannot, in general, be solved. There is no logical "interpolation" or "extrapolation" either. These terms refer to the case in which exact matching is not available, but two or more similar entities would serve as the basis for some tentative action or planning process. (Also, for example, some of our prejudices may be the results of certain logical "extrapolations.")

On the other hand, in a *nonexact associative memory*, the above restrictions do not apply. Associations connect statistically related entities, too. A metric may be defined to measure the strength of the latter type of linkages. The same retrieval search may yield results only some of the time, or the results so obtained may vary. Also, the storing process could contain stochastic components. The concepts of spatial and temporal nearness, similarity, and rank ordering play important roles.

Biological systems, of course, incorporate both kinds of associative memories. Remembering a person's telephone number or a chemical formula should be the task of the exact associative memory whereas most of our nonnumerical experiences are stored in the nonexact one. We should conjecture here that, while the elements of information are identically represented in the two kinds of associative memory, the connecting linkages and storage and retrieval processes are different in nature.

As can be seen, the number of questions that can be raised is practically unlimited. A successful simulation model may not only provide insight to these problems but valuable guidelines should also be obtainable by it for the design of various types of information systems. Quillians' work [2, 3] somewhat related to ours, clearly indicates this point.

It appeared to us that even list processing languages may not be powerful enough for the task at hand. Another computer language was needed of which we speak in the next section.

III. An Associative Memory, Parallel Processing Language: AMPPL–II

In contrast with conventional, word-oriented machines, computers with *associative memories* are *content-addressable*. These terms refer to the interrelationship between data as well as to the fact that a memory word or words can be accessed by matching with a selectable field of a special word, rather than by an address. *Parallel processing*, a related idea and distinct from multiprocessing, allows command sequences to be executed simultaneously over large numbers of data sets.

It was intended to develop a language which incorporates, from the programmer's viewpoint, these facilities in addition to the previously available algebraic, list-processing and string-manipulating facilities.

For understandable reasons, embedding seemed to be an economical and fairly efficient approach, which also achieves a reasonably high level of machine independence. The presently described version is an extension of SLIP, itself being embedded in FORTRAN IV. (The internal mechanism of SLIP had to be modified to a small extent, but the user need not be aware of this fact.) There are only two AMPPL subprograms written in assembly language now.

We shall describe here only three important characteristics of AMPPL-II: the structure and dynamic allocation of the memory, the "Search and Flag" operation, and the Relations.

Unlike the expensive and inflexible associative memories presently built in hardware, the size of the Simulated Associative Memory (SAM) is determined by the programmer according to his needs. In fact, he has to specify the ratio between the sizes of SAM and of the Available Space List (AVSL) of SLIP at the beginning of his program. The sum of SAM and AVSL equals the storage area left unused after the compilation of the FORTRAN program.

The programmer can also build into the program trap points at which a part of SAM or AVSL is dynamically reassigned to the other part if there is a need for it, i.e., if the size of one memory type decreases below a certain prespecified threshold value. Memory contraction, coupled with a specific form of garbage collection, takes place in SAM at this instance. There is an efficient and fast flow of information between any two of the SAM, AVSL, and FORTRAN memory.

It will be helpful in understanding the organization of AMPPL-II if we consider the diagram in Figure 1.

The main block is the *memory matrix*, which consists of r SAM words,* each having $2n$ bit positions. There are four special words, the short registers, each n bits long. (On the CDC 6400, there are $n = 60$ bits in a word.) Two of these serve as Argument Registers 1 and 2. The other two represent Mask Registers 1 and 2. There are also three long registers, vertical columns r bits in length and 1 bit in width. Two of these are called Response Register 1 and Response Register 2. The third one is the Availability Register. (The role of the words FIRST and LAST in Figure 1 is explained later.)

To the AMMPL programmer, SAM appears to contain information in a manner that permits certain basic processes, including reading and writing, to be carried out simultaneously in particular cells. These designated cells contain responding pieces of information and were selected by a previous "Search and Flag" operation or were deliberately flagged by a special flagging instruction. The "Search and Flag" operations locate and mark SAM words according to various criteria. Subsequent processes may then be performed on these again and the results can represent Boolean combinations, AND's, OR's, and NOT's of consecutive searches.

The basis of comparison is usually† put into one of the Argument Registers. The search is carried out only over those fields of SAM words that are marked by bits" 1 " in the relevant Mask Register. The success of a search is indicated by flags (bits " 1 ") at the level of the corresponding SAM word in the relevant Response Register. Those SAM words that have not been used or are no longer necessary are denoted by a tag (bit " 1 ") in the Availability Register.

Two points should be mentioned here. In order to speed up the search processes in SAM, one-directional pointers link flagged SAM words (see Figure 2) and end markers indicate the addresses of the SAM words first and last flagged in the two Response Registers (the contents of the FORTRAN variables FIRST and LAST on Figure 1).

Two other FORTRAN variables, PØINT1 and PØINT2 contain the SAM addresses of the last SAM word searched, whether successfully or otherwise, with reference to Response Register 1 and Response Register 2, respectively.

---

* As will be seen later, every SAM word consists of two actual memory words.

† If, for example, those numbers are searched for that are greater than a given one. However, if the criterion of search is, for example, "maximum," the Argument Registers are ignored.

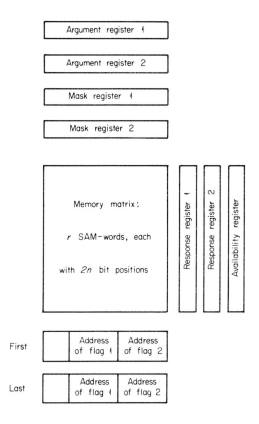

FIGURE 1. The structure of the Simulated Associative Memory and Parallel Processor.

(Compare the possible values of the argument WHICH of the subroutine **SERFLG**.)

The actual form of the major instruction performing the above described processes is

SERFLG (BØØLE, WHICH, CRITER, IARG, IMASK, IRESP)

where

$$
BØØLE = \begin{cases} \text{NEWRSP} \\ \text{ANDRSP} \\ \text{ØRRSP} \\ \text{NØTRSP} \end{cases}
$$

i.e., the resulting flags in IRESP are

regardless of previous status of the Response Register,
AND-ed with flags in the other Response Register,
OR-ed with flags in the other Response Register,
NOT-ed and left in the same Response Register;

WHICH =
- SAMADR — i.e., flags are put in IRESP if CRITER is satisfied for — a certain SAM-addressed word,
- FIRST — the first SAM word,
- NXT — the next-after-PØINT word,
- LAST — the last SAM word,
- ALL — all SAM words,
- ANY — any single SAM word;

CRITER =
- NEXTHI — next higher than the one in Argument Register,
- NEXTLØ — next lower than the one in Argument Register,
- NEXT — nearest in absolute value to the one in Argument Register
- MAX — of largest value,
- MIN — of lowest value,
- GTEQ, — i.e., search for the word(s) — greater than or equal to the one in Argument Register,
- EQU — equal to the one in Argument Register,
- LTEQ — less than or equal to the one in Argument Register,
- BITSHI — with the highest number of bits matched with string in Argument Register,
- BITSLØ — with the lowest number of bits matched with string in Argument Register,
- GRPØFM — with the highest number of matching groups of $M (= 2 - 8)$ bits regardless of group position, starting from the left.

IARG =
- 1 — i.e., the number of the relevant
- 2 — Argument Register;

IMASK =
- 1 — i.e., the number of the relevant
- 2 — Mask Register;

IRESP =
- 1 — i.e., the number of the relevant
- 2 — Response Register.

A few words of comment are needed here. Two subsequent "Search and Flag" operations with CRITER = GTEQ and LTEQ yield responsive words of values between given limits. NEXTHI can be performed by two subsequent searches with criteria GTEQ and MIN, similarly NEXTLØ is done with criteria LTEQ and MAX. The value of one of NEXTHI and NEXTLØ, that is nearer to the value in the Argument Register, yields NEXT. The criteria BITSHI and BITSLØ are useful in comparing nonnumerical data and selecting the "most similar" or "least similar" pieces of information, respectively. The number of matching bits can be found as the values of special FORTRAN variables. GRPØFM finds, for example, misprints caused by transposition, missing, and added characters. The character set can be represented by groups of 2–8 bits. Since the matching process ignores the position of the groups being matched, there are extra facilities to identify transposition errors. Also, the number of the matching groups is accessible.

There are safeguards to prevent a SAM word of the wrong information mode from becoming respondent if its contents happens to be the right bit configuration.

Finally we are going to describe the third salient feature of AMPPL, the *Relations*. The following formula, analogous to algebraic functions, defines a Relation (REL) between an Object (ØBJ) and a Value (VAL):

$$REL(ØBJ) = VAL.$$

The first entity REL is always symbolic; the other two, ØBJ and VAL, can be either symbolic or numeric, simultaneously or separately. Regardless of which type, a further classification is possible as to whether an entity is a single item or one of different kinds of lists. The first kind of list simply contains various equivalent names of the same item. (One can think of synonyms within the given context.) This is called the *Equivalence List*. The second kind of list bears the names of a number of subunits any processing on which is always uniform. An example of these lists may be the students of a class, who always have the same teacher, always stay in the same classroom, etc. Distinguishing processes, such as grading of individual exams, are not to be carried out on the elements of so designated lists. Finally, the third kind of list has distinct and, in some respect, independent elements. An example of this could be the pieces of furniture in a certain room if one would like to, say, paint them different colors. The internal representation of a SAM word containing a Relation is shown in Figure 2.

We have stated before that items on the Equivalence List can be considered as context-dependent synonyms. As a logical extension of this idea, names of various types of sublists may also appear on an Equivalence List. Here we discuss only two of these.*

* Work is still going on at the time of writing this paper to make these concepts quite general and flexible.

CODE NUMBER 1	CODE NUMBER 2	CODE NUMBER 3
0 | 1 | 0 | 1 | 1 | 1 | unused	Address of downward nearest flag in Response Register 1	0

59 · · · · 54

FIGURE 2. SAM word as a Relation Descriptor.

In this example, all the three entities are symbolic. Therefore, bit positions 56, 55, and 54 carry a bit 1. The SAM word is not available—bit position 59 contains 0. A previous "Search and Flag" operation has left a flag in Response Register 1—bit position 58 contains 1, and the first pointer field carries the address of the downward nearest flag, also in Response Register 1. Since Response Register 2 has no flag, bit position 57 is 0 and the second pointer field is empty.

1. Let us define Reverse Relation REVREL. If

$$\text{REL1}(\text{ØBJ}) = \text{VAL} \qquad \text{and} \qquad \text{REVREL}(\text{REL1}) = \text{REL2},$$

then

$$\text{REL2 (VAL)} = \text{ØBJ}.$$

Note also that

$$\text{REVREL}(\text{REVREL}(\text{REL1})) = \text{REL1}.$$

Examples are given in Table I.

TABLE I

REVERSE RELATIONS

REL	REVREL
husband of	wife of
parent of	child of
spouse of	spouse of
greater than	less than
above	below
inside	outside
left of	right of
superset of	subset of
similar to	similar to

* Work is still going on at the time of writing this paper to make these concepts quite general and flexible.

2. The second type of sublist of the Equivalence List refers to a more general concept, Defined Entity. It is constructed of Primitive Entities, possibly other Defined Entities, and connecting operators. The operators are listed in Table II. Only the last one needs special mention before examples clarify the meaning of all of them. The left hand side operand of ↓ is considered to be in Teutonic genitive (the possessive case denoted with an apostrophe and the letter "s"). The possessed item is the right hand side operand. Let us also define a special entity SELF in order to be able to exclude self-referencing in unwanted cases. The symbol ⇒ (programmer's notation: .DEF.) is to mean "defined as."

TABLE II

Various Operators for Defined Entities

Symbolic notation	Type	Representing	Programmer's notation
¬		Boolean NOT	.NØT.
←		reverse	.REV.
<		less than	.LT.
≤		less than or equal to	.LE.
>	unary	greater than	.GT.
≥		greater than or equal to	.GE.
Max		maximum	.MAX.
Min		minimum	.MIN.
=		equivalent or synonymous	.EQ.
∧		Boolean AND	.AND.
∨	binary	Boolean OR	.ØR.
↓		concatenated	.CØN.

Examples follow:

(i) $\text{PARENT} \Rightarrow \text{FATHER} \vee \text{MOTHER}$

that is, a parent is defined as a father or mother;

(ii) $\text{CHILD} \Rightarrow \leftarrow \text{PARENT}$

that is, the child is defined as the reverse of the parent;

(iii) $\text{GRANDFATHER} \Rightarrow (\text{FATHER} \vee \text{MOTHER}) \downarrow \text{FATHER}$

that is, the grandfather is defined as the father's or mother's father;

(iv) $\text{HUSBAND} \Rightarrow \text{SPOUSE} \wedge \neg \text{WIFE}$

that is, the husband is defined as a spouse but (and) not wife;

(v)   BROTHER $\Rightarrow$ ((MOTHER $\wedge$ FATHER) $\downarrow$ SON) $\wedge$ $\neg$SELF

that is, the brother is defined as the mother's and father's son but (and) not self; if we wish to include half-brothers as well, we can put

BROTHER $\Rightarrow$ ((MOTHER $\vee$ FATHER) $\downarrow$ SON) $\wedge$ $\neg$SELF

that is, the mother's *or* father's son but (and) not self.

(vi)   If V is a scalar describing quality, we can say

$$\begin{aligned}
\text{GØØD} &\Rightarrow > V1 \\
\text{BAD} &\Rightarrow < V2 \\
\text{BEST} &\Rightarrow \text{Max } V \\
\text{WØRST} &\Rightarrow \text{Min } V
\end{aligned}$$

(vii)   If L is a scalar describing persons' height, we can define

$$\begin{aligned}
\text{TALL} &\Rightarrow > L1 \\
\text{SHØRT} &\Rightarrow < L2 \\
\text{MEDIUM BUILT} &\Rightarrow \leq L1 \wedge \geq L2
\end{aligned}$$

(viii)   GRANDFATHER $\Rightarrow$ = GRANDPA $\wedge$ = GRANDAD

that is, the grandfather is synonymous with grandpa and grandad.

There are altogether seven basic questions a retrieval system for Relations can answer. These are as follows:

a. Is a particular relation between a given object and value true?

b. What is (are) the value(s) belonging to a given relation–object pair, if any? REL (ØBJ) = ?

c. What is (are) the object(s) belonging to a given relation-value pair, if any? REL(?) = VAL

d. What is (are) the relation(s) that connect(s) a given object-value pair, if any? ?(ØBJ) = VAL

e. What relation–object pair(s) belong(s) to a given value, if any? ?(?) = VAL

f. What relation–value pair(s) belong(s) to a given object, if any? ?(ØBJ) = ?

g. Finally, what object–value pair(s) belong(s) to a given relation, if any? REL(?) = ?

The answers are obtainable by using one simple instruction in every case.

Another high level retrieval process can be accomplished by the function

FIND (A, B, C, K)

After its execution, the value of **FIND** is equal to the name of a list containing all X's for which it is true that

$$A : B = C : X.$$

The sign ":" may be verbally interpreted as "is related to." It is assumed that there are at least two Relation Descriptors in one of the following six forms:

$$\begin{bmatrix} Q(A) = B \\ Q(C) = X \end{bmatrix}, \quad \text{or} \quad \begin{bmatrix} A(Q) = B \\ C(Q) = X \end{bmatrix}, \quad \text{or} \quad \begin{bmatrix} A(B) = Q \\ C(X) = Q \end{bmatrix}, \quad \text{or}$$

$$\begin{bmatrix} Q(B) = A \\ Q(X) = C \end{bmatrix}, \quad \text{or} \quad \begin{bmatrix} B(Q) = A \\ X(Q) = C \end{bmatrix}, \quad \text{or} \quad \begin{bmatrix} B(A) = Q \\ X(C) = Q \end{bmatrix}.$$

Here, Q is an entity common to the two (or more) Relation Descriptors both in content and in position (same type of entity). Further, the type of the entities A and C, and also B and X are identical. (This refers to REL, ØBJ, or VAL, and to whether symbolic or numerical.) K can be 0 or 1 but its role does not concern us here.

The following three examples should make this whole idea clear.

1. Suppose in SAM, we have Relation Descriptor words standing for

$$\begin{array}{cccc} : & : & : & : \\ \end{array}$$
MOTHER TONGUE OF (JEANNE) = FRENCH
$$\begin{array}{cccc} : & : & : & : \\ \end{array}$$
MOTHER TONGUE OF (JOSÉ)   = SPANISH
$$\begin{array}{cccc} : & : & : & : \\ \end{array}$$

If A = JEANNE, B = FRENCH, and C = JOSÉ, the resulting X will be SPANISH since Jeanne's relation to French is the same as that of José's to Spanish—these are the mother tongues of the people in question (Q = MOTHER TONGUE OF).

2. Let SAM now contain

$$\begin{array}{cccc} : & : & : & : \\ \end{array}$$
UNCLES OF (JACK) = {JOE, BILL, PETER}
$$\begin{array}{cccc} : & : & : & : \\ \end{array}$$
AUNTS OF (JACK) = {MARY, CARON}
$$\begin{array}{cccc} : & : & : & : \\ \end{array}$$

If A = UNCLES OF, B = {JOE, BILL, PETER}, and C = AUNTS OF, the resulting X will be the list with {MARY, CARON} since {JOE, BILL, PETER} are the uncles of the same person (Q = JACK) whose aunts are {MARY, CARON}.

3. Suppose SAM contains the appropriately coded information about the following diagram:

FIND should answer the question coded in the necessary manner: "The small square is related to the big square in the same way as the small triangle is to which object?"

IV. An Overview

We have tried to give two somewhat disjoint descriptions of our interpretation of living and machine associative memories. We have listed some of the major problems to be studied and a few ideas that may be helpful in the first category. We have also outlined a rather powerful tool for this endeavor in the second category.

AMPPL-II is, we feel, more than "just another computer language;" it represents another philosophy of, another approach to, problem solving. After all, it is only the sequential design of the von Neumann-type machines that has imposed upon the computing community the presently prevalent, but often quite unnatural computational methods. Even using these conventional methods, AMPPL-II (a) should decrease the length of written programs and (b) should simplify the writing, debugging, and understanding of programs. (It has very powerful diagnostic facilities.) There is, however, a significant trend to develop new algorithms and techniques that make use of content addressability and parallel processing, expose latent parallelism, and introduce computational redundancy. We hope AMPPL-II will enhance this trend.

We expect to save considerable programming effort in using AMPPL-II whenever:

1. Data are to be addressed by a combination of various sets of reference properties.
2. Data elements satisfying the above reference properties are scattered throughout the memory in a sparse and random manner.
3. Data elements dynamically change their location in the memory as a consequence of the information processes acting on them.
4. Identical sequences of processes manipulate on distinct, noninteracting data elements.

5. The ratio between concurrently and serially executable processes is reasonably high.

These criteria of language applicability occur to some extent with practically every complex programming problem. The availability of a conventional algebraic language with the AMMPL-cum-SLIP package renders the approach efficient.

ACKNOWLEDGMENTS

The work reported here has been supported by the National Science Foundation, Grant GJ-658.

REFERENCES

1. Findler, N. V., and McKinzie, W. R., On a New Tool in Artificial Intelligence Research. *Proc. Internat. Joint Conf. on Artificial Intelligence, Washington, May 1969*, pp. 259–270.
2. Quillian, M. R., Word Concepts: A Theory and Simulation of Some Basic Semantic Capabilities. *Behav. Sci.* **12**, 410–430 (1967).
3. Quillian, M. R., The Teachable Language Comprehender: A Simulation Program and Theory of Language. *Comm. ACM* **12**, 459–476 (1969).

On Syntactic Pattern Recognition

K.-S. Fu and P. H. Swain

PURDUE UNIVERSITY
LAFAYETTE, INDIANA

I. Introduction

This chapter is primarily a review and evaluation of the state of the art of syntactic pattern recognition, a subject of considerable current interest due to the increasing need for powerful new approaches to pattern recognition problems of great complexity. Aspects of the syntactic approach that seem to be in urgent need of attention are also discussed at some length. It is hoped that this chapter will provide an enlightening introduction and unifying background for the other chapters and at the same time will provide a contribution in its own right to the further development of syntactic pattern recognition.

Early attempts at machine generation and analysis of handwriting (Eden, 1961, 1963) demonstrated that a set of primitive elements together with a set of rules for combining the primitives could be used to generate script which was virtually indistinguishable from human handwriting. These studies had important implications for handwriting recognition since they suggested a method for (1) describing complicated two-dimensional patterns in a one-dimensional format well suited for input to communication and data processing systems and (2) distilling the essential information from complex patterns so as to reduce to practical levels the amount of information to be transmitted or processed. A serious obstacle to the recognition of handwriting remained in the problem of ambiguity, i.e., the fact that handwritten words apparently could not be partitioned into unique sequences of the primitives considered, particularly when the handwriting was far from " textbook " script. But it was postulated that contextual considerations could be helpful in solving this problem.

The concept of describing patterns in terms of primitive elements, subpatterns, and their relationships can be applied to other forms of pattern data for which concise numerical descriptions are often not easily obtainable, (e.g., nuclear bubble-chamber tracks, human speech, geometric figures, games, digital display data, etc.). With respect to such data, one can often formulate a hierarchical structure of subpatterns analogous to the syntactic structure of languages. Syntactic pattern recognition is an attempt to adapt the techniques of formal language theory, which provide both a notation (grammars) and an analysis mechanism (parsing) for such structures, to the problem of representing and analyzing patterns containing a significant syntactic content. As this apparently includes many kinds of patterns of interest, syntactic pattern analysis has recently become the focus of an increasing amount of pattern recognition research.

Regardless of the precise form of the data, syntactic analysis can proceed only if a grammatical model for the data generation and/or analysis process can be formulated. (This does not necessarily imply that the data is actually generated by a mechanism which operates in the same way as the model.) A related practical problem is the development of efficient analysis procedures based on the grammatical model. The available literature concerning syntactic pattern recognition deals almost exclusively with the formulation of grammatical models, although the development of analysis algorithms is currently receiving more attention. The following sections discuss the problem of selecting pattern primitives which can be used to describe patterns of interest, methods for assembling the primitives and their relationships into pattern grammars, and techniques for actually performing pattern analysis in terms of the grammars. Finally some problems involved in dealing with "real life" patterns containing the inevitable distortion and noise are noted and an approach to such problems is proposed.

It might be worth mentioning at the outset that the terms "linguistic" and "syntactic" are used almost interchangeably herein, as has become common practice in the literature, although the former is a somewhat broader term. Strictly speaking, "syntactic" refers only to the structural aspects of languages; analytical techniques have been considered, both for natural languages (Shank and Tesler, 1969) and for patterns (Fischler, 1969) which may be construed as linguistic but not syntactic.

II. Grammars, Syntax, Parsing, and Concatenation

Since some of the terminology of formal language theory will be used extensively throughout this paper, a necessarily brief introduction to the terminology is in order. Some additional material in this respect will be provided as needed.

The central idea of formal language theory is the generation and/or analysis of the strings (sentences) of languages in terms of grammars, typically *phrase-structure grammars* as defined informally in Figure 1. The structural description of the language (note that a language is just a set of strings over the set of terminals—often referred to herein as "primitives"—of the grammar) in

A <u>Phrase-Structure Grammar</u> is a four-tuple

$$G = (V_N, V_T, P, S)$$

V_N: finite set of "nonterminals" or variables

V_T: finite set of "terminals"

$S \in V_N$:   "start" symbol or "sentence" symbol

P: finite set of "productions" or rewriting rules

Productions have the general form

$$\alpha \rightarrow \beta$$

where α and β are strings over

$$V_N \cup V_T,$$

and "→" is read "is replaced by."

$L(G)$ denotes the language (set of strings) generated by G.

Example: $V_N = \{S, A\}$ $V_T = \{0, 1\}$

P: $S \rightarrow 0A$ $A \rightarrow 1A$

$A \rightarrow 0A$ $A \rightarrow 11$

$L(G) = \{x \mid x \in V_T^* \text{ and } x \text{ begins with } 0, \text{ ends with } 11\}$

Sample generation: $S \Longrightarrow 0A \Longrightarrow 00A \Longrightarrow 001A \Longrightarrow 0010A \Longrightarrow 001011$

FIGURE 1. A phrase-structure grammar.

terms of a grammar is called a *syntax* of the language. Analysis in terms of this structure is called *syntactic analysis,* or often simply *parsing.*

In formal language theory, the only relation between the elements in a string, either a terminal string or an intermediate string containing nonterminals, is concatenation, i.e., the juxtaposition of adjacent elements. It will be seen throughout this chapter that a crucial point involved in adapting the techniques of formal language theory to pattern analysis is the generalization of this simple notion to include other (almost arbitrary) relationships and mechanization of the resulting, considerably more general, formalism in as systematic a way as has been done for formal "string" languages and grammars.

III. Selection of Pattern Primitives

The first step in formulating a syntactic model for pattern analysis is the determination of a set of primitives in terms of which the data of interest may be described. This will be largely influenced by the nature of the data, the specific application in question, and the technology available for implementing the analysis. The primitives should provide an adequate description of the data, i.e., the primitive descriptions of patterns from different classes should be distinguishable by whatever method is to be applied to analyze the descriptions. In addition to this obvious requirement, the primitive descriptions should be readily obtainable from the raw data and should be compact enough so as not to overtax the memory and processing capacities of the analysis system. In many instances these may be conflicting requirements, and it may be necessary to find an acceptable trade-off among them.

One of the earliest papers describing the decomposition of patterns into primitives (Grimsdale et al., 1959) presented a conceptually appealing method which allowed the recognition system to determine the primitive elements by inspection of training samples. Each primitive consisted of an observed point set (i.e., part of a pattern) the horizontal extent of which displayed no sudden changes on successively scanned lines (quantitatively, "sudden" meant within a user-specified tolerance set to account for noise in the pattern). Such primitives are easily detected by a simple raster scan of the pattern. The analysis scheme developed was apparently quite successful, allowing for such annoyances as varied pattern size, pattern rotation, etc., but required an impractical amount of processing time and a large dictionary to remember the valid pattern structures. Simpler pattern descriptions and analysis procedures may have been achieved (possibly at the expense of increased hardware complexity) if explicit consideration could have been given to formalizing the pattern syntax.

More recent efforts concerned with the primitive selection problem may be grouped roughly as follows: general methods emphasizing boundaries, general methods emphasizing regions, and special methods which take advantage of the peculiarities of specific applications. A set of primitives commonly used to describe boundaries is the chain code due to Freeman (1961). Under this scheme, a rectangular grid is overlaid on the two-dimensional pattern and straight line segments are used to connect the grid points falling closest to the pattern (see Figure 2). Each line segment is assigned an octal digit according

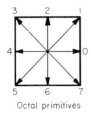

Octal primitives

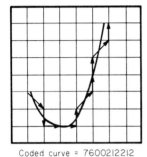

Coded curve = 7600212212

FIGURE 2. Freeman's chain code.

to its slope. The pattern is thus represented by a (possibly multiply connected) chain or chains of octal digits. This coding scheme has some useful properties. For example, patterns coded in this way can be rotated through multiples of 45; simply by adding an octal digit (modulo 8) to every digit in the chain (although only rotations by multiples of 90° can be accomplished without some distortion of the pattern). Other simple manipulations such as expansion, measurement of curve length, and determination of pattern self-intersections are easily carried out. Also, the code is a "saturated" three-bit code (i.e., there are 8 possibilities for each digit) which makes it both economical and easy to manipulate. Finally, any desired degree of resolution can be obtained by adjusting the fineness of the grid imposed on the patterns. Of course, this method is not limited to closed boundaries; it can be used for coding arbitrary two-dimensional figures composed of straight or curved lines and line segments.

Notable works using Freeman's chain code include efforts by Knoke and Wiley (1967) and by Feder (1967). Knoke and Wiley attempted to demonstrate that linguistic principles can usefully be applied to describe structural relationships within patterns (hand-printed letters). After preprocessing of a CRT-input pattern to obtain a Freeman-code description of the pattern, they use a "transformational grammar" to reduce irregularities (i.e., to smooth the pattern). The result of this step is a description of the pattern in terms of a list of vertex interconnections and the shapes of the corresponding connecting arcs, which constitutes a sentence in the pattern language (see Figure 3). The

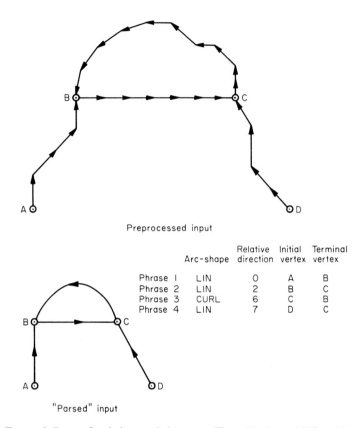

FIGURE 3. Parse of a chain-encoded pattern. (From Knoke and Wiley, 1967.)

sentence is then checked against a dictionary of prototypes and "recognized" if a match is found. Although some limited success has been achieved in applying this method to character recognition, the authors readily admit some serious difficulties, namely, (1) it has not been possible to find a pattern grammar which generates all and only valid patterns; (2) it is necessary to restrict the allowable length of pattern sentences; (3) it has not been possible to utilize context; (4) the syntactic analysis is slow and inefficient; and, (5) only connected patterns are considered.

Feder's work considers only patterns which can be encoded as strings of primitives (the Knoke and Wiley vertex–arc shape–vertex scheme can deal with multiply connected chains of primitives). Several bases for developing pattern languages are discussed, including equations in two variables (straight lines, circles and circular arcs, etc.), pattern properties (self-intersection, convexity, etc.) and various measures of curve similarity. Much of the work is taken up with determining the computational power (automaton complexity) required to detect the elements of these languages (which are mostly context-sensitive but not context-free), a problem considerably complicated by the facts that (1) the chain code yields only a piecewise linear approximation of the original pattern, and (2) the coding of a typical curve is not unique, depending to a degree on its location and orientation with respect to the coding grid. Unfortunately, little attention is given to how one would actually synthesize a pattern recognizer based on the proposed pattern languages.

The efforts of Knoke and Wiley and Feder provide confirmation for the hypothesis that the linguistic approach may be applied to pattern recognition, although some serious problems need further attention. On the negative side, however, it appears that although Freeman's chain-encoding method is one of the simplest ways to present patterns to data processing equipment, patterns so encoded usually must undergo considerable preprocessing (essentially data reduction, smoothing, and a sort of feature extraction), which helps to emphasize structural relationships (syntax), before syntactic analysis can be effectively applied. In this sense the Freeman encoding may be "too primitive" in much the same way as the binary elements in the familiar "photocell array" encoding used in some character recognition devices. The required preprocessing may not necessarily be best achieved by linguistically oriented techniques [for example, see Zahn (1969)].

A set of primitives for encoding geometric patterns in terms of regions has been proposed by Pavlidis (1968). In this case, the basic primitives are half-planes in the pattern space (this could be generalized to halfspaces of the pattern space). If can be shown that any arbitrary polygon may be interpreted as the union of a finite number of convex polygons. Each convex polygon can in turn be interpreted as the intersection of a finite number of halfplanes. By defining a suitable ordering on the convex polygons composing the arbitrary polygon, it is possible to determine a unique minimal set of maximal (in an appropriate sense) polygons, called *primary subsets*, the union of which is the given polygon. Pavlidis' approach provides a formalism for describing the syntax of polygonal figures and more general figures which can be approximated reasonably well by polygonal figures. However, his analysis procedures require the definition of suitable measures of similarity between polygons. The similarity measures he has considered are quite sensitive to noise in the patterns and/or are very difficult to implement practically on a digital computer.

Another approach to the analysis of geometric patterns is discussed by Guzmán (1967, 1968). This approach assumes that a picture can be reduced by preprocessing to a list of vertices, lines, and surfaces. Various heuristics, based primarily on the analysis of types of intersections of lines and surfaces, are applied to this list to compose its elements into two- or three-dimensional regions. In effect, this amounts to a data compression process after which further processing for the purpose of, say, pattern recognition can be greatly simplified. Some candidate pattern recognition schemes are investigated (Guzmán, 1967), all of which involve methods for matching the reduced pattern descriptions against a prototype dictionary.

The chapter by Rosenfield and Strong proposes another selection of pattern primitives based on regions and apparently of a somewhat more general nature than those previously discussed. Interesting examples of rather specialized selections of pattern primitives include Eden (1963), Ledley *et al.* (1965), and the chapter by Pavlidis.

One aspect which most of the foregoing approaches share is a concern with the reduction of the pattern to be analyzed into some sort of string representation. This is partly due to the relative ease with which string representations can be handled, but it may also be attributed to a desire to take advantage of the existing results in formal language theory, since to use these results it is necessary either to develop effective methods to accomplish the reduction of patterns to strings of concatenated primitives or to extend the existing theory to include syntactic relations more general than concatenation. The former has, to date, been the most common approach. One effort to formulate generalized syntactic relations has recently been undertaken by Anderson (1968) for the syntactic analysis of handwritten mathematical expressions. Anderson has proposed an entity called a *syntactic unit* as the multidimensional analog of the one-dimensional syntactic variable (he defines both terminal and nonterminal syntactic units). A syntactic unit is a subscripted variable, say A_p, where A is the name of the unit and p is an ordered set of coordinates specifying the location of the subpattern named A in the pattern space. A pattern described as a list of syntactic units differs in a very fundamental way from the conventional string: Since each syntactic unit contains its own location information, the position of the unit in the list no longer has any particular significance. This gives considerably more flexibility and power to the corresponding grammars than one might expect. It also complicates the analysis. More will be said about this work in Section IV,B.

There is a group of syntactic pattern recognition researchers which is not particularly concerned about string-encoding of patterns because they are primarily interested in developing equipment capable of processing all elements of a digital picture array in parallel (Narasimhan, 1964, 1966; McCormick, 1963; Narasimhan and Mayoh, 1963). Under their picture-processing formalism, entire picture arrays are treated as operands of picture-processing operations which produce a new picture array as a resultant. Pictures can thus serve as syntactic primitives and higher-order syntactic constructs as well. Near the top of the hierarchy, however, their syntactic elements are very much like Anderson's syntactic units, each construct consisting of a name and an attribute list [see especially Narasimhan (1966)]. Interestingly, Rosenfeld and Pfaltz (1966) have noted that many (perhaps most) useful picture transformations which have been defined under parallel processing formalisms involve local operations (i.e., functions which define a value for each element in the new picture in terms of the values of the corresponding element and a small set of its neighbors in the original picture), and they have proved that parallel processing of this sort is computationally equivalent to sequential processing. In other words, there are no local parallel processing functions which cannot be accomplished by local sequential processing, and vice versa. What is perhaps more surprising is that sequential processors can be significantly more efficient in terms of the total number of operations involved (the number of points times the number of operations per point) than parallel processors in performing many useful types of picture processing. In fact, parallel processors are sometimes forced to simulate sequential processing and can do so only very inefficiently. But one can still expect that, in general, parallel processing will yield a significant time advantage over sequential processing in spite of the relative computational efficiency of the latter.

IV. Pattern Grammars and Syntax-Directed Analysis

Now if one assumes that a satisfactory solution of the " primitive selection " problem is available for a given application, the next question is: How does one carry out the analysis of the primitive pattern description? (Of course, this is not to imply that the primitive selection and pattern analysis aspects can be separated in practice; but the fact that they cannot will not prohibit a dichotomous survey of the work that has been attempted.) Before plunging too far into this part of the problem, it would be well to recall a bit more terminology commonly associated with methods of syntactic analysis.

A convenient way to exhibit syntactic structure is by means of a *parsing tree*. The root of the tree, conventionally displayed at the top, is labeled with the start symbol; the terminating branches, at the bottom, are labelled with terminal symbols the union of which (concatenation in the case of string languages) is a sentence of the language. The structure leading from root to terminating branches describes how the sentence is derived from the start symbol by successive applications of the productions in the grammar.

Some parsing techniques develop the parse by proceeding downward from the root of the tree, i.e., by attempting to synthesize the pattern through use of the syntactic productions. These are called *top-down* methods. Other methods work upward from the bottom of the tree by attempting to decompose the pattern by applying the productions in reverse. These are called *bottom-up* methods. There has been considerable debate among formal linguists as to the relative merits of the two approaches for automatic parsing, but from a practical point of view the best approach generally depends on the particular form of the grammar involved (Griffiths and Petrick, 1965).

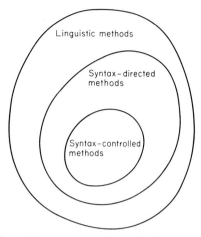

FIGURE 4. Hierarchy of linguistic analysis techniques.

One can describe a "hierarchy" of linguistic or syntactic analysis procedures (Figure 4). Any procedure which is at least incidentally concerned with decomposing a pattern into primitive components (alternatively, synthesizing it from primitive components) will be called a *linguistic* procedure. A procedure which utilizes in any way the syntactic description of an entity (sentence, pattern) is a *syntax-directed* procedure. If the grammar on which such a description is based is intimately associated with the procedure (e.g., the grammar may in some manner direct the analysis), then the procedure is said to be *syntax-controlled*. [This terminology is analogous to that used with respect to syntax directed compilers (Floyd, 1964a, b).] For example, a pattern categorization procedure might consist of matching the parse of an unknown against various prototype parses. This is syntax-directed but not syntax-controlled pattern recognition. A top-down or bottom-up procedure might have the category names as higher-order syntactic elements so that a successful parse necessarily accomplishes the categorization. This procedure would constitute syntax-controlled pattern recognition.

Surprisingly, some of the approaches which have been taken to syntactic pattern analysis are hardly syntax-directed, much less syntax-controlled. For example, in Pavlidis' work mentioned earlier, cognizance is taken of the fact that a syntactic model may be formulated for the composition of polygonal figures from halfplanes; but although higher-level constructs are defined in terms of the intersections of the primitive halfplanes, the syntactic analysis stops at that point, with no consideration given to the relationships at the higher level. This is like terminating the analysis of a FORTRAN statement once it has been ascertained to consist of additive terms and divisor terms without determining specifically how the terms are related. Such a scheme may be sufficient for a class of problems involving fairly elementary patterns and distinct pattern classes, but it is probably not an adequate model for more complicated situations.

On the other hand, a successful application of syntax-controlled pattern recognition is the FIDAC system (Film Input to Digital Automatic Computer) developed by Ledley *et al.* (1965) for the detection and classification of chromosome types in photomicrographs. In this case a set of primitives was determined (line segments of various shapes) which was at once adequate for the characterization of the patterns of interest and readily detectable by a suitable combination of hardware and computer software. Furthermore, the primitive-encoded patterns amounted to strings which could be generated by a fairly simple context-free phrase-structure grammar (Figure 5). The syntax-controlled analysis system permits rapid and dependable processing (according to its developers) of sufficient numbers of chromosome photomicrographs for statistical studies of chromosome variability.

Most attempts at syntactic pattern analysis fall somewhere between the two extremes cited above in terms of the degree to which they exploit the " syntactics " of the problem. Sometimes the syntactic structure is more readily definable than for Pavlidis' polygon figures, but only occasionally can it be defined as directly as appears to have been the case for FIDAC. General solutions for the primitive selection, grammar formulation, and analyzer synthesis problems have not yet appeared. The primitive selection problem has been discussed in the previous section. Research pertaining to the formulation of pattern grammars and some approaches to the synthesis of syntax-directed pattern analyzers will now be considered. It is in this area that one hopes to take advantage of the body of results available from research in formal language theory and syntax-directed compilers and perhaps some results from automata theory. Some references which may be of particular interest in this respect are included in the bibliography.

Much of the work yet to be mentioned can be conveniently described in terms of the following generalized syntactic formalism (GSF).

A *generalized syntactic element* (GSE) is a construct consisting of two parts; a *name*, which is actually a convenient way of referring abstractly to sets of invariant properties and property relationships; and an *attribute list*, which is a set of modifiers or variable properties which take on values associated with specific occurrences of the GSE.

A *generalized syntactic production* (GSP) is a rule which specifies how a syntactic element is composed from or generates other (usually more primitive) syntactic elements. A GSP also consists of two parts; the first part indicates the relationship of names; the second specifies the necessary relationships of attributes.†

To illustrate, consider three GSE's defined as follows. CEE(RADIUS, DIRECTION) represents the set of semicircular arcs (invariant property)

---

†In fact, a GSP may express a relationship of predicates in the sense of Evans (1967), Banerji (1968), or Sherman and Ernst (1969), thereby providing possibly the most general type of syntactic formalism.

$V_T = \{a,b,c,d,e\}$

$V_N = \{S, T, Bottom, Side, Armpair, Rightpart, Leftpart, Arm\}$

P: S → Armpair · Armpair

  T → Bottom · Armpair

  Armpair → Side · Armpair

  Armpair → Armpair · Side

  Armpair → Arm · Rightpart

  Armpair → Leftpart · Arm

  Leftpart → Arm · c

  Rightpart → c · Arm

  Bottom → b · Bottom

  Bottom → Bottom · b

  Bottom → c

  Side → b · Side

  Side → Side · b

  Side → b · d

  Arm → b · Arm

  Arm → Arm · b

  Arm → a

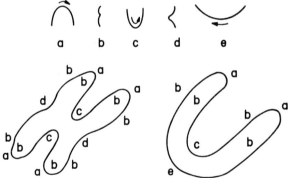

FIGURE 5. The grammar for FIDAC. From Ledley *et al.*, 1965. Used with the permission of Dr. Robert H. Ledley, National Biochemical Research Foundation, Silver Spring, Maryland.

of arbitrary radius and orientation (variable properties). BAR(LENGTH, DIRECTION) represents the set of straight line segments of arbitrary length and orientation. And DEE(HEIGHT, DIRECTION) represents the set of D-shaped figures of arbitrary size and orientation. The GSP

$$DEE(a, b) \rightarrow BAR(a, b) \, CEE(a/2, b)$$

describes how a D-shaped figure is composed of (or generates) a semicircular arc and straight line segment of suitable size and orientation.

This example may be far too simple to be realistic; for example, no connectivity specifications are given. But any such additional properties could be added to the attribute lists as desired. In fact, deciding how complex to make the attribute list and how much structure to subsume as part of the invariant property set associated with the GSE name constitutes a critical aspect of the selection of suitable syntactic elements and relations. This decision affects at once the form of the productions, the adequacy of the model, and the nature of the analysis algorithm. In practice the selection must be such that the required analysis is achievable within any specified cost and efficiency (processing speed) limitations.

A. Pattern Grammars

The Picture Description Language (PDL) developed by Shaw (1968, 1969) is actually a pattern grammar which appears to be a reasonably general and flexible formalism for the description and analysis of picture data (and possibly other forms of multidimensional data with syntactic content). The PDL is a generalized syntactic formalism and also a string grammar, so that there is reason to hope not only that it can be applied to a large class of pattern data, but also that some of the results and techniques of formal linguistics and/or automata theory can be brought to bear through it to assist in the realization of efficient pattern analysis techniques.

By means of the PDL formalism, one-, two-, and three-dimensional data can be put into string form. This is accomplished by requiring that all syntactic elements (pictures, subpictures, and primitives as well) have a *head* and a *tail*; concatenation can occur only at the head and tail of syntactic elements (head to tail). All pictures are assumed connected, which is made to hold even for pictures with disjoint elements by the definition of suitable *blank* primitives. A *null point* primitive is also defined which consists only of coincident head and tail. Four binary operators are defined which, together with the null point primitive, are sufficient to describe all possible concatenations of syntactic elements (Figure 6). Two unary operators are defined, one of which acts as a *reverser* (head-to-tail interchange), the other specifying superposition of primitives. The superposition operator in conjunction with the definition of blank primitives and *label operators* provide the PDL the ability to describe multiply connected figures. Thirteen context-free productions generate all valid PDL sentences. A PDL grammar for a particular application results when a set of suitable primitives and applicable productions is specified (Figure 7). Shaw gives several examples.

Possibly the most severe limitations of the PDL is its restriction to context-free languages. There is a strong feeling in some quarters that context-free

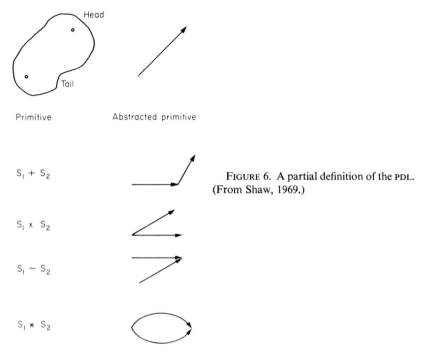

Primitive   Abstracted primitive

$S_1 + S_2$

$S_1 \times S_2$ FIGURE 6. A partial definition of the PDL.
                                                   (From Shaw, 1969.)

$S_1 - S_2$

$S_1 * S_2$

Binary concatenations

languages cannot be expected to provide adequate models for a very general class of complex pattern analysis problems. But this is an open question. The full potential of the PDL deserves to be investigated in this respect. The PDL has some other relatively minor limitations which are discussed by Shaw but do not seem insurmountable. It is significant that the PDL has proved useful in at least one practical application (Shaw, 1968) for which a picture analyzer based on the PDL has been implemented. The nature of this implementation is interesting and will be discussed in Section IV,B.

The *web grammars* due to Rosenfeld and Pfaltz (1969) appear to offer a natural two-dimensional generalization of string grammars. A *web* is a directed graph with nodes bearing labels from a vocabulary of symbols. Since a string is a special case of a graph, a string of symbols is a special case of a web. A web grammar consists of a vocabulary with terminal and nonterminal elements, and a set of rewriting rules (productions)—much like the familiar phrase-structure string grammar. However, the productions of the web grammar are more complicated: Each rule specifies the replacement of a subweb in the original web by another subweb to form the rewritten web. The

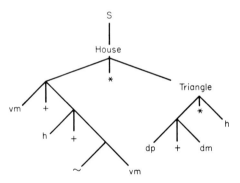

$$V_T = \{ \ dp \quad , \quad dm \quad , \quad h \quad , \quad vm \ \}$$

$$V_N = \{Triangle, \ House, \ S, \ A\}$$

P: S → A
    S → House
    House → ((vm + (h + (∼ vm))) * Triangle)
    A → (dp + (Triangle + dm))
    Triangle → ((dp + dm) * h)

S ⟹ ((vm + (h + (∼ vm))) * ((dp + dm) * h))

FIGURE 7. A PDL grammar and example. (From Shaw, 1969.)

rule must specify precisely how the new subweb is to be "embedded" in the "host" web. This can be done in any number of ways as long as the embedding rule does not depend on the host web, a requirement which assures that the rule can be applied to any occurrence of the variable (subweb) being rewritten (see Figure 8).

Context-sensitive and context-free web grammars are defined. A web grammar is a generalized syntactic formalism, the embedding rules constituting at least part of the attribute relationship. Shaw's PDL is a special case of a web grammar, but the unrestricted web grammar formalism seems to provide a more natural way of representing multiply connected graphs. Although the practical applicability of web grammars remains to be demonstrated, there would seem to be no reason why this formalism should not be at least as useful as the PDL. Thus, web grammars represent another step toward the

$$G = \{V_N, V_T; S, P\}$$

where

$$V_N = \{A\} \qquad \text{nonterminal vocabulary}$$

$$V_T = \{a,b,c\} \qquad \text{terminal vocabulary}$$

$$S = \{\overset{\cdot}{A}\} \qquad \text{initial web}$$

P:

productions

where the embedding rule for both productions is

$$E = \{(p,a) \mid (p,A) \text{ is an edge of the host web}\}$$

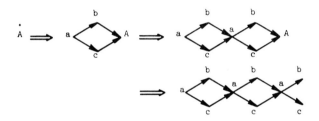

FIGURE 8. A simple web grammar. (From Rosenfeld and Pfaltz, 1969.)

generalization of phrase-structure grammatical concepts from strings to more general syntactic entities.

B. Pattern Analysis Mechanisms

Evans (1968a, b) has developed a "grammar-controlled pattern analyzer" (a LISP program) which he describes as a very useful tool for testing pattern grammars. Utilizing a GSF, the analyzer accepts as input both the pattern grammar (syntactic elements, productions, and predicates which define the syntactic relationships) and patterns to be analyzed (expressed in terms of the primitive syntactic elements). The output of the system consists of all hierarchical descriptions possible under the specified grammar, which amounts to an accounting of all possible subpatterns (GSE's) detected and their relationships. The grammar could be constructed so that part of this accounting would be the name(s) of any pattern class(es) to which the pattern might belong.

There is virtually no restriction on the form of the grammars acceptable by Evans' analyzer. They may be finite-state, context-free, or context-sensitive in form, i.e., in the same sense as is usually defined for string grammars. However, a string language generated by a generalized syntactic formalism grammar which is, say, context-free in this sense may *not* be a context-free string language, i.e., capable of being generated by a context-free string grammar (see Anderson, 1968, Chapter 10). Unfortunately, as Evans remarks, "the price paid for this generality may preclude any practical application of the system so that its principal use may be as an experimental tool in the choice of the primitives to be included in particular special purpose systems." This is not surprising considering the inefficiency of the general parsing techniques which have been developed for string languages and grammars. Again what appears to be needed is a generalization of some of the special string grammars for which there exist very efficient analysis procedures (Floyd, 1964; Wirth and Weber, 1966; Crespi-Reghizzi and Presser, 1969).

Anderson (1968) uses a top-down analysis procedure to parse handwritten mathematical expressions (see the discussion of his formalism in Section II). His grammars are GSF's which have been carefully formulated to enhance parsing efficiency, which is essential since top-down syntactic analysis procedures often tend to be very inefficient, particularly in rejecting "ungrammatical" sentences. He takes advantage of the fact that mathematical expressions tend to be written in a left-to-right manner and also utilizes to a limited extent some of the techniques of precedence analysis (Wirth and Weber, 1966). The idea is to arrange the grammar and the analysis procedure so that it becomes obvious as quickly as possible that the analysis is proceeding down an invalid branch of the parsing tree. Although Anderson provides no precise timing information, he indicates that his analysis prodecure is fast enough for the application even though it has not been rigorously optimized. This provides an indication that sufficiently specialized syntactic analysis procedures can be designed which are practical to implement.

Another interesting aspect of Anderson's work is an evaluation of the possible benefits of parallel processing. He shows that even two processors working in parallel on different branches of the parsing tree would yield a dramatic overall efficiency advantage over strictly serial processing. The efficiency gains tend to level off quickly as the number of parallel processors increases. Note that this "procedure-parallel" processing is considerably different from the "picture-parallel" processing concept of Narasimhan discussed earlier.

To implement an analysis system based on PDL, Shaw (1968) uses a syntax-controlled, top-down, goal-oriented picture parsing algorithm. As a top-down algorithm, the analyzer uses a PDL grammar to try to synthesize a PDL description of the input pattern. (A bottom-up algorithm would try to reduce groupings of syntactic variables and terminals into successively higher-level variables by reverse application of the productions in the grammar.) The algorithm is goal oriented because at each stage of the analysis it tries to attain a specific goal, namely, to determine whether a specific syntactic construct—the right-hand side of the production being applied—describes part of the input pattern. A successful generation of a PDL description of the input pattern indicates that the pattern belongs to the pattern class of interest. The analysis may also yield additional useful information about the pattern depending on any semantic analysis carried out in conjunction with the syntactic analysis.

As pointed out by Shaw, a goal-oriented procedure of this nature has some important advantages over other approaches. The logic of the syntactic analysis is straightforward, consisting primarily of stepping through the pattern grammar, with backtracking as necessary in case false goals are generated at higher levels in the analysis. [There has been some skepticism in the past regarding the use of top-down analysis for practical analysis schemes because of the inefficiency that results from a large amount of backtracking [see, for example, Griffiths and Petrick (1965)]. But Shaw's experience indicates that, assuming due care in defining the PDL grammar, the total time consumed by the syntactic analysis tends to be negligible compared to that required for the detection of primitives in the raw data.] Also, it is helpful to use a goal-oriented procedure in dealing directly with unpreprocessed pattern data because the syntax specifically prescribes which primitives must be located in the pattern and what relationship these primitives must have to the rest of the pattern. This is, in effect, one way of utilizing context to aid in the recognition process which, as a result, may not need to be as precise as methods which must search out arbitrary primitives (the job of some preprocessors, for instance, is to compile a list of possible primitives in the pattern without reference to the syntax). It should be clear that this may also reduce to some degree the effects of noise in the data.

A few restrictions must be imposed on the precise form of the PDL grammar to be implemented. For example, left-recursive productions are prohibited because top-down parsers can get into infinite loops when processing grammars with left-recursive productions. However, most of the restrictions are automatically satisfied if the grammar is transformed into Shaw's PDL *standard form*. Shaw believes, although he has not been able to prove, that any PDL grammar can be so transformed.

Shaw's work is the most convincing demonstration yet to appear that syntactic pattern analysis is a feasible approach to problems involving complexly structured data. It will be interesting to see if equally or more effective analysis algorithms can be developed employing the web grammars discussed earlier.

V. "Learning" Pattern Grammars by Grammatical Inference

The researcher's intuition and familiarity with the data are relied on heavily at present in formulating grammars for specific applications. The grammar synthesis procedure is now largely trial and error, sometimes aided by user-interactive computer graphics (Knoke and Wiley, 1967; Evans, 1968b). Clearly a facility is needed for automatically inferring grammars from representative samples of the languages in question, much as the training procedures of "conventional" pattern recognition technology are used to synthesize pattern classifiers from "training samples" of known classification. This is apparently a rather difficult problem which has only recently begun to receive attention in the literature (Gold, 1967; Sherman and Ernst, 1969; Rosenfeld et al., 1969; Sauvain and Uhr, 1969). A more comprehensive consideration of the problem is the subject of the chapter by Evans.

VI. The Roles of Probability in Syntactic Pattern Analysis

The syntactic pattern analyzers found in the literature are generally well shielded from the "real world" by extensive preprocessing of the raw patterns (smoothing, gap-filling, thinning, etc.) intended to extract pure patterns and eliminate noise [for example, see works by Ledley et al. (1965), Narasimhan (1964), Knoke and Wiley (1967), and Evans (1968b).] The preprocessing techniques commonly used make little or no use of the pattern syntax even though the syntax could be of great assistance in distinguishing noise and detecting distortions of pure patterns. Unfortunately, however, it is precisely distortion and noise which make quite difficult the description of "real life" patterns by means of familiar nonprobabilistic grammatical models. Recalling that probabilistic approaches have often yielded some success in dealing with distortion and noise, one is led to consider the formulation of a probabilistic model for syntactic analysis.

In attempting to build a universal theoretical foundation for "grammatical analysis of patterns," Grenander (1967a) has proposed a model called a *probabilistic deformation grammar*. The model is somewhat vaguely specified in order to maintain generality, but it essentially involves a set of deformation transformations applied to the syntactic variables. A probability measure is defined over the set of deformation transformations. This model appears to be applicable only to the variety of syntactic analysis procedures which do not depend on a parse of the patterns but only on the description of the patterns in terms of primitives and deformations. These procedures sometimes turn out to be variations on the familiar minimum distance recognition rule.

In another work Grenander (1967b) has suggested the possibility of defining a probability distribution over the productions of a context-free pattern grammar. This in turn impresses a probability distribution on the set of parsing trees which may be generated by the grammar and thence on the language generated by the grammar. The model turns out to be a multitype branching process which has been studied in some detail (Harris, 1963). Grenander has investigated the constraints on the probability measure over the set of terminating parsing trees generated by context-free grammars [see also Booth (1969)]. This model comes much closer in spirit to the concept of syntax-controlled pattern analysis than does the probabilistic deformation grammar (although only empirical studies can be expected to demonstrate which model is truly most appropriate for a given problem). In addition to the work by Grenander and Booth, Kherts (1968) has defined and studied briefly the entropy of stochastic context-free grammars; and Fu and Li (1969) have described the realization of a stochastic finite-state automaton which recognizes a stochastic finite-state language, and have shown how such an automaton can be synthesized if a grammar generating the language is known. The remainder of this section will summarize the limited progress which has been made toward developing stochastic grammars and mention some problems which must be faced in order to develop an adequate model for stochastic syntactic analysis.

Following the formulation of Kherts (1968), the simplest type of stochastic grammar is defined as follows.

A stochastic finite-state grammar with independent production probabilities is a five-tuple (V_N, V_T, P, D, S), where V_N is a finite nonterminal vocabulary; V_T is a finite terminal vocabulary; P is a finite set of productions, each having one of the following forms:

$$A_i \to a_j A_k \qquad \text{or} \qquad A_i \to a_j,$$

where $A_i, A_j \in V_N$; $S \in V_N$ is the distinguished sentence symbol; D is a probability measure over P. The probability associated with $A_i \to a_j A_k$ is denoted by p_{jk}^i; the probability associated with $A_i \to a_j$ is denoted by p_{j0}^i.

Clearly it is necessary that $0 \leq p_{jk}^i \leq 1$. It is also required that

$$\sum_j \sum_k p_{jk}^i = 1$$

for each i such that $A_i \in V_N$. Moreover, it is desirable that the probability distribution over the productions impress a valid probability distribution over the language generated by the grammar. The probabilities of the terminal strings generated by the grammar should sum to unity. This is not automatically true. Grenander (1967b) has shown that a valid distribution over the language is obtained if each nonterminal of the finite-state grammar is contained in at least one string derivable with nonzero probability from the sentence symbol and each nonterminal generates with nonzero probability at least one string containing only terminals.

Unfortunately, this delightfully simple model is of little practical utility, failing by far to describe a sufficiently broad class of languages of interest. One might argue that for practical problems the maximum number of possible patterns which could be observed is certainly bounded (in most cases) and that finite-state grammars are capable of describing such situations. Indeed this is a theoretically valid observation, but the finite-state grammars which are necessary whenever the number of possible patterns is large and/or their structure is at all nontrivial are unwieldly and by no means revealing of the significant pattern structure. The reader may prove this to his satisfaction by trying to write a finite-state grammar for the language

$$L = \{a^n b^n c^n d^n \mid 0 < n \le m\}$$

for m equal to, say, ten. This language might represent a family of squares with sides of length $1, 2, \ldots, 10$. Also, refer to the example at the end of this section.

The stochastic grammatical model can be generalized in either or both of two ways: by extension to more powerful grammar forms (context-free, context-sensitive), or by the use of more complex probabilistic mechanisms, e.g., various forms of conditional probabilities [see Booth (1969)]. The use of more powerful grammar forms seems to be the most direct approach [see Swain (1970) for a more detailed discussion of this point].

A stochastic context-free grammar can be defined in much the same manner as in the finite-state case. Grenander (1967b) and Booth (1969) have specified the conditions for a valid set of context-free production probabilities, which again involve guaranteeing that every derivation (or generation) from the grammar terminates with unit probability. Some successful applications of (nonprobabilistic) context-free grammars have been described earlier in this chapter, which attests to their greater practical utility as compared with finite-state grammars for pattern analysis purposes. But they still lack the descriptive power available to context-sensitive grammars which are generally most capable of producing the types of structural descriptions most useful for pattern analysis purposes.

The increasing descriptive power of the context-free and context-sensitive grammars is paid for in terms of increased complexity of the analysis system (Hopcroft and Ullman, 1969). Whereas deterministic finite-state automata are capable of recognizing finite-state languages, nonfinite nondeterministic devices are required, in general, to recognize the languages generated by context-free and context-sensitive grammars. This is at worst a theoretical difficulty, however, which is unlikely to cause serious problems in practice as long as some care is exercised in developing the required grammars. This is especially true when the languages of interest are actually finite-state even though the form of the grammars may be context-sensitive (possibly the most likely situation), or when the languages may be approximated by finite-state languages (Booth, 1969). An important step yet to be carried out is the development of a characterization of stochastic context-sensitive grammars; for example, the conditions required to guarantee a valid probability distribution over the productions and terminal strings have yet to be determined. Another practical problem is the complicated and altogether unintuitive manner with which context-sensitive phrase-structure grammars must perform routine operations such as maintaining counters which are essential to the derivations. Such "roundabout" operation tends to obscure the structural relationships within the derived sentences, relationships which are of paramount importance. Fortunately, this problem can be alleviated to a considerable extent by using special types of grammars which have only recently been defined and investigated. Examples include programmed grammars (Rosenkrantz, 1967) and indexed grammars (Aho, 1968). Stochastic versions of such specialized syntactic formalisms, once characterized, should constitute a step in the direction of the sort of compact and efficient grammatical models needed for practical analysis of real data. The authors are currently investigating the properties and potential applications of stochastic programmed grammars and expect to publish some results in the near future.

The following simple nonprobabilistic example illustrates some of the points discussed above, particularly the increased power of the productions of the more general classes of grammars.

EXAMPLE. It is desired to construct a grammar to generate the finite-state language $L = \{a^n b^n c^n \mid 1 \leq n \leq 3\}$. This might be the language describing, say, the set of equilateral triangles of side-length one, two, or three units. So that the grammar will be compatible with a top-down goal-oriented analysis procedure, the grammar must produce terminals in a strictly left-to-right order and at most one terminal may be produced by a single application of any production. Nonterminals may not appear to the left of terminal symbols, but the generation of nonterminals is otherwise unrestricted.

1. A finite-state grammar: $G_1 = (V_N, V_T, P, S)$, where

$$V_N = \{S, A_1, A_2, B_{10}, B_{20}, B_{30}, B_{21}, B_{31}, B_{32}, C_1, C_2, C_3\}$$

is the nonterminal vocabulary and $V_T = \{a, b, c\}$ the terminal vocabulary.

$$
\begin{array}{ll}
P: & S \to aA_1 \\
& S \to aB_{10} \\
& A_1 \to aA_2 \\
& A_1 \to aB_{20} \\
& A_2 \to aB_{30} \\
& B_{10} \to bC_1 \\
& B_{20} \to bB_{21}
\end{array}
\qquad
\begin{array}{l}
B_{21} \to bC_2 \\
B_{30} \to bB_{31} \\
B_{31} \to bB_{32} \\
B_{32} \to bC_3 \\
C_1 \to c \\
C_2 \to cC_1 \\
C_3 \to cC_2
\end{array}
$$

2. A context-free grammar (in Greibach normal form): $G_2 = (V_N, V_T, P, S)$, where

$$V_N = \{S, A_1, A_2, B_1, B_2, B_3, C\}, \qquad V_T = \{a, b, c\}$$

$$P: \quad S \to aA_1 C \qquad\qquad B_3 \to bB_2$$
$$A_1 \to b \qquad\qquad\quad B_2 \to bB_1$$
$$A_1 \to aB_2 C \qquad\quad B_1 \to b$$
$$A_1 \to aA_2 C \qquad\quad C \to c$$
$$A_2 \to aB_3 C$$

3. A programmed grammar†: $G_3 = (V_N, V_T, J, P, S)$ where $V_N = \{S, B, C\}$ is the nonterminal vocabulary, $V_T = \{a, b, c\}$ the terminal vocabulary, and $J = \{1, 2, 3, 4, 5\}$ the production labels.

P: Production label	Production core	Success branch	Failure branch
1	$S \to aB$	2,3	$\in$
2	$B \to aBB$	2,3	$\in$
3	$B \to C$	4	5
4	$C \to bC$	3	$\in$
5	$C \to c$	5	$\in$

† The programmed grammar operates as follows: Production 1 is applied first; in general, if one tries to apply production k to rewrite a nonterminal N and the current string contains at least one N, then the leftmost N is rewritten by k and the next production is selected from the "success branch" field; if the current string does not contain N, then k is not used and the next production is selected from the "failure branch" field (of k); if the applicable branch field contains $\in$, the derivation halts.

DISCUSSION. Even for this simple case, the context-free grammar is considerably more compact than the finite-state grammar. For this example, a context-sensitive grammar would not be much different from the context-free grammar and hence has not been given. However, the programmed grammar is still more compact than the context-free grammar.

VII. Summary and Further Remarks

Syntactic pattern analysis and recognition have been found to offer an approach to dealing with pattern data which cannot be conveniently described numerically or are otherwise so complex as to defy analysis by conventional techniques. It has often been observed that such data are highly structured and that the structural descriptions contain the essential information for recognition while being perhaps orders of magnitude more convenient to process than the raw patterns. Research in syntactic pattern recognition appears to have demonstrated the feasibility of this approach, at least for some nontrivial applications. However, some formidable hurdles remain to be cleared before syntactic pattern recognition can be widely applied. Some problems and areas of promise include:

1. A systematic approach to the determination of appropriate syntactic elements. Researchers presently depend largely on intuition to select reasonable sets of pattern primitives and higher-order syntactic elements (a situation analogous to that which has existed with respect to feature extraction in conventional pattern recognition techniques). The selection of syntactic elements affects the form of the pattern grammar and hence both the efficiency and the computational complexity of the analyzer, not to mention the pattern recognition accuracy. Certainly some sort of interaction between the primitive selection procedure and the evaluation of recognition performance is needed, both to optimize the performance and to minimize the analyzer complexity.

2. Grammar synthesis based on samples of pattern data (grammatical inference). Here again intuition is relied on heavily at present. A pattern grammar must be hypothesized and then iteratively tested by simulation and improved by the designer. User-interactive computer graphics aid considerably in this respect, but it is not difficult to imagine pattern recognition problems for which computer graphics could not be conveniently employed. Grammatical inference techniques are needed by which analyzers could learn grammars from sets of training patterns.

3. Generalization of concatenation to multiple dimensions and more complex syntactic relationships. A better generalization seems almost essential if efforts in formal linguistics and automata theory are to be brought to bear on the problems of syntactic pattern recognition. Shaw's PDL and the web grammars due to Pfaltz and Rosenfeld appear promising in this respect.

4. Development of special pattern languages and grammars which lend themselves to efficient parsing. Presently attainable processing speeds need to be improved by as much as several orders of magnitude.

5. Detailed formulation of a stochastic syntactic pattern analysis model capable of processing patterns with distortion and noise. Given future development of training methods for determining the necessary stochastic grammars (including vocabularies, productions, and production probabilities), one can imagine a syntax-controlled pattern recognition scheme such as the following. A stochastic grammar is found for each individual pattern class; for each pattern to be classified, a parse and its associated probability are obtained

(whenever possible) according to each class grammar; based on the parse probabilities (and any *a priori* information available), the classification is then made according to a criterion such as minimum risk (Bayes). Such a scheme has the advantage of applying syntactic analysis directly to the raw data rather than going through an initial "noise cleaning" stage which makes little or no use of the wealth of prior information stored in the pattern grammar.

6. Further contributions of automata theory to the syntactic analysis problem. Work is continuing on characterization of the classes of languages recognizable by various types of automata [see especially Jones (1968)]. As mentioned in Section VI, stochastic finite-state automata can be synthesized based on stochastic finite-state grammars and can recognize the languages generated by such grammars. It has recently been shown that stochastic automata can recognize some languages that are context-free but not finite-state (Salomaa, 1968); it has been conjectured that stochastic automata also may recognize nonfinite-state languages which are not context free (Fu and Li, 1969). There is room for speculation that stochastic automata theory may eventually provide both a theoretical foundation for stochastic syntactic analysis and an alternative approach to the realization of analytical mechanisms based on stochastic grammars.

The range of important problems to which syntactic pattern analysis could be applied and which otherwise appears to be beyond the scope of presently known techniques will continue to stimulate research in this new direction.

ACKNOWLEDGMENTS

This work was supported by NSF Grant GK-1970, AFOSR 69-1776, USDA Contract No. 12-14-100-9549(50), and NASA Contract No. NGR 15-005-112.

REFERENCES

Aho, A. V. (1968). "Indexed Grammars—An Extension of Context-Free Grammars." *J. Assoc. Comput. Mach.* **15**, 647–671.

Aho, A. V. and Ullman, J. D. (1968). "The Theory Languages." *Math. Systems Theory* **2**, 97–125.

Anderson, R. H. (1968). "Syntax-Directed Recognition of Hand-Printed Two-Dimensional Mathematics." Ph.D. Dissertation, Harvard Univ., Cambridge, Massachusetts.

Banerji, R. B. (1963). "Phrase Structure Languages, Finite Machines, and Channel Capacity." *Information and Control* **6**, 153–162.

Banjeri, R. B. (1966). "Some Studies in Syntax-Directed Parsing." *In* "Computation in Linguistics: A Case Book." (P. L. Garvin and B. Spolsky, eds.), Chapter 4. Indiana Univ. Press, Bloomington, Indiana.

Banjeri, R. B. (1968). "A Language for Pattern Recognition." *Pattern Recognition* **1**, 63–74.

Booth, T. L. (1967). "Sequential Machines and Automata Theory." Wiley, New York.

Booth, T. L. (1968). "Discrimination between Discrete Random Processes Using Sequential Testing Techniques." *Proc. Ann. Conf. Information Sci. and Systems, 2nd, Princeton, 1968,* pp. 214–218.

Booth, T. L. (1969). "Probabilistic Representation of Formal Languages." *IEEE Conf. Record, 9th Ann. Symp. Switching and Automata Theory, Univ. of Waterloo, Ontario, Canada, 1969.*

Chartres, B. A., and Florentin, J. J. (1968). "A Universal Syntax-Directed Top-Down Analyzer." *J. Assoc. Comp. Mach.* **15,** 447–464.

Chomsky, N. (1956). "Three Models for the Description of Languages." *IRE Trans. Information Theory,* **2,** 113–124.

Crespi-Reghizzi, S., and Presser, L. (1969). "Extensions to Precedence Techniques for Syntactic Analysis." *Proc. Purdue Centennial Year Symp. on Information Processing, Purdue Univ., 1969.* Purdue Univ., Lafayette, Indiana.

Eden, M. (1961). "On the Formalization of Handwriting." *Proc. Symp. Appl. Math.* **12,** 83–88. Am. Math. Soc., Providence, Rhode Island.

Eden, M. (1963). "Handwriting and Pattern Recognition." *IRE Trans. Information Theory* **8,** 160–166.

Evans, T. G. (1967). "A Formalism for the Description of Complex Objects and Its Implementation." *Proc. Internat. Congr. Cybernetics, 5th Namur, Belgium, 1967.*

Evans, T. G. (1968). "A Grammar Controlled Pattern Analyzer," *In* "Information Processing 68." North-Holland Publ., Amsterdam.

Evans, T. G. (1969a). "Descriptive Pattern Analysis Techniques: Potentialities and Problems." in *"Methodologies of Pattern Recognition"* (S. Watanabe, ed.). Academic Press, New York, 1969.

Evans, T. G. (1969b). "Grammatical Inference Techniques in Pattern Analysis." *Internat. Symp. Comput. Information Sci., 3rd, Bal Harbour, Florida, 1969.* Academic Press, New York. See also his chapter in this book.

Feder, J. (1967). "Languages, Automata, and Classes of Chain-Encoded Patterns." Tech. Rep. 400–165. N.Y.U. Lab. for Electroscience Res.

Fischler, M. A. (1969). "Machine Perception and Description of Pictorial Data." *Proc. Joint Internat. Conf. Artificial Intelligence, Washington, D.C., 1969.*

Floyd, R. W. (1964a). "Bounded Context Syntactic Analysis." *Comm. ACM* **7,** 62–67.

Floyd, R. W. (1964b). "The Syntax of Programming Languages—A Survey." *IEEE Trans. Electronic Computers* **13,** 346–353.

Friedman, J. (1969). "Directed Random Generation of Sentences." *Comm. ACM* **12,** 40–46.

Freeman, H. (1961). "On the Encoding of Arbitrary Geometric Configurations." *IRE Trans. Electronic Computers* **EC10,** 260–268.

Fu, K. S., and Li, T. J. (1969). "On Stochastic Automata and Languages." *Information Sci.* **1,** 237–256.

Gilbert, P. (1966). "On the Syntax of Algorithmic Languages." *J. Assoc. Comput. Mach.* **13,** 90–107.

Gold, E. M. (1967). "Language Identification in the Limit." *Information and Control* **10,** 447–474.

Grenander, U. (1967a). "Foundations of Pattern Analysis." Preliminary Version, Tech. Rep. No. 2 (Project Graphics). Div. of Appl. Math., Brown Univ., Providence, Rhode Island.

Grenander, U. (1967b). "Syntax-Controlled Probabilities." Div. of Appl. Math., Brown Univ., Providence, Rhode Island.

Griffiths, T. V., and Petrick, S. R. (1965). "On the Relative Efficiencies of Context-Free Grammar Recognizers." *Comm. ACM* **8,** 289–300.

Grimsdale, R. L., Summer, F. H., Tunis, C. J., and Kilburn, T. (1959). "A System for the Automatic Recognition of Patterns." *Proc. IEE (London) Pt. B* **106**, 210–221.

Guzmán, A. (1967). "Some Aspects of Pattern Recognition by Computer." Project MAC Rep. No. MAC-TR-37. M.I.T., Cambridge, Massachusetts.

Guzmán, A. (1968). "Decomposition of a Visual Scene into Three-Dimensional Bodies." *Proc. Fall Joint Comput. Conf., 1968*, Thompson, Washington, D.C.

Harris, T. E. (1963). "The Theory of Branching Processes." Springer, Berlin.

Harrison, M. A. (1965). "Introduction to Switching and Automata Theory." McGraw-Hill, New York.

Hopcroft, J. E., and Ullman, J. D. (1969). "Formal Languages and Their Relation to Automata." Addison-Wesley, Reading, Massachusetts.

Irons, E. T. (1963). "An Error-Correcting Parse Algorithm." *Comm. ACM* **6**, 669–673.

Jones, N. D. (1968). "Classes of Automata and Transitive Closure." *Information and Control* **13**, 207–229.

Kherts, M. M. (1968). "Entropy of Languages Generated by Automated or Context-Free Grammars with a Single-Valued Deduction." *Nauch. Tekh. Inform. Ser. 2*, pp. 29–34.

Kirsch, R. A. (1964). "Computer Interpretation of English Text and Picture Patterns." *IEEE Trans. Electronic Computers* **EC13**, 363–376.

Knoke, P. J., and Wiley, R. G. (1967). "A Linguistic Approach to Mechanical Pattern Recognition." Appl. Res. Lab., Curry, McLaughlin and Len, Inc., Syracuse, New York; also *Proc. IEEE Comput. Conf. 1st Chicago, 1967*, pp. 142–144.

Ledley, R. S., Rotolo, L. S., Golab, T. J., Jacobsen, J. D., Ginsburg, M. D., and Wilson, J. B. (1965). "FIDAC: Film Input to Digital Automatic Computer and Associated Syntax-Directed Pattern Recognition Programming System." *In* "Optical and Electro-Optical Information Processing Systems." (J. Tippet, D. Beckowitz, L. Clapp, C. Koester, and A. Vanderburgh, Jr., eds.), Chapter 33. M.I.T. Press, Cambridge, Massachusetts.

McCormick, B. H. (1963). "The Illinois Pattern Recognition Computer (Illiac III)." Digital Comput. Lab. Rep. No. 148. Univ. of Illinois, Urbana, Illinois.

McLaren, R. W. (1968). "A Technique for Generating the Structure of an Automaton to Satisfy a Given Input/Output Relationship." *Proc. Ann. Conf. Information Sci. and Systems, 2nd, Princeton, 1968*, pp. 209–213.

McMurty, G. J., and Fu, K. S. (1964). "On Learning Behavior of Finite-State Systems in Random Environments." *Proc. 2nd Ann. Allerton Conf. on Circuits and System Theory, Univ. of Illinois, 1964*.

Mattews, G. H. (1963). "Discontinuity and Asymmetry in Phrase Structure Grammars." *Information and Control* **6**, 137–146.

Miller, W. F., and Shaw, A. C. (1968). "Linguistic Methods in Picture Processing—A Survey." *Proc. Fall Joint Comput. Conf., 1968*.

Narasimhan, R. (1964). "Labeling Schemata and Syntactic Descriptions of Pictures." *Information and Control* **7**, 151–179.

Narasimhan, R. (1966). "Syntax-Directed Interpretation of Classes of Pictures." *Comm. ACM* **9**, 166–173.

Narasimhan, R., and Mayoh, B. H. (1963). "The Structure of a Program for Scanning Bubble Chamber Negatives." Digital Computer Lab. File No. 507. Univ. of Illinois, Urbana, Illinois.

Nasu, M., and Honda, N. (1968). "Fuzzy Events Realized by Finite Probabilistic Automata." *Information and Control* **12**, 284–303.

Pavlidis, T. (1968). "Analysis of Set Patterns," Tech. Rep. No. 25. Dept. of EE, Information Science and Systems Lab., Princeton Univ., Princeton, New Jersey. See also *Pattern Recognition* **1**, 165–178.

Pavlidis, T. (1969). "Linguistic Analysis of Waveforms." *Internat. Symp. Computer and Information Sci., 3rd, Bal Harbour, Florida, 1969*. Academic Press, New York. See also his chapter in this book.

Paz, A. (1966). "Some Aspects of Probabilistic Automata." *Information and Control* **9**, 26–60.

Rabin, M. O. (1963). "Probabilistic Automata." *Information and Control* **6**, 230–245.

Rosenfeld, A. (1969). "Picture Processing by Computer." *Computing Surveys* **1**, 147–175.

Rosenfeld, A., and Pfaltz, J. L. (1966). "Sequential Operations in Digital Picture Processing." *J. Assoc. Comput. Mach.* **13**, 471–494.

Rosenfeld, A., and Pfaltz, J. L. (1969). "Web Grammars." *Proc. Joint Internat. Conf. Artificial Intelligence, Washington, D.C. 1969*.

Rosenfeld, A., and Strong, J. P. (1969). "A Grammar for Maps." *Internat. Symp. Computer and Information Sci., 3rd, Bal Harbour, Florida, 1969*. Academic Press, New York. See also his chapter in this book.

Rosenfeld, A., Huang, H. K., and Schneider, V. B. (1969). "An Application of Cluster Detection to Text and Picture Processing." *IEEE Trans. Information Theory* **15**, 672–681.

Rosenkrantz, D. J. (1967). "Programmed Grammars—A New Device for Generating Formal Languages." Ph.D. Dissertation, Columbia Univ., New York. Also *IEEE Conf. Record Ann. Symp. Switching and Automata Theory, 8th Austin, Texas, 1967* (summary of thesis).

Salomaa, A. (1968). "On Languages Accepted by Probabilistic and Time-Variant Automata." *Proc. Ann. Conf. Information Sci. and Systems, 2nd, Princeton, March 1968*. Princeton Univ., Princeton, New Jersey.

Sauvain, R. W., and Uhr, L. (1969). "A Teachable Pattern Describing and Recognizing Program." *Pattern Recognition* **1**, 219–232.

Shank, R. C., and Tesler, L. G. (1969). "A Conceptual Parser for Natural Languages." *Proc. Joint Internat. Conf. on Artificial Intelligence, Washington, D.C., 1969*.

Shaw, A. C. (1968). "The Formal Description and Parsing of Pictures." SLAC. Rep. No. 84. Stanford Linear Accelerator Center, Stanford Univ., Stanford, California.

Shaw, A. (1969). "A Formal Picture Description Scheme as a Basis for Picture Processing Systems." *Information and Control* **14**, 9–52.

Sherman, R., and Ernst, G. W. (1969). "Learning Patterns in Terms of Other Patterns." *Pattern Recognition* **1**, 301–313.

Swain, P. H. (1970). "On Nonparametric and Linguistic Approaches to Pattern Recognition." Ph.D. Dissertation, Purdue Univ., Lafayette, Indiana, June, 1970.

Tou, J. T. (1969) "On Feature Encoding in Picture Processing by Computer." *Proc. Ann. Allerton Conf. on Circuits and System Theory, 7th, Univ. of Illinois, 1969*.

Wirth, N., and Weber, H. (1966). "Euler: A Generalization of Algol, and Its Formal Definition." *Comm. ACM* **9**, 13–25.

Zahn, C. T. (1969). "A Formal Description for Two-Dimensional Patterns." *Proc. Joint Internat. Conf. Artificial Intelligence, Washington, D.C., 1969*.

Grammatical Inference Techniques in Pattern Analysis

*Thomas G. Evans**

AIR FORCE CAMBRIDGE RESEARCH LABORATORIES
BEDFORD, MASSACHUSETTS

I. Introduction

The principal object of this chapter is to describe some recent studies of methods for the automatic inference of pattern grammars. However, to explain what we mean by this and to motivate these developments and place them in context, we shall start further back and attempt a brief exposition of a broader subject. In the past few years, there has been increased research interest in "description-based" approaches to pattern recognition problems; that is, in the development of formalisms for representing the structure of patterns and of techniques for treating problems of pattern recognition, analysis, and manipulation by means of the generation and processing of pattern descriptions expressed in such formalisms. Various arguments for such an approach, especially as contrasted with some of the more "orthodox" approaches to pattern recognition, have been put forward by a number of authors [for example, see Minsky (1961), Kirsch (1964), Narasimhan (1964)]. For brevity, we refer the reader to those sources and to others listed at the end of this chapter, as well as to the survey by Fu and Swain in this volume, for exposition of the reasoning underlying the choice of a description-based approach.

Motivated by some of the reasoning just alluded to, a number of investigators, faced with pattern analysis problems in which the structural aspects appeared important, devised their own representations for the relevant structures and developed programs capable of doing the analysis in question by working with such representations of patterns. Early programs taking a descriptive approach to character recognition include those of Grimsdale *et al.* (1959), Sherman (1959), and Marill *et al.* (1963) (the CYCLOPS-1 program described in the last-cited reference was capable of disentangling quite complex cases of overlapping characters on the basis of descriptions of their stroke

* The author is also associated with Project MAC, Massachusetts Institute of Technology.

structures). The work of Eden (1961) on the analysis of handwriting in terms of strokes is well known. The work of Roberts (1963) on a program capable of developing plausible computer representations of three-dimensional scenes (composed of relatively simple objects) from a photograph is of great interest and has influenced much of the work on "scene analysis" that is central to the vision aspects of the "robot projects" under way at, most prominently, M.I.T., Stanford, and Stanford Research Institute [see especially Guzman (1968) in this regard]. The work on figure-analogy problems reported by Evans (1964) furnishes a particularly clear (since highly stylized) example of a class of problems in which manipulation of pattern descriptions seems to be an essential part of any effort to construct procedures to solve the problems in question. The preceding citations are by no means an attempt at completeness but rather point to a few examples to indicate the flavor of the approach we have in mind.

A significant point about these instances is that in each case the work of developing appropriate descriptions and the machinery to process them began more or less from scratch. Eventually, the notion arose that perhaps it was possible to design (1) a descriptive formalism and (2) machinery for processing a pattern according to a specification expressed in that formalism that would be sufficiently general to permit convenient specialization to any of a wide variety of pattern analysis tasks (while still retaining sufficient processing efficiency to make the use of this more general framework feasible). The notion of picture grammar had been discussed in the early 1960s by, among others, Kirsch and Narasimhan, but it is only in the past several years that most of the work that has been done in this area has appeared in the literature. Since a relatively detailed description of the formalism employed in one such system will appear in Section III as a necessary prerequisite to the principal business of this chapter and since comprehensive surveys exist (Fu and Swain, this volume; Miller and Shaw, 1968), no attempt will be made here to discuss the work in this research area, which has been variously called "linguistic-approach," "syntax-directed," or "grammatical" pattern recognition.

It is perhaps of interest that among those pursuing this approach are some investigators whose principal interest is human pattern perception and who see in this work potentially useful formalisms for modeling human perceptual processing of complex patterns.

II. Learning

A major theme in pattern recognition research since its beginning has been the study of "learning," in the sense that a device capable of improving its pattern classification performance by making internal adjustments on the basis of exposure to a set of labeled examples can be said to learn. In work with the traditional classification model, these internal adjustments have usually taken the form of modifications in the weighting assigned to the results of the various property filters by the decision-making mechanism. Other forms of modification have also been considered and some work has been done on limited cases of generation of new and better property filters starting from the initial given set. The reader is referred to the surveys by Nagy (1968) and Rosenfeld (1969) and to Nilsson's book (1965) for detailed discussion and extensive bibliographies pertaining to work on learning in the framework of the classification model.

It is natural to ask if there is some analog of the notion of learning in the classification model that we can pursue in working with picture grammars. Broadly speaking, we would like to have an automatic procedure that, given a set of instances of patterns, is capable of generating a grammar that in some sense fits those instances well. Virtually no work on this problem has been reported; one of the closest approaches in the pattern recognition literatures is that of Sauvain and Uhr (1969), who describe a program that goes as far as it can in analyzing a given pattern in terms of the composition rules and relationships available to it, then interacts with a human "teacher," who can examine its results and tell it to introduce new rules, which it will then use (thus the program in effect "learns" a grammar by being told what to do at key points in the analysis of examples). Another is that of Sherman and Ernst (1969), who discuss the application of an EPAM-like memory organization to the problem of efficiently selecting from a large set of previously learned patterns a few in terms of which a new pattern to be learned can be described.

Since the string grammars of formal linguistics have been studied longer than the more complex "pattern grammars" with which we are concerned, we might expect more help from that source on the problem of inferring grammars from examples. In fact, there does exist a small body of work. Solomonoff (1959), Gold (1967), Feldman (1967, 1969), Feldman et al. (1969), and Horning (1969) have been concerned primarily with theoretical aspects (decidability results, properties of various complexity measures, etc.) of this problem for various classes of grammars, while Miller and Stein (1963, 1966) have studied human performance at tasks of this nature. However, in the development of programs for grammatical inference (to be described later), using a certain fixed class of pattern grammars, we were able to find very little in this body of theory in its present state of development directly relevant to our aims. The most closely related work is that in one portion of Feldman et al. (1969), which is devoted to discussion of programs which carry out a form of grammatical inference for two simple types of string grammars (finite state and pivot), fitting given sets of terminal strings. The grammars we work with in Section IV are more complex and present additional problems;

however, the flavor of the methods discussed by Feldman *et al.* (1969) is much the same as those we shall discuss. Horning (1969) develops an elaborate "enumerative Bayesian" procedure for inferring context-free string grammars based on an assumed probability structure expressed in terms of stochastic grammars.

There is considerable reason to expect that further development of the theory of grammatical complexity along the lines indicated in the work of Feldman and his associates will produce results applicable to constructing grammatical inference systems on a sounder basis than is presently possible.

There is another body of work that should be mentioned at this point, if only to clarify some differences. This is the area of "concept formation," where one is also concerned with the problem of learning a "concept" from a set of instances. However, in this work, "concept" has meant some Boolean function of a set of properties of the instances. Human performance on such tasks has been studied intensively, especially by Bruner *et al.* (1956), and computer programs implementing various strategies for attacking a number of variants of "concept formation" tasks have been developed and studied by, among others, Hunt and Hovland (1961), Kochen (1961), and Hunt *et al.* (1966). The last-cited is a thorough investigation and comparison of various strategies. The principal difference between the "concept formation" approach and that with which we are concerned is that the former is essentially "one-level"—given a set of instances of objects and a list of properties with the values of these properties for each of the instances, it tries to characterize the set of instances in terms of these values. In our case, we are concerned with the "internal structure" of the instances we are given and attempt to characterize that structure by building it up in as many levels as needed in terms of given lowest level "building blocks" and given relational predicates.

We conclude these remarks by noting that the argument has been made that what we have been calling [after Feldman (1967)] "grammatical inference" is an attractive paradigm for the process of inductive inference in general. For example, this point of view has been well stated by Minsky (1961).

III. Pattern Description Formalism

To describe our experiments in automatic generation of pattern grammars, we must first explain in some detail the underlying grammatical formalism. It is one we have described earlier (Evans, 1968) and works as follows: we assume there is available to us a certain set of terminal (lowest-level) object types—in the analysis of a pattern according to a grammar in our formalism, the input pattern (after preprocessing) would consist of a list of constituents, each of which is identified as belonging to exactly one of these object types.

We also assume a set of predicates expressing properties of objects and relations among them. As with the set of lowest-level object types, what predicates we use depends on the class of patterns we are interested in and the purpose for which we are processing them. If the subject matter, as it will in our examples below, consists of line drawings, reasonable lowest-level objects might be, say, line segments, arcs, etc., and a useful predicate might be, say, *above*[x;y] (which, when applied to some pair of objects, would have the value "true" if x was indeed "above" y, in whatever exact sense had been assigned to that notion). Finally we have a grammar, which is just a finite set of rules (productions) each of which consists of three parts:

1. The (arbitrary) name of the construct being defined.
2. A list of "dummy variable" names for the parts of which it is composed, so that they can be referenced in (3).
3. A condition (written in terms of the available predicates) that must be satisfied by the constituent parts in order that we have an instance of the pattern object being defined.

This differs in two ways from the formalism described by Evans (1968); First, part 2 of a rule could specify, as well as a list of constituent objects, a list of "context" objects. The condition of part 3 could then be written in terms of both lists of objects. Thus, it became possible to write a "context-dependent" form of rule, a considerable addition to the power of the formalism. Here, we shall ignore this possibility; while it seems perfectly feasible to extend our inference procedures to the "context-dependent" case, we shall simplify our task by restricting the discussion to the "context-free" case. Second, the grammar rules had a fourth part, which specified, when an instance of the construct defined by the rule was successfully recognized, what information, in terms of the information attached to each of the constituents (if a terminal, at input; if a nonterminal, at a previous stage of the pattern analysis process) should be attached to the newly-found object for subsequent use. This feature is an important convenience in the use of the formalism, but can always logically be eliminated, at the cost of additional complexity in the programs that implement the predicates, and it will be dispensed with here.

Two more remarks about the grammar rules are necessary:

1. Any number of alternate rules defining a given object type may be included.
2. Grammar rules may be recursive; that is, an object type may be defined using itself as one of the constituents, either directly or through a chain of rules.

A simple-minded example of a grammar of this type may help clarify some of the foregoing discussion. Suppose we want to describe a stylized line drawing of a face like that in Figure 1a by a grammar in terms of some set of available predicates. Let us assume they are *inside*[*x*;*y*], meaning "object *x* is inside object *y*," *left*[*x*; *y*], meaning "object *x* is on the left of object *y*" (in some reasonable sense), *above*[*x*; *y*], meaning similarly "object *x* is above

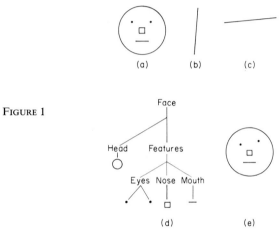

FIGURE 1

object *y*," and *horiz*[*x*], which means "*x* is approximately horizontal," defined for, say, line segments and arcs in terms of their end-point coordinates and with a meaning exemplified by "the line in Figure 1b is not horizontal, while that in Figure 1c is horizontal." Further, suppose the types of lowest-level objects we have available to start with are circles, squares, dots, and line segments. Then, one possible way of describing the face by a set of rules would be

$$\text{face} \rightarrow (x, y): \text{features}(x), \text{head}(y): inside[x, y]$$
$$\text{head} \rightarrow (x): \text{circle } (x)$$
$$\text{features} \rightarrow (x, y, z): \text{eyes}(x), \text{nose}(y), \text{mouth}(z): above[x, y] \wedge$$
$$above[x, z] \wedge above[y, z]$$
$$\text{eyes} \rightarrow (x, y): \text{dot}(x), \text{dot}(y): left[x, y]$$
$$\text{nose} \rightarrow (x): \text{square}(x)$$
$$\text{mouth} \rightarrow (x): \text{lineseg}(x): horiz[x].$$

where the first rule can be read as: a "face" is defined to be an object (pattern) made up of two constituents (call them *x* and *y*) such that *x* is of object type "features" and *y* is of object types "head" and the predicate *inside*[*x*; *y*] is satisfied. Note that we could have written this grammar in any number of ways. Note also that this grammar is extremely simple in that it has no recursion and only defines one structure, namely one that we can diagram as in Figure 1d.

If we gave an input pattern containing, among other things, one or more sets of terminal objects satisfying the above rules to the analysis program described by Evans (1968), after having made available to it the grammar exhibited above, we would get back the equivalent of such a tree for each instance of a "face" that it found. Note that, depending on the meanings we gave to our relational predicates, a wide variety of possible instances might or might not be accepted. For example, Figure 1e might or might not qualify, depending on how permissive our definition of *left* is. We remark finally that the input pattern is given as a list of lowest-level constituents, where each has attached to it its object type and any other information that may be desired. This is the information that will be retrieved and used in evaluating the predicates. For example, "center-of-mass" coordinates and an approximate size (say, a radius about the object's center of mass and just containing the entire object) might be supplied for each object. Reasonable computations for *above* and *left*, say, could be defined using this information.

So far, to use this formalism we must first write a grammar specifying the structures we are interested in. Now we go on to discuss the task of automatic generation of grammars in this formalism to fit sets of examples.

IV. Grammatical Inference

We are now in a position to specify a somewhat more precise formulation of the inference task alluded to in Section II.

Suppose we have a fixed set of predicates and also a fixed list of terminal object types available to us. Now, suppose we are given a set of input patterns (we will call them "scenes") $\{S_1, \ldots, S_n\}$. Each consists of a list of the terminal objects in that scene, together with perhaps for each some information attached to it (for example, for a line segment it might include end-point coordinates)—this information is not directly visible to the inference procedure, but enters indirectly through its effect on the values of the predicates.

Our task is to produce a "good" set of grammar rules written in terms of the available predicates that "fits" the given set of scenes. Leaving aside the qualification "good," what this means (at least if we are to produce a grammar to assign a structure to the whole scene) is relatively clear; we must produce a grammar such that, if each of the scenes were fed as input to the analyzer and analyzed according to that grammar, one or more structural descriptions of that scene would be returned as output. This is a grammar which "fits" the set of scenes, which is not at all the same as a "good fit." For example, suppose one had separately inferred a grammar to fit each scene, i.e., a G_i for scene S_i.

Then $\bigcup_i G_i$ is a grammar which "fits" all the S_i in the above sense (and may be, in certain cases, about as well as one can do, when the scenes do not have any appreciable amount of common structure). However, we are interested in the case where the scenes have a lot in common and we will be satisfied only with grammars that are "reasonable" from this point of view. While we do not yet have any theoretically satisfactory measure of how well a grammar of the class we are considering fits a set of examples—this question, for much simpler classes of (string) grammars, is treated to some extent in the work of Feldman's group—the inference procedure to be described is constructed with the goal of finding common structure among the scenes wherever possible and seems to us to produce results, at least on the fairly simple cases where it has been tried to date, which are intuitively rather satisfactory—in some cases as well as it seems possible to do.

After these preliminaries, we can discuss a basic version of the procedure. (It should be understood that this work on inference procedures has included numerous experiments with alternate versions of virtually every portion of the programs which carry out the inference task. Because of space limitations and because further experimentation is still in progress, it is impossible to give a complete account of the results here. Rather, what follows is a brief description of just one version—a relatively simple one—among many, together with some examples of its performance on some simple scenes.) The first step in the process is carried out independently for each of the input scenes to find all the structure that is imposed by the predicates. Namely, for a given scene, each predicate is applied in turn to each n-tuple of objects from the input list (where n is the appropriate number of arguments for that predicate—and predicate symmetry information is used to shorten the task, where applicable). Each time one or more predicates turn out true, a new "object" is created, and the information about its constituents and the satisfaction of the predicate is recorded (in the form of a grammar rule, with a new unique name generated from the syntactic type). Then, a new pass is made applying the predicates to the n-tuples made up from these newly-created objects and the input objects, and so on until nothing new can be built up (of course, on each pass only the n-tuples involving at least one object created on the previous pass need to be looked at) and only one object is recorded if two potential objects differ only by argument order in a symmetrical predicate, etc. Also, each time a new "object" is to be recorded, it is checked to verify that no subobject occurs twice in its composition; if so, it is rejected.

Once all the object-building passes are complete, there is a check to determine which of the objects found have *all* the terminal objects of the scene as their constituents. All objects which are not either in this set or among the constituents of a member of this set are discarded. (That is, all the generated grammar rules not used in the generation of these objects are dropped.) So, in effect, we are left with the equivalent of one or more structural-description-like trees (or perhaps none, in which case the present procedure admits failure—although there are some reasonable alternatives as to how one could proceed in this case). Some further cleanup is then done on those trees. For example, all reference to specific terminal objects is replaced by reference to object types only; if this renders two or more trees equal, deletion is made of the redundant one(s).

So far, what we have for each scene is a set of one or more grammars, each corresponding to a different structural description assignable to the scene. The only nonterminal object type occurring in more than one of these grammars is the one corresponding to the top level—the entire scene (call it S). Now, we proceed as follows. We choose a grammar for scene 1, then one for scene 2, and so on, and form their union. In the experiment being described we do it in all possible ways. Thus, if there were three scenes and scene 1 had 2 structural descriptions (grammars), scene 2 had 3, and scene 3 had 1, we would be generating $2 \times 3 \times 1 = 6$ grammars.

To each of these grammars we independently apply the grammar rewriting procedure to be described next, resulting in (for each) a modified grammar. Then we choose the "best" of these by some criterion. Essentially, we prefer a "short" grammar, since this suggests we really have a common grammar for the examples, not just a collection of special cases. However, we would like the rules of this grammar to be as specific as possible about object types and relations. A grammar consisting of rules that have been weakened in the rewriting by having all the detail removed suggests that two structural descriptions without really much in common were involved; therefore, it seems plausible that some criterion combining these two heuristics should be used to make a final choice or ranking of the alternative proposed grammars.

The rewriting procedure is as follows:

1. If there are multiple occurrences of any rule in G, eliminate the redundant one(s). (G is the grammar being rewritten.)

2. Look for a pair of nonterminals such that identifying them (that is, uniform substitution of one for the other throughout the grammar) would result in some multiple rule occurrence(s). If there are alternate possibilities, choose the one that causes the largest number of multiple rule occurrences. Make the substititution and go to (1).

3. Look for a pair (N, n, say) consisting of one nonterminal N and a terminal n such that addition of the rule $N \rightarrow n$ (if not already in) and some selective substitution of N for n in G results in a net reduction in the number of grammar rules after elimination of multiple occurrences of rules. If there are alternatives, take the one that results in the greatest reduction in the number of rules. Go to (1).

4. [So far we have talked about transformations on a grammar that identify nonterminal object types or substitute a nonterminal for a terminal. Now we introduce transformations that work on object types and relations. The idea is that we want to be cautious about throwing detail out of a set of rules so that they collapse into one; if we do this too freely, we can wind up with grammars that "fit" practically everything; that is, have little discriminatory power— compare the situation in matching figure transformation rules in Evans (1964). The simple compromise adopted here is to set a threshold.] Suppose the value of the threshold is N (it has been $N = 3$ in most of our experiments). This means that if there are n rules, all of which would collapse into one either directly or by an identification as in 2 or 3 if we disregarded any relational information contained in them, then if $n \geq N$, we do the rewrite and go to (1). A slightly more sophisticated alternative is to weight the alternatives according to the amount of relational information that must be discarded to cause the collapse.

5. Similarly, we have a threshold for object types. If we have n rules that would be identical except for differences in object types of the terminal components and n is greater than or equal to the threshold value, we rewrite the n rules as one, using the special pseudo-object type ANY, which means "any terminal type" (it should be noted that the analyzer described by Evans (1968) will not accept such a grammar without some modification) and go to (1). When no more rewrites are possible, the process stops.

(Note that this procedure produces only one output grammar. We could, of course have chosen to branch under certain conditions and carry out alternate reductions, resulting in a number of new grammars as output.)

After this process has been executed on each of the candidate grammars, resulting in a new set of grammars, we must choose the "best" of them. (We are guaranteed by the restrictions we put on rewriting the grammars, each of which originally "fit" all the scenes, since it was a union of grammars of which the ith "fit" the ith scene, that the resulting grammars will also "fit" each scene.) Representative of the criteria tried is the following, based on the two criteria mentioned earlier, length of the grammar and "strength" of the rules. We define the strength of a rule to be the sum of the number of its components that are terminals (other than ANY, which does not count) and the number of property or relation terms in the "rule part 3" condition. For example, a rule like face $\rightarrow (x, y)$: features(x), circle(y): *inside*$[x, y]$ would have strength 2 (if circle is a terminal). The strength S_G of a grammar G is defined to be simply the sum of the strengths of its rules. Finally, the figure of merit we use is $S_G/(N_G)^2$, where N_G is the number of rules in the grammar. (Thus, we penalize number of rules heavily). This is an extremely simple-minded measure, but even it seems to do the job fairly well on a number of examples.

Now that we have described a version of the inference process in some detail, it is time to give some examples to indicate the sort of things it can do and perhaps clarify further what happens during the process of discovering a grammar to fit some given instances.

Example 1. Here, we shall consider a case where only one scene is presented. The purpose is to show in some detail how the first phase, the buildup of the allowed structural descriptions, takes place. In the later examples, we shall say less about this portion and concentrate on the grammar reduction process.

The input pattern is the scene shown as Figure 2a.

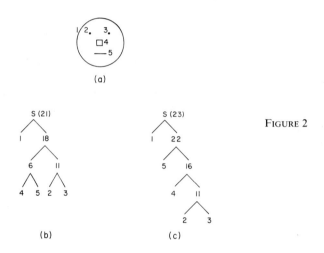

FIGURE 2

The terminal object types that occur are circle, dot, square, and line segment. Suppose the available predicates are

$left[x:y]$ (true if x is to the left of y);
$above[x;y]$ (true if x is above y);
$inside[x;y]$ (true if x is inside y).

As a more concrete indication of how such predicates might be implemented, suppose each input object has associated with it a center (as a pair of coordinates) and a size (as, say, a pair of numbers, the dimensions of a rectangle about the center that would just contain the object). Then, $left[x;y]$, say, might just be a test that the size rectangles of x and y do not overlap and that the angle between the line from the center of x to the center of y and the horizontal axis is less than, say, $10°$, in absolute value. This defines $left$ on terminal object types. If we make some reasonable definition of center and size for composite (that is, nonterminal) objects in terms of their constituents, *left* will thereby be extended to them as well.

The process begins by finding all instances of a set of objects in the input [in our case, the input is a list of five objects of object types dot (two), circle, square, and line segment] that satisfy one or more predicates from the available list and are interrelated in the sense that a chain of satisfied predicates leads from any object in the set to any other. For example, objects O_1, O_2, O_3, O_4 such that $P_1(O_1, O_2)$ and $P_2(O_3, O_4)$ were the only predicates satisfied would not qualify, while an additional $P_3(O_2, O_3)$ would make it qualify. Then, as explained earlier, we call each such instance a new object and see what we can build out of them and the originals, then use those to build more, etc., till no more can be generated. Then, we throw away all those objects that are not components of some object that contains every terminal object of the scene. In our example, this looks as follows. (The input objects are numbered from 1 to 5, as shown in Figure 2a. As we find new objects, we will number them from 6 on up.) First, for example, we find *above*[4;5] is true and therefore generate an object #6 consisting of 4 and 5. The full list of what can be produced from the input objects (assuming, of course, a particular implementation of the predicates) is

    6: (4, 5): *above*[4; 5]
    7: (1, 2): *inside*[2; 1]
    8: (1, 3): *inside*[3; 1]
    9: (1, 4): *inside*[4; 1]
   10: (1, 5): *inside*[5; 1]
   11: (2, 3): *left*[2; 3]
   12: (1, 2, 3): *left*[2; 3] ∧ *inside*[2; 1] ∧ *inside*[3; 1]
   13: (1, 4, 5): *above*[4; 5] ∧ *inside*[4; 1] ∧ *inside*[5; 1].

In the next stage:

   14: (1, 6): *inside*[6; 1]
   15: (1, 11): *inside*[11; 1]
   16: (4, 11): *above*[11; 4]
   17: (5, 11): *above*[11; 5]
   18: (6, 11): *above*[11; 6].

Next,

   19: (1, 16): *inside*[1; 16]
   20: (1, 17): *inside*[1; 17]
  *21: (1, 18): *inside*[1; 18]
   22: (5, 16): *above*[16; 5]
  *23: (1, 22): *inside*[22; 1].

The two objects indicated by the asterisk correspond to the two structural descriptions that we were able to construct for the scene. Represented as trees they are shown as Figures 2b,c (S is the entire scene). Finally, we translate each structural description we have made into a grammar, completely straightforwardly (we use $G1$, $G2$, $G3$, ... as needed as the names of the nonterminal object types above and replace each terminal by its object type).

Thus, the two grammars look like:

$S \;\rightarrow (x, y)$: $G1(x)$, circle(y): *inside*$[x; y]$
$G1 \rightarrow (x, y)$: $G2(x)$, lineseg(y): *above*$[x; y]$
$G2 \rightarrow (x, y)$: $G3(x)$, square(y): *above*$[x; y]$
$G3 \rightarrow (x, y)$: dot(x), dot(y): *left*$[x; y]$

and

$S \;\rightarrow (x, y)$: $G4(x)$, circle(y): *inside*$[x; y]$
$G4 \rightarrow (x, y)$: $G5(x)$, $G6(y)$: *above*$[x; y]$
$G5 \rightarrow (x, y)$: dot(x), dot(y): *left*$[x; y]$
$G6 \rightarrow (x, y)$: square(x), lineseg(y): *above*$[x; y]$.

A few remarks might be useful at this point. First, note that the procedure exhibited will produce only grammar rules in which each constituent is involved in at least one predicate. This will not necessarily be true in the grammar we end up with after applying our rewriting procedures, since they may, on sufficient provocation, weaken rules by removing predicate information. Another point to note is that the two grammars produced in our example consist entirely of rules with two constituents satisfying one predicate. It should be emphasized that this is an accident of the example, not a general property of the process. Finally, note that we have assumed, reasonably enough, that 2 and 4, say, are not in the relation *above*$[2; 4]$. Similarly, *above*$[3; 4]$ is false. However, once 2 and 3 are built into object 11, *above*$[11; 4]$ ought to be true, as has been assumed above. This is perhaps not in itself an especially convincing example of one of the reasons for the power of hierarchically-structured descriptions; no amount of looking at the input-level objects would reveal that relationship, which is only uncovered in a context of assumptions about higher-level structure.

Example 2. Suppose the available primitive object types are square, triangle, circle, and dot and suppose the only available predicate is *inside*$[x; y]$. Then, presented with the scenes of Figure 3, our first phase will produce the (one-rule) grammars:

$$S \rightarrow (x, y)\text{: triangle}(x), \text{square}(y)\text{: }inside[x, y]$$

for scene (a),

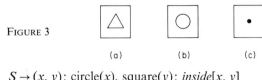

FIGURE 3

(a)   (b)   (c)

$$S \rightarrow (x, y): \text{circle}(x), \text{square}(y): \textit{inside}[x, y]$$

for scene (b), and

$$S \rightarrow (x, y): \text{dot}(x), \text{square}(y); \textit{inside}[x, y]$$

for scene (c).

When we apply our reduction process to the grammar formed as the union of these three, we find no possible reductions until we come to the object type-weakening case. Then, since we have three instances, and we will assume that this is the value of our threshold, we rewrite these three rules as the single one:

$$S \rightarrow (x, y): \text{any}(x), \text{square}(y): \textit{inside} \ [x;y]$$

(where "any" is the special pseudo-object mentioned earlier) and this one-rule grammar is the result.

Example 3. Suppose the only primitive object type is square and the predicates available are *left*[x; y], *above*[x; y], and *inside*[x; y].

Then in Figure 4, scene (a) gives us

$$S \rightarrow (x, y): \text{square}(x), \text{square}(y): \textit{above}[x, y],$$

scene (b) gives

$$S \rightarrow (x, y): \text{square}(x), \text{square}(y): \textit{left}[x, y],$$

and scene (c) gives

$$S \rightarrow (x, y): \text{square}(x), \text{square}(y): \textit{inside}[x, y].$$

The reduction process applied the predicate-weakening rule (we assume our threshold value for this rule is three), resulting in the final one-rule grammar

$$S \rightarrow (x, y): \text{square}(x), \text{square}(y).$$

That is, all our inference process could find in common to the three scenes is that each consists of two squares; this is the generalization it ends up with.

Example 4. Here we have a rather more interesting case. Suppose the only primitive object type is line segment (we will call it seg) and the available predicates are *join*[x; y] and *close*[x; y], which apply to any object x, y made up of a sequence of line segments and test for situations like those shown in Figures 5a and 5b, respectively (that is, "meet at one end" and "meet at both ends"). The two "scenes" we shall consider are the triangle and rectangle shown as Figures 6a and 6b.

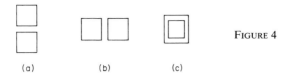

FIGURE 4

(a)   (b)   (c)

The grammar for (a) looks like

1: $S \rightarrow (x, y)$: seg(x), $G1(y)$: *close*[x, y]
2: $G1 \rightarrow (x, y)$: seg(x), $G2(y)$: *join*[x, y]
3: $G2 \rightarrow (x, y)$: seg(x), seg(y): *join*[x, y]

and for (b) it is

4: $S \rightarrow (x, y)$: seg(x), $G3(y)$: *close*[x, y]
5: $G3 \rightarrow (x, y)$: seg(x), seg(y): *join*[x, y].

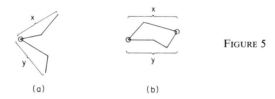

FIGURE 5

(a)   (b)

We take the union of these two and begin the reduction process. The first reduction is the identification of $G3$ and $G1$, eliminating rule 4, so the grammar now looks like

1′: $S \rightarrow (x, y)$: seg(x), $G1(y)$: *close*[x, y]
2′: $G1 \rightarrow (x, y)$: seg(x), $G2(y)$: *join*[x, y]
3′: $G2 \rightarrow (x, y)$: seg(x), seg(y): *join*[x, y]
4′: $G1 \rightarrow (x, y)$: seg(x), seg(y): *join*[x, y].

The next reduction identifies $G2$ and $G1$, eliminating rule 3′ (note the recursion introduced). Now we have

1″: $S \rightarrow (x, y)$: seg(x), $G1(y)$: *close*[x, y]
2″: $G1 \rightarrow (x, y)$: seg(y), $G1(y)$: *join*[x, y]
3″: $G1 \rightarrow (x, y)$: seg(x), seg(y): *join*[x, y]

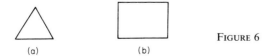

FIGURE 6

(a)   (b)

and no further reduction takes place. The result is a grammar that will recognize any polygon. This is the generalization of the two scenes that the inference process arrives at.

Example 5. In the work by Feldman *et al.* (1969), a procedure for finding finite-state grammars is successfully applied to the seven strings.

$$\{caaab, bbaab, caab, bbab, cab, bbb, cb\}.$$

The final grammar found is of form

$$x \to cz|bz_4$$
$$z_1 \to b|az_1$$
$$z_4 \to bz_1 .$$

The grammatical formalism used here can be specialized to work with strings by introducing a predicate $adj[x; y]$ which is true if the substring x is immediately left-adjacent to the substring y, then defining syntactic types in the usual way in terms of constituents, using the adj predicate. Thus, it is possible to attempt the same task with our procedure (except that we shall be inferring a context-free grammar for the set of strings rather than a strictly finite-state one).

Our first phase produces for each scene a grammar for each alternative possible structural description. To shorten the discussion, we shall look only at a 7-tuple of grammars that will reduce to the final grammar.

They are as follows, taking the strings in the order given above and writing in the usual notation for string grammars—for example, we write $C \to AB$ instead of $C \to (x, y): A(x), B(y): adj [x, y]$. (The terminal object types are a, b, and c and the only predicate is adj.)

(a) $S \ \to cG1$
        $G1 \to aG2$
        $G2 \to aG3$
        $G3 \to ab$
(b) $S \ \to bbG4$
        $G4 \to aG5$
        $G5 \to ab$
(c) $S \ \to cG6$
        $G6 \to aG7$
        $G7 \to ab$
(d) $S \ \to bbG8$
        $G8 \to ab$
(e) $S \ \to cG9$
        $G9 \to ab$
(f) $S \ \to bbb$
(g) $S \ \to cb.$

The first set of reduction steps identifies $G3$, $G5$, $G7$, $G8$, and $G9$. The resulting grammar is

$$S \rightarrow cG1$$
$$G1 \rightarrow aG2$$
$$G2 \rightarrow aG3$$
$$G3 \rightarrow ab$$
$$S \rightarrow bbG4$$
$$G4 \rightarrow aG3$$
$$S \rightarrow cG6$$
$$G6 \rightarrow aG3$$
$$S \rightarrow bbG3$$
$$S \rightarrow cG3$$
$$S \rightarrow bbb$$
$$S \rightarrow cb.$$

The next pair of reductions identifies $G1$, $G3$, and $G6$, resulting in

$$S \rightarrow cG1$$
$$G1 \rightarrow aG2$$
$$G2 \rightarrow aG1$$
$$G1 \rightarrow ab$$
$$S \rightarrow bbG4$$
$$G4 \rightarrow aG1$$
$$G1 \rightarrow aG1$$
$$S \rightarrow bbG1$$
$$S \rightarrow bbb$$
$$S \rightarrow cb.$$

Identifying $G1$, $G2$, and $G4$ results in

$$S \rightarrow cG1$$
$$G1 \rightarrow aG1$$
$$G1 \rightarrow ab$$
$$S \rightarrow bbG1$$
$$S \rightarrow bbb$$
$$S \rightarrow cb.$$

The next reduction introduces $G1 \rightarrow b$ and selectively substitutes $G1$ for b in rules 3, 5, and 6. So we have

$$S \rightarrow cG1$$
$$G1 \rightarrow aG1$$
$$S \rightarrow bbG1$$
$$G1 \rightarrow b,$$

the final result (or in notation more like that of Feldman *et al.* (1969) denoting *S* by *X* and *G*1 by *Y*),

$$X \to c\,Y \mid bb\,Y$$
$$Y \to a\,Y \mid b.$$

V. Some Miscellaneous Remarks

1. Perhaps the most unsatisfactory aspects of the approach described above is that, while it generates grammars to fit the given instances, these grammars must be written in terms of a fixed set of predicates. Just as we have a potentially quite broad class of grammars available from which the procedure we have discussed selects one, we would like to have a rich formalism for expressing predicates in terms of some primitives and combining rules which would permit the generation of appropriate new predicates as part of the inference procedure. This is a quite difficult problem—the most elaborate approach tried so far has been to allow a family of predicates depending on some parameter or parameters, where suitable values for the parameter(s) are to be determined, as in Sauvain and Uhr (1969). Certainly, a sophisticated grammatical inference program should have such facilities for manipulating predicate descriptions and its inference strategy should be able to take advantage of an interaction between grammar-making and predicate-making.

2. We show the program only positive instances, i.e., scenes to be fit by the final grammar, not a mixture of scenes labeled "yes" and "no," meaning that they satisfy and do not satisfy, respectively, the grammar to be found. Negative instances play a large role in the Boolean concept formation studies we have mentioned; furthermore, some of Gold's results on an abstract model of grammatical inference exhibit interesting differences in what can in principle be achieved when negative instances are or are not included.

It is not very clear how best to use negative-instance information in the inference task we have been considering, but the capability of doing so should also be part of a sophisticated grammatical inference machine and experiments with various approaches are part of our ongoing work, though this is not reflected in the simple scheme we have chosen to describe.

3. The approach discussed in Section IV can be summarized as "given some examples of scenes, find a generalization of them by building a grammar that reflects the structure they have in common." Another possible approach is to work directly with the structural descriptions of the individual scenes to arrive at a generalization in the form of a "common structural description" for all the scenes. Winston (1970) takes this approach.

4. As in most of the work to date with the "linguistic" approach, we are dealing here with idealized "noise-free" input and statistical considerations

are ignored, as a simplification permitting us to concentrate on the grammar-constructing procedures in this simpler environment. Certainly, a "real-life" inference system must be able to cope with statistically variable input. The survey by Fu and Swain in this volume emphasizes this area, covering the work to date and discussing some possible directions for future work.

REFERENCES

Bruner, J. S., Goodnow, J. J., and Austin, G. S. (1956). "A Study of Thinking." Wiley, New York.

Eden, M. (1961). "On the Formalization of Handwriting." *In* "Structure of Language and Its Mathematical Aspect." *Proc. Symp. Appl. Math., 12th,* pp. 83–88. Amer. Math. Soc., Rhode Island.

Evans, T. G. (1964). "A Heuristic Program to Solve Geometric-Analogy Problems." *Proc. Spring Joint Comput. Conf.,* pp. 327–338.

Evans, T. G. (1968). "A Grammar-Controlled Pattern Analyzer." *Proc. IFIP 68 Congr.*

Feldman, J. (1967). "First Thoughts on Grammatical Inference." Artificial Intelligence Memo. No. 55. Computer Science Dept., Stanford Univ., Stanford, California.

Feldman, J., Gips, J., Horning, J., and Reder, S. (1969). "Grammatical Complexity and Inference." Artificial Intelligence Memo. No. 89. Computer Science Dept., Stanford Univ., Stanford, California.

Feldman, J. (1969). "Some Decidability Results on Grammatical Inference and Complexity." Artificial Intelligence Memo. No. 93. Computer Science Dept., Stanford Univ., Stanford, California.

Gold, M. (1967). "Language Identification in the Limit." *Information and Control* **10,** 444–474.

Grimsdale, R., Sumner, F., Tunis, C., and Kilburn, T. (1959). "A System for the Automatic Recognition of Patterns." *Proc. Inst. Elec. Eng. Part B* **106,** 129–135.

Guzmán, A. (1968). "Decomposition of a Visual Scene into Bodies." *Proc. Fall Joint Comput. Conf.,* pp. 291–304.

Horning, J. (1969). "A Study of Grammatical Inference." Artificial Intelligence Memo. No. 98. Computer Science Dept., Stanford Univ., Stanford, California.

Hunt, E. B., and Hovland, C. I. (1961). "Programming a Model of Human Concept Formulation." *Proc. Western Joint Comput. Conf.,* pp. 145–155.

Hunt, E. B., Marin, J., and Stone, P. J. (1966). "Experiments in Induction." Academic Press, New York.

Kirsch, R. A. (1964). "Computer Interpretation of English Text and Picture Patterns." *IEEE Trans. Electronic Computers* **EC13,** 363–376.

Kochen, M. (1961). "An Experimental Program for the Selection of 'Disjunctive Hypothese'." *Proc. Western Joint Comput. Conf.,* pp. 571–578.

Marill, T., Hartley, A., Evans, T., Bloom, B., Park, D., Hart, T., and Darley, L. (1963). "Cyclops-1: A Second-Generation Recognition System." *Proc. Fall Joint Comput. Conf.,* pp. 27–33.

Miller, G., and Stein, M. (1963). "Grammarama Memos." Center for Cognitive Studies, Harvard Univ., Cambridge, Massachusetts.

Miller, G., and Stein, M. (1966). "Grammarama Memos." Center for Cognitive Studies, Harvard Univ., Cambridge, Massachusetts.

Miller, W. F., and Shaw, A. C. (1968). "Linguistic Methods in Picture Processing—A Survey." *Proc. Fall Joint Comput. Conf.,* pp. 279–290.

Minsky, M. L. (1961). "Steps Toward Artificial Intelligence." *Proc. IRE* **49**, 8–30.

Nagy, G. (1968). "State of the Art in Pattern Recognition." *Proc. IEEE* **56**, 836–862.

Narasimhan, R. (1964). "Labeling Schemata and Syntactic Descriptions of Pictures." *Information and Control* **7**, 151–179.

Nilsson, N. J. (1965). "Learning Machines." McGraw-Hill, New York.

Roberts, L. (1963). "Machine Perception of Three-Dimensional Solids." Ph.D. Thesis, Dept. of Elec. Eng., M.I.T., Cambridge, Massachusetts.

Rosenfeld, A. (1969). "Picture Processing by Computer." *Comput. Surveys* **1**, 147–176.

Sauvain, R. W., and Uhr, L. (1969). "A Teachable Pattern Describing and Recognizing Program." *Pattern Recognition* **1**, 219–232.

Sherman, H. (1959). "A Quasi-Topological Method for Machine Recognition of Line Patterns." *Proc. Int. Conf. Inform. Processing* (UNESCO).

Sherman, R., and Ernst, G. (1969). "Learning Patterns in Terms of Other Patterns." *Pattern Recognition* **1**, 301–313.

Solomonoff, R. (1959). "A New Method for Discovering the Grammars of Phrase Structure Languages." *Proc. Int. Conf. Inform. Processing (UNESCO)*.

Tou, J. T. (1969). "On Feature Encoding in Picture Processing by Computer." *Proc. Ann. Allerton Conf. on Circuits and System Theory 7th*. Univ. of Illinois, Urbana, Illinois, 1969.

Winston, P. (1970). "Learning Structural Descriptions from Examples." Ph.D. Thesis, Dept. of Elec. Eng., M.I.T., Cambridge, Massachusetts.

Linguistic Analysis of Waveforms

T. Pavlidis

PRINCETON UNIVERSITY
PRINCETON, NEW JERSEY

I. Introduction

If one looks at the development of research in pattern recognition during the last fifteen years, he may notice that at different periods different mathematical techniques were thought to be more promising in helping to solve its problems. The most recent such effort is the development of the linguistic approach. One may date its origin with the papers of Kirsch [1] and Narasimhan [2]; however, it had been used in an informal way earlier than that.

Although the major thrust has been in the development of linguistic models for the recognition of two-dimensional pictures, there is in our opinion, another area where such models may prove quite useful. This is the analysis of patterns represented by functions of one variable. In the past, such patterns were treated through various forms of series expansions, and in many instances such an analysis is quite meaningful. However, there are cases where such an approach fails, the best known among them being the analysis of electrocardiograms. To the best of our knowledge, the only actively used implementations of ECG analysis are based on what we may call empirical linguistic techniques (for example, see Bonner *et al.* [3]). Therefore, it is desirable to study in a systematic way the application of linguistic techniques in waveform analysis.

In general, the output of such an analysis will be a one-dimensional string of primitives, and therefore the subsequent application of linguistic analysis will be much easier than in the case of two-dimensional pictures, where one is faced with the necessity to generalize the notion of concatenation. Instead, one may concentrate his attention to some other very important problems involved in the application of the automata and formal-language theories in pattern recognition. Some of these are the need for a grammatical inference theory [4], and the need for "fuzzy" matching algorithms. Otherwise, the applications of the rather rigid linguistic theories to the very fuzzy pattern recognition problems is not really justified. This has been one of the major criticisms on the merits of the linguistic approach [5].

Of course, the primary problem is to develop efficient coding techniques in order to represent functions of a single variable as one-dimensional strings over a finite alphabet. This is comparable to the classical problem of measurements selection, although it might be easier to solve. This, of course, is the main hope behind the recent interest in linguistic techniques. One can reasonably expect that an efficient encoding will make the subsequent steps of the analysis much easier in the same manner that a good selection of measurements in the classical approach resulted in strong clustering and therefore easy class detection without the use of complicated statistical techniques. This problem will be the main subject of our discussion.

II. Fundamental Considerations

In general, the distinguishing features determining class membership of a function of a single variable will be of two types: either spread out throughout its domain or concentrated in small subsets of it. In the most common case of time functions, we may speak of narrowband and wideband features. For the case of the spreadout features, it is obvious that a promising approach will be to represent the original function as the (weighted) sum of simpler functions. This is the essence of the various serious expansions and spectral analysis techniques. However, such an approach will be quite inappropriate for the analysis of features defined only in small subsets of the domain of the original function.

For the latter case, we propose that the original function should instead be represented as the concatenation of simpler functions. This takes us right away to the segmentation problem in numerical analysis.

A standard problem in numerical analysis is the approximation of a given function by a polynomial (of fixed degree) or a rational function while minimizing some error norm over the domain of interest. A variant of this problem is to subdivide the domain in a fixed number, say n, of subintervals and use a different approximating function in each one of them with certain constraints on the continuity of the approximation at the junctions of the subintervals. The theory of splines is dealing with this problem, especially in the case when the subdivisions are fixed (e.g., Ahlberg *et al.*, [6]). It is obvious that the degree of approximation will be improved if the points of subdivision are allowed to vary. Then the problem becomes one of dynamic programming and more complex than before [7–10]. Some approximate techniques without using dynamic programming have been also proposed and they seem easier to use [11–13].

Unfortunately, none of these techniques is directly applicable to our problem since they all assume that the number of subdivisions is known *a priori* and this is an assumption which can hardly be justified in pattern recognition problems. Of course, if one leaves the number of subdivision intervals free, the error minimization problem becomes absurd. The best solution will obviously be obtained for the largest number of segments allowed. One might try to minimize instead a weighted sum of the error norm and a cost function depending on the number of subdivisions. This, however, is a very difficult problem to solve, as anyone familiar with optimization theory knows. One alternative is to fix the error allowed and then attempt to minimize the number of subdivisions to achieve this error by varying their endpoints. This may be quite acceptable in pattern recognition applications.

It may be argued that the segmentation problem is the most important problem in pattern recognition, especially if it is generalized for multidimensional patterns. What one attempts to do is to find a partition of a given figure (or object) in general so that in each part the figure can be represented in some simple fashion. Although in this chapter we are dealing primarily with functions of one variable, the method can be trivially extended to two-dimensional pictures with two levels of illumination only by applying the segmentation procedure on their boundary. On the other hand, its extension to the analysis of, say, photographs is more difficult. There, one might have to partition first according to the level of illumination and then according to shape. The mathematical formulation of this problem can be as follows.

Find regions $x_1, x_2, \ldots, x_n$ of the domain of $f(\mathbf{x})$ such that in each one of them the error norm of the approximation of $f(\mathbf{x})$ by some function $g(\mathbf{x})$ (from a prespecified family of functions) is less or equal to δ, while the number of partitions n is minimized. In this way, one could have

$$f(\mathbf{x}) \sim \sum_{k=1}^{m_j} a_k{}^j \phi_k{}^j(\mathbf{x}) = g(\mathbf{x}, j), \qquad \mathbf{x} \in x_j.$$

In the rest of the chapter we will deal only with the case when $\mathbf{x}$ is just a scalar and $\phi_k{}^j(t) = t^k$.

One may also attempt to use for $\phi_f{}^j(t)$ other functions, like Chebyshev polynomials, for example (see [14]). However, it does not seem likely that the additional computational effort is worthwhile.

Figure 1 illustrates the "desired" results of a segmentation algorithm in a number of examples.

Before proceeding in the implementation of this approach, one has to make a decision about what type of error norm to use. In the usual minimization problems, this choice is not very crucial. However, it is very important here, where the error is fixed. Since we are interested in features which are in general of very short "duration," we may not use any integral norms. Therefore, a decision was made in favor of using the maximum absolute value of the errors (over the whole domain) as the error norm.

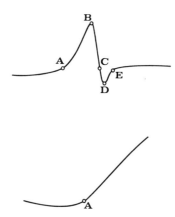

FIGURE 1. Examples of desirable segmentations: In the top figure, the points A, B, D, and E or the points A, C, and E may be used for two possible segmentations. In the bottom part of the figure, the point A is the obvious choice.

III. Fixed Error Approximations

The solution to the above problem would have been very easy if one could express the coefficients $a_0, a_1, a_2, \ldots, a_n$ of the best approximating polynomial of nth order as functions of the end points of the interval of approximation. Then the error norm could be expressed as a function of the end points $E(t_a, t_b)$. The following simple algorithm would then give the minimum number of segments.

If T_i is the left end of the interval, calculate $E(T_i, t)$ for all $t > T_i$ and find the smallest t_0 such that $E(T_i, t_0) = \delta$ and $E(T_i, t_0 + \varepsilon) > \delta$ for all $\varepsilon > 0$. Choose then as a separation point $T_{i+1} = t_0$ and repeat the above procedure using T_{i+1} instead of T_i.

If the total interval is $(0, T)$ and one chooses $T_0 = 0$, the above procedure will provide the minimum number of segments m such that in each interval the error norm does not exceed δ. In general, the last interval will have error norm less than δ and the overall approximation could be improved by modifying the junction points while minimizing the error norm under the assumption of a fixed number of intervals m.

However, this method is applicable only in a few special cases. If the error norm is the integral square error, then the coefficients of the best nth order approximating polynomial are given by the expression

$$a = B^{-1}m,$$

where $a = (a_0, a_1, \ldots, a_n)$, B is a matrix whose generic element b_{kj} is given by

$$b_{kj} = (t_1^{k+j+1} - t_1^{k+j+1})/(k+j+1),$$

and **m** a vector whose generic element m_j is given by

$$m_j = \int_{t_1}^{t_2} f(t)t^j \, dt.$$

Then the problem can be solved.

For the case when the error norm is the maximum absolute value of the error, explicit expressions can be found only in the case when $f(t)$ is convex or concave and the approximation is linear. The method can be modified and used also when $f(t)$ is not convex or concave. The following is an outline of this procedure.

We assume that $f(t)$ is continuous and differentiable. In the case when $f(t)$ is given as a discrete sequence of points sampled from some continuous process, the above assumptions will be substituted by the requirement that the function has a modulus of continuity which is much smaller than the value of the error of approximation. If this condition is not satisfied, no significant data reduction will be achieved. There is no need to assume differentiability because one can always take the first difference of the discrete function.

Let T_i be a junction point. We form the following function defined for t greater than T_i:

$$G(t) = f(t) - f(T_i) - (t - T_i)f'(t). \tag{1}$$

Obviously, $G(T_i)$ is zero. If $f(t)$ is linear, then $G(t)$ is identically zero. It is also easy to verify that, unless $f(t)$ has an inflection point, $G(t)$ is also monotonic. If $f(t)$ has inflection points, then $G(t)$ has extrema at these points.

Consider now the following procedure:

A. Find the smallest t greater than T_i such that the absolute value of $G(t)$ equals 2δ, where δ is the error of approximation. Suppose this happens for $t = y$.

B. Find the new junction point T_{i+1} by solving the equation

$$[f(T_{i+1}) - f(T_i)]/(T_{i+1} - T_i) = f'(y). \tag{2}$$

C. The linear approximation for $f(t)$ will then be given by

$$l(t) = f'(y)(t - T_i) + \tfrac{1}{2}G(y) + f(T_i). \tag{3}$$

The following theorem is proven in Appendix 1:

Theorem 1. If $f(t)$ is continuous and differentiable, and has no inflection points, then (1) Eq. (2) always has a solution and it is unique; (2) The procedure described by steps A, B, and C gives the minimum number of points separating the domain of $f(t)$ in segments where its linear approximation results in maximum absolute error less than δ.

Of course, in all practical examples one is faced with inflection points and therefore the above procedure is not applicable. However, it can be modified to allow one to achieve a reasonable segmentation, although the number of segments is no longer the minimum. The following is one possible procedure:

A'. Define $G(t)$ as before and proceed again to find the first point (greater than T_i) where either the absolute value of $G(t)$ equals 2δ or where $G(t)$ has an extremum. In the first case, take this point as a separating point T_{i+1}. In the second case, continue the computation as before but compare $G(t)$ to $2\delta - Z$ instead of 2δ, where Z is the absolute value of the extremum.

B'. Set the slope of the linear approximation equal to

$$a = [f(T_{i+1}) - f(T_i)]/(T_{i+1} - T_i). \tag{4}$$

C'. Solve the equation

$$f'(t) = a. \tag{5}$$

It will have one more root than the number of inflection points of $f(t)$ in the interval (T_i, T_{i+1}).

D'. If y is the only root of Eq. (5), then set the constant term b of the approximation equal to $G(y)/2$. If there are two roots y_1 and y_2, then set the constant term equal to the quantity $[G(y_1) + G(y_2)]/2$. In both cases, also add to the constant term the quantity $f(T_i)$.

The following theorem is proven in Appendix 1:

Theorem 2. The procedure described in steps $A–D$ above results in a piecewise approximation with error less than δ in absolute value, provided $f(t)$ has at most one inflection point in each subinterval.

There is an intuitive interpretation of the above approach: Equation (1) can be rewritten as

$$\frac{G(t)}{t - T_i} = \frac{f(t) - f(T_i)}{t - T_i} - f'(t) = \frac{1}{t - T_i} \int_{T_i}^{t} f'(s)\, ds - f'(t). \tag{6}$$

The right-hand side represents the difference between the derivative at t and its average value over the interval (T_i, t). By requiring that its absolute value is less than $2\delta/(t - T_i)$, we guarantee that at no point of the interval does the derivative deviate from its average value by more than 2δ. A direct proof of this is given in Appendix 1. The major drawback of this method is the need to estimate derivatives (or differences), and this makes it too sensitive to noise.

An alternative approach is to calculate the coefficients of the optimal polynomial that minimizes the integral square error and then use them in the calculation of the intervals, i.e., in the linear approximation case,

$$E(T_i, t) = \sup_{T_i \le x \le t} |f(x) - a(x) \cdot (x - T_i) - b(x)|.$$

If the discrete form of f is used, then the argument can be taken to be integer n and the coefficients will be given by

$$a(n) = [12 \sum_n f(n)n/(n-1)n(n+1)] - [6 \sum_n f(n)/(n-1)n], \tag{7}$$

$$b(n) = [(4n+2) \sum_n f(n) - 6 \sum_n f(n)n]/(n-1)n. \tag{8}$$

This will not give an optimal solution, but in general it will be fairly close to it.

It seems that the most interesting result of this section is not the development of the fixed error approximation procedures but the fact that the segmentation resulting in the minimum number of segments is the same or close to the segmentation that guarantees that the derivative does not deviate significantly from its average value. This result seems also to hold for higher-order approximations, i.e., in order to obtain the minimum number of segments for an approximation with nth-order polynomials, one has to look for segments where the nth derivative is approximately constant. However, no formal proof for this statement exists as yet.

IV. Optimization of the Segmentation

At this point, one can proceed in two ways. Either use the segmentation obtained with the coefficients given by Eq. (3) [or Eq. (4) and step D' above] or attempt to improve upon them by further processing. If the data are smooth, then the assumptions of Theorems 1 and 2 usually hold and additional analysis is not necessary. On the other hand, if the data are noisy, then this will not be true. Although a prefiltering of the waveform might be used, this is not always a good solution because it may result in the loss of valuable information.

One form of further processing may be obtained by using a modification of an algorithm proposed by Lawson ([11], see also Esch and Eastman [12]) dealing with maximum error minimization when the number of segments is fixed.

It is well known that the error of approximation of $f(t)$ in an interval $(0, T)$ by an nth-order polynomial satisfies the following relation:

$$|e(t)| \le [T^{n+1}/(n+1)! 2^{2n+1}] \sup_{0 \le t \le T} |f^{(n+1)}(t)| \tag{9}$$

provided that the $(n+1)$th derivative exists ([14, pp. 5–7]; [15, Chapter III]; [16, pp. 190–191, 226–229]).

For an approximation in the interval $(-T, T)$, the following is true:

$$|e(t)| \cong [T^{n+1}/(n+1)!\, 2^n] f^{(n+1)}(0) \qquad (10)$$

provided that $f^{(n+1)}(0)$ is not zero and T is sufficiently small ([17, p. 60]).

On the basis of the above, Lawson suggested that the maximum error e_m in the mth interval of the segmentation is given by

$$e_m = c_m h_m^{n+1}, \qquad (11)$$

where h_m is the length of the interval, c_m an undetermined constant, and n the order of the approximating polynomial ([12, pp. 122–123]).

In view of the above, one might suggest that Eq. (9) or Eq. (11) could have been used to obtain a fixed error approximation. This, however, is not possible: Eq. (9) gives too conservative an estimate, while Eq. (11) cannot be used at all because the value of the constant is unknown.

However, once a segmentation has been achieved, then one may solve a system of equations, determine c_m, and, furthermore, adjust the ends of the intervals in such a way that the maximum error in each interval is the same throughout the segmentation. This is called a balanced error solution and for the given number of segments gives an optimal solution. Because Eq. (11) is only approximately correct, this solution is not achieved in one step but rather through repetition ([12, pp. 122–123]). Although for smooth functions such a procedure converges quickly to the solution, there are a number of difficulties in its practical application, especially in connection with the problems discussed in this chapter.

A rather minor problem is that, due to quantization of both the domain and the range of $f(t)$, cycling may occur, i.e., the algorithm does not converge, but oscillates between two (unbalanced) solutions. This may be corrected by choosing the solution with the smallest maximum error after cycling is detected.

A more important problem is the following: If, at a given step, the error in an interval is very small compared to the rest, the algorithm will tend to extend that interval over the whole domain This is undesirable especially from our viewpoint because an error close to zero means a virtually perfect match and this can be a very important feature.

Therefore, the following procedure is suggested:

A". After a segmentation has been obtained by the methods of the previous section, proceed by applying Lawson's algorithm* modified only to take into account the possibility of cycling.

* This refers to the above-described technique for segmented approximation. Lawson has also proposed another algorithm for nonsegmented minimax approximation [18].

B". If one segment is found with error below a certain level (which should be considered as equal to zero for all practical purposes), then this segment is removed from consideration and the optimization is considered on each of the two remaining intervals.

C". The process terminates under one of the following conditions: (1) All the intervals have zero error; (2) balanced error solutions are achieved in groups of intervals separated by intervals with zero error; (3) cycling occurs in groups of intervals; (4) a mixture of both (2) and (3) above.

Table I shows two typical examples of the results of this procedure.

TABLE I

Segment no.:	1	2	3	4	5	6	7	8	9	10	11
Original:	0	36	46	88	105	125	138	156	164	259	281	300
(errors)	↓ 2.33	↓0.70	↓0.49	↓1.97	↓1.89	↓1.08	↓1.67	↓1.12	↓ 0.85	↓ [0.50]	↓ [0.50] ↓
Improved:	0	22	33	76	86	96	109	123	143	169	271	300
(errors)		1.54	0.00	2.15	0.00	1.17	1.27	1.43	0.00	1.55	0.00	0.00

Segment no.:	1	2	3	4	5	6	7	8	9	10	11	12	13	14
Original:	0	20	40	64	109	117	127	152	188	207	226	242	261	288	300
(errors)	↓ 0.71	↓0.37	↓2.09	↓4.90	↓0.43	↓4.50	↓0.77	↓0.92	↓1.23	↓1.33	↓0.00	↓0.47	↓0.78	↓0.46↓
Improved:	0	52	70	77	98	111	116	132	185	196	226	242	263	286	300
(errors)		1.27	1.67	1.64	0.00	0.46	0.00	4.50	0.00	1.59	1.50	0.00	0.47	0.47	0.46

One possible improvement can be achieved if for intervals where the error is not close to zero an approximation by a higher-order polynomial is attempted, i.e., after the step C" is completed, one goes back to step A" but using, say, quadratic approximation instead of linear.

Also, at the end of the procedure, adjacent intervals with zero error may be merged if the approximating coefficients are very close, or very narrow intervals may be omitted. This editing can be done under the string representation described in the next section.

V. Waveform Editing

The analysis of the previous section shows that one can represent a function $f(t)$ through an array of $N(n + 2)$ numbers, where N is the number of segments and n the degree of the approximating polynomial. For each segment, one has the $n + 1$ coefficients and its duration $T_{i+1} - T_i$. For a given quality of approximation, one may expect that for large n the number of segments N should be small and vice versa. A large n may not be very desirable because of the computational effort involved. In many practical cases, one attempts only a piecewise linear approximation.

This restriction seems to have the disadvantage of overlooking certain complex features which may be characteristic of many waveforms and also of requiring too long representations (because of the high value of N). These defects can be overcome by editing of the first results of the analysis. Editing is also necessary in order to remove the effects of noise. Although it is quite possible to prefilter the original data, this may not be enough. In general, one may use a low-pass filter to remove high-frequency noise due to the recording instruments or other filters specifically designed to remove noise due to interference, etc. [3]. However, there may be other sources which are not as easy to get rid of. We should emphasize that because of the type of our approach, it is not desirable to tamper too much with the signal before the analysis. For example, a low-pass filter will smooth sharp peaks which may be among the distinguishing features we are looking for.

We shall try to illustrate the editing process by describing the grammatical representation of a simple case. Let $n = 1$ and let us assume that W is a (finite) set which consists of slope values that are allowed for the representation. For example,

$$W = \{\tan(n\phi) \mid \phi = 1°, \quad n \text{ integer between } -89 \text{ and } +89\}.$$

Then each segment may simply be represented by the value of its slope approximated by a member of W, w, and its duration approximated by a, say, two-digit integer n. In this way, the string representation of the wave form will be of the following form:

$$w_1 n_1 w_2 n_2 \cdots w_N n_N.$$

The following trivial grammar will produce such strings:

$$\$ \to wn$$
$$\$ \to \$wn,$$

where $\$$ is a generic string, w any member of W, and n any two-digit integer (including expressions like 05, 00, etc.). We may now add more rules:

1. $\$w_1 n_1 w_2 n_2 \$' \to \$wn\$'$

provided that

    (i) $n_1, n_2 \le k$ (k is a small integer, say, 3);
    (ii) $w_1 w_2 < 0$;
    (iii) $|w_1 + w_2| < c$ (some constant);
    (iv) $n = n_1 + n_2$;
    (v) $w = (w_1 n_1 - w_2 n_2)/n$.

This represents the removal of a short-duration [because of (i)] peak and its substitution by a straight line with slope given by (v). This may be considered as noise filtering.

On the other hand, the following rules detect particular complex symbols:

2. $\$w_1 n_1 w_2 n_2 \$' \to \$Qn\$'$

provided that

(i) $|n_1 - n_2| < 1$;
(ii) $w_1 w_2 < 0$;
(iii) $|w_1 + w_2| < d$;
(iv) $n = n_1 + n_2$;
(v) Q is the symbol for a "peak" if $w_1 > 0$ or the symbol for a "valley" if $w_1 < 0$.

3. $\$w_1 n_1 w_2 n_2 w_3 n_3 \$' \to \$Rn\$'$

provided that

(i) $|n_1 - n_3| < 1$;
(ii) $w_1 w_3 < 0$;
(iii) $|w_2| < e$ (e a small constant, say 0.02);
(iv) $|w_1 + w_3| < d$;
(v) $n = n_1 + n_2 + n_3$;
(vi) R is the symbol for a "hat" if $w_1 > 0$ or the symbol for a "cup" if $w_1 < 0$.

All these reductions can be performed automatically very easily. Obviously, one can elaborate considerably on these rules. For example, symbols for "peaks" of various sizes may be introduced.

However, it is not always desirable to introduce all these rules *a priori*. Ideally, one would like to have a process that would allow the system to "learn" these rules from various samples. This is even more important for rules that will characterize the various patterns.

VI. Applications and Discussion of the Method

The linguistic approach is of interest in cases where the data under consideration are time signals containing pulses of short duration which contain the important information. Besides the case of the electrocardiograms, another important example concerns the signatures of reciprocating-engine vibrations. Figure 2 shows examples of such a waveform. They were obtained by an accelerometer, stored on analog magnetic tape, and then digitized by using a LINC-8 computer. They were subsequently filtered to eliminate high-frequency noise. Figure 3 shows a printout of the results of the analysis performed by the implementation of a simplified version of steps A–D of Section III on a LINC-8 computer.

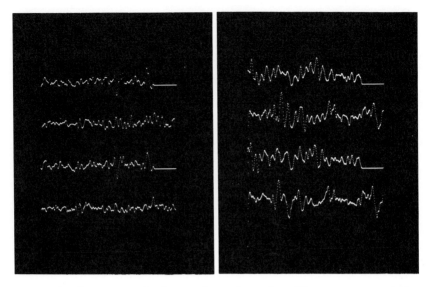

FIGURE 2. Vibration records of two reciprocating engines: There are two records from four cycles (two from each engine). Each record is in two lines starting from lower left and ending at the upper right.

Another application of the method involved topographical data. There, the main problem is one of data compression, but one might also be interested in the recognition of certain terrain features. A segmented approximation is ideally suited in both cases. For the data compression case, it picks out "flat" regions from "rough" regions. For the recognition case, the analysis determines the form of the various segments. It should be mentioned that there is a difference between the methods described here and the better known data compression techniques [19]. In the latter, the data are known sequentially, while in the former, one has knowledge of the whole record. This additional knowledge allows for further improvement, not only by permitting the variation of the junction points (as described in Section IV) but also by allowing a "look ahead" as in the first procedure of Section III.

The data used for the analysis were produced by the Army Map Service and their form has been described often in the literature [20, 21]. Figure 4 shows an example of a close approximation produced without junction optimization and using programs APPREX and ARRANGE (see Appendix 2 for a discussion of these). Figures 5 and 6 show larger segments of terrain profiles segmented while using junction optimization. In Figure 5, the first segmentation was performed while using steps A'–D' of Section III (program APPREX), while in Figure 6, the first segmentation used as error norm is the mean integral square error (program INTGRL). In general, the first gives a finer

```
+0450
A +2502/B +2415
  +2013 -0017/ +0006= -0002
  +2021 +0052/ +0006= +0008
  +2030 +0021/ +0007= +0003
  +2036 -0036/ +0006= -0006
  +2046 -0031/ +0008= -0003
  +2053 -0002/ +0005= -0000
  +2061 +0047/ +0006= +0007
  +2074 -0049/ +0011= -0004
  +2104 +0018/ +0008= +0002
  +2115 +0018/ +0009= +0002
  +2124 -0032/ +0007= -0004
  +2135 +0039/ +0009= +0004
  +2152 -0030/ +0013= -0002
  +2160 -0008/ +0006= -0001
  +2172 +0042/ +0010= +0004
  +2204 -0028/ +0010= -0002
  +2212 +0001/ +0006= +0000
  +2217 +0022/ +0005= +0004
  +2225 -0019/ +0006= -0003
  +2236 -0023/ +0009= -0002
  +2250 +0028/ +0010= +0002 +0021 SEGMENTS

+0454
A +2502/B +2416
  +2012 -0007/ +0005= -0001
  +2021 +0042/ +0007= +0006
  +2030 -0001/ +0007= -0000
  +2040 -0043/ +0008= -0005
  +2051 -0011/ +0009= -0001
  +2057 +0050/ +0006= +0008
  +2066 -0020/ +0007= -0002
  +2074 -0024/ +0006= -0004
  +2103 +0017/ +0007= +0002
  +2110 +0016/ +0005= +0003
  +2115 +0007/ +0005= +0001
  +2123 -0031/ +0006= -0005
  +2133 +0033/ +0003= +0004
  +2155 -0032/ +0018= -0001
  +2167 +0042/ +0010= +0004
  +2176 -0010/ +0007= -0001
  +2206 -0021/ +0008= -0002
  +2220 +0029/ +0010= +0002
  +2227 -0044/ +0007= -0006
  +2235 +0011/ +0006= +0001
  +2242 +0035/ +0005= +0007 +0021 SEGMENTS
```

FIGURE 3. Results of the application of the method of Section III to a segment (near the top dead center) of the vibration patterns shown in Figure 2. Each line displays the separation point, the quantities $f(T_{i+1}) - f(T_i)$, $T_{i+1} - T_i$, and their ratio. All or part of this information can be used for further processing.

segmentation; however, one may notice that in both cases certain outstanding features are picked out. The segments of Figure 6 correspond to the ones of Figure 5 roughly in the following way:

Original integral: 1   2   3   4
Original minimax: 1   2, 3   4, 5   6

Another area of application is on the one-dimensional transformation of two-dimensional figures. One such transformation, called integral projection

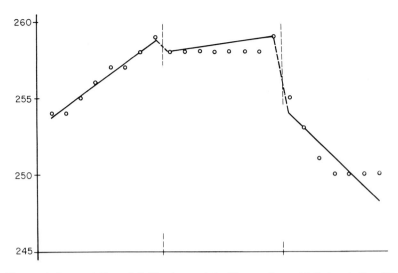

FIGURE 4. Segmentation of digitized map data. The numbers at left denote the altitude in arbitrary units.

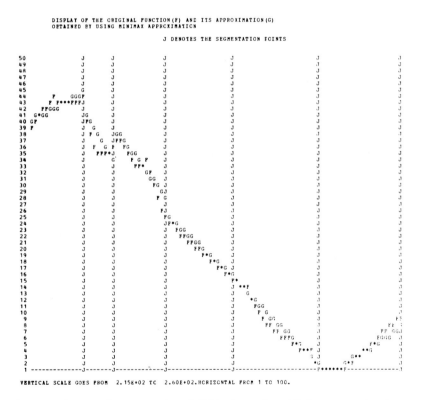

FIGURE 5. Large-scale segmentation of digitized map data. Minimax approximation was used in the original analysis. The vertical lines denote the boundaries of the segments.

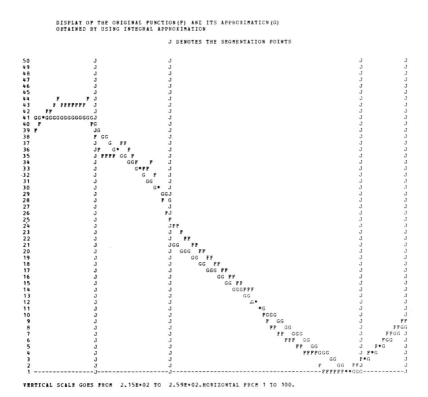

FIGURE 6. Same as Figure 5, but with integral approximation.

has been described elsewhere [22]. Figure 7 shows an example. Again here one tries to detect peaks at certain locations as an indication of the type of the picture.

In all such cases, the result of the processing described in the previous section will be an array of triplets (slope, constant term, duration) rather than a one-dimensional array of primitives. There are two ways, among others, to find the latter.

In the more complicated cases (as in the example of engine signatures), one proceeds to quantize the slopes and present them as a one-dimensional string representation of the original waveform, possibly adding the duration as described in the previous section.

In the simpler cases (like the integral projections), one may decide to look only at certain parts of the waveform and, depending on the presence or absence of certain features, to set certain binary variables equal to one or zero. In this way, the linguistic approach may be reduced to the classical approach

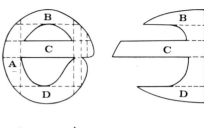

FIGURE 7. Integral projections of a letter
"e". (Adapted from Pavlidis [22].)

of measurements. On the other hand, one could define certain "truth" functions implementing our knowledge of the structure of a pattern.

Table II shows the results of this method in comparison with separation by
hyperplanes.

TABLE II

Description	Design Test			Testing set			Total		
	Size	C.C.[a]	Percent	Size	C.C.[a]	Percent	Size	C.C.[a]	Percent
Truth functions	260	260	100.00	2280	2230	97.81	2540	2490	98.03
Hyperplanes	261	261	100.00	2279	2221	97.45	2540	2482	97.71
	660	658	99.70	1880	1847	98.24	2540	2505	98.62

[a] Correctly classified.

VII. Concluding Discussion

There is obviously a long way to go before a complete theory for linguistic
analysis of pattern recognition becomes available. Probably the only area where
satisfactory progress has been made is the analysis of graphlike figures (e.g.,
bubble chamber photographs) [2, 23–25]. In most other areas, there exist
either theories which have not been implemented or quite empirical implementations. In general, one expects that a linguistic or, to use a synonym [26],
structural analysis will be more difficult to implement than most measure-
ment-taking techniques. This is so because one has to process the whole
pattern rather than only part of it. Even if this is not the case, the segmentation
often turns out to be quite complicated. In the particular case of waveforms,

one might compare the more or less straightforward series expansions to the segmentation problem in numerical analysis, which we showed to be quite involved. Note that all our analysis has been without continuity conditions at the end points. If this was also required, then one would have been faced with a linear programming problem on top of everything else [12].

The approach described in this chapter is quite general in the sense that it does not require any *a priori* knowledge about the nature of the waveform. It is based simply on a numerical analysis optimization problem and it was also shown that it can be justified intuitively as a segmentation according to regions of approximately constant slope. A knowledge of the physical properties, when available, will obviously be helpful. An effort in that direction for the case of speech analysis has been made by Resnikoff and Sitton [27].

During the final writing of this chapter, a report by Patrick *et al.* [28] was published which discussed the waveform segmentation problem. However, the suggested approach is feasible only for integral square-error approximations since only in this case is it possible to achieve a precise solution of the fixed-error approximation problem. In the case of a uniform approximation (i.e., with the maximum absolute error taken as the error norm), their approach would require repeated applications of Lawson's algorithm instead of only one as described in this chapter.

Appendix 1

A. Proof of Theorem 1

If $f(t)$ is convex or concave and differentiable in an interval $(0, T)$, then it is easy to verify that its best uniform linear approximation $l(t)$ will be given by the equation

$$l(t) = \frac{f(T) - f(0)}{T} t + \frac{f(y) - yf'(y) + f(0)}{2},$$ (12)

where y is determined from the equation

$$f'(y) = [f(T) - f(0)]/T.$$ (13)

Equation (12) has a unique solution according to the mean value theorem for convex (or concave) functions. The maximum error has an absolute value equal to the absolute value of

$$[f(y) - yf'(y) - f(0)]/2.$$ (14)

The same is true if $f(t)$ is concave. In both cases, the maximum error occurs at the ends of the interval and for $t = y$.

But (14) is the same as $\frac{1}{2}G(t)$ [Eq. (1)] and since $|G(y)| = 2\delta$, then the maximum error will be δ. If it so happens that $T_k = T$ for some k, then this is a "balanced error" solution [11] and, therefore, is the best uniform approximation for k subintervals. Hence, k is the minimum number of intervals that allow a piecewise linear approximation with error less than δ. If in the last interval the error is less than δ, then again k is also the minimum number of segments, although the subdivisions do not give the minimum error. The optimal subdivisions could then be found on the assumption of a fixed number of intervals k. In order to show that k is the minimum number, consider a subdivision by $k - 1$ intervals. Then, a simple argument can show that at least two of them must contain intervals of the subdivision in k segment (compare Lemma 3 by Lawson [11]). By assumption, at least one of these intervals must be one with error norm equal to δ. Hence, any interval that contains it will have error norm larger or equal to δ. The only case where equality might occur requires a function with inflection points ([17, pp. 59–60]). Since this is not the case here, the error norm should exceed δ. Hence, k is the minimum number of segments such that the error does not exceed δ.

B. PROOF OF THEOREM 2

It is easy to construct a formal proof that the error of approximating $f(t)$ by the line $a(t - T_i) + b + f(T_i)$ is less than δ. Here, we simply give its outline: Because $f(t)$ was assumed to be continuous and with at most one inflection point z, $G(t)$ will be increasing (or decreasing) for $t < z$. Hence, $G(z)$ and $G(T_{i+1})$ will be of opposite signs (see Figure 8). $G(z)$ will be zero when $f'(t) = f(t)/t$ (point A at Figure 8). The line BC is parallel to the linear approximation, and we assume without any loss of generality that A lies above BC. This means that $f''(t)$ is positive in that region. The first derivative will then be increasing and since $f'(y_1)$ equals the slope of BC, it will lie to the right of A. In this way, we can show that $G(y_1)$ and $G(y_2)$ are of opposite sign. Hence, because of the construction described in (A'), one has

$$|G(y_1)| + |G(y_2)| < 2\delta. \qquad (15)$$

Therefore, $|b|$ is less than δ.

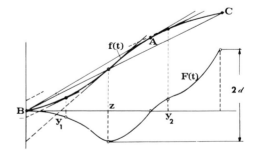

FIGURE 8. Construction for the proof of Theorem 2.

The approximation error is given by

$$e(t) = f(t) - a(t - T_i) - b - f(T_i) \tag{16}$$

and it is easy to verify that at the end points it equals $-b$. The extrema of $e(t)$ occur obviously at y_1 and y_2 and it is easy to verify that

$$e(y_1) = -e(y_2) = \tfrac{1}{2}[G(y_1) - G(y_2)]. \tag{17}$$

Again, because of Eq. (15) one can see that the RHS of Eq. (17) is less than δ.

C. PROOF OF THE AVERAGE-SLOPE APPROXIMATION

To show that the procedures described in Section III determine sections where the derivative does not deviate significantly from its average value, we proceed as follows. For simplicity, we consider a function of a discrete variable $F(i)$ and let $S(k)$ be its average value for $i = 1, 2, \ldots, k$. One proceeds by checking the following inequality for increasing values of i:

$$|F(i) - S(i - 1)| < h(i)\delta, \tag{18}$$

where $h(i)$ is a positive decreasing function of i satisfying condition (28) below. This is essentially a discrete version of Eq. (6). If Eq. (18) is not satisfied, then i is taken as the start for a new interval. If Eq. (18) holds, then we proceed to the next point, updating $S(i)$ according to the well-known formula for arithmetic averages

$$S(i) = [(i - 1)/i]S(i - 1) + (1/i)F(i). \tag{19}$$

We will show next that this procedure guarantees that

$$|F(i) - S(n)| < \delta, \qquad i = 1, 2, \ldots, n. \tag{20}$$

From Eq. (19), we have for some arbitrary i and $j < i$

$$S(i) - F(j) = S(i - 1) - F(j) - (1/i)[S(i - 1) - F(i)] \tag{21}$$

or

$$|S(i) - F(j)| \le |S(i - 1) - F(j)| \times (1/i)|S(i - 1) - F(i)|.$$

Because of Eq. (18), the above inequality gives

$$|S(i) - F(j)| \le |S(i - 1) - F(j)| + [h(i)/i]\delta. \tag{22}$$

By a similar argument, we can prove that

$$|S(i - 1) - F(j)| \le |S(i - 2) - F(j)| + [h(i - 1)/(i - 1)]\delta \tag{23}$$

and so obtain $i - j + 1$ inequalities of this form, the last of which can be obtained directly from Eq. (19) as

$$S(j) - F(j) = [(i - 1)/i][S(j - 1) - F(j)]$$

or

$$|S(j) - F(j)| \leq |S(j - 1) - F(j)|. \tag{24}$$

Substituting (23) into (24) strengthens the inequality, and by doing this for all of them until $i = j - 1$, we obtain

$$|S(i) - F(j)| \leq |S(j - 1) - F(j)| + \sum_{p=j+1}^{i} \frac{h(p)}{p} \delta. \tag{25}$$

Because of Eq. (18), the above becomes

$$|S(i) - F(j)| \leq \delta \sum_{p=j}^{n} \frac{h(p)}{p}. \tag{26}$$

Since the right-hand side of Eq. (26) is an increasing function of the number of terms in the sum and since $S(n)$ is the final value of the average, we may write

$$|S(n) - F(j)| \leq \delta \sum_{p=1}^{n} \frac{h(p)}{p}. \tag{27}$$

Then it is obvious that Eq. (20) will be satisfied if the function h is chosen in such a way that

$$\sum_{p=1}^{n} \frac{h(p)}{p} \leq 1. \tag{28}$$

One possible choice for $h(p)$ is

$$h(p) = (6/\pi^2)(1/p).$$

This will satisfy Eq. (28) because

$$\lim_{n \to \infty} \sum_{p=1}^{n} \frac{1}{p^2} = \frac{\pi^2}{6}.$$

This completes the proof that the procedure based on Eq. (18) determines intervals over which $F(i)$ does not differ more than δ in absolute value from its average.

Equation (6) is a special case of the above with $f'(t)$ taken for $F(t)$.

Appendix 2

Figure 9 shows the main parts of a PL/I program available for the waveform processing.

FILTER is a simple low-pass digital filter.

SCAN implements in a "quick and dirty way" the analysis described in Section III. It should be used only on very smooth input.

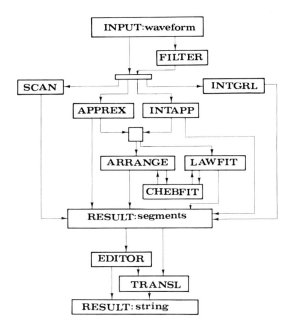

FIGURE 9. Block diagram of the program for waveform analysis.

APPREX implements the steps A′–D′ of Section III. A number of modifications are possible by the setting of the appropriate control parameters.

INTAPP is the same as APPREX except that it uses the coefficients of the integral approximation [Eq. (7) and (8)].

INTGRL implements the fixed error segmentation by minimizing the mean-square error.

ARRANGE determines the coefficients of the minimax polynomial without changing the segmentation points. This results in an improvement over the approximation by coefficients given by Eq. (4) and step D in Section III if there is more than one inflection point in a subinterval.

LAWFIT implements the analysis described in steps A″–C″ in Section IV.

CHEBFIT* determines the minimax polynomial on a given interval and it is called by both APPREX and LAWFIT.

EDITOR and TRANSL encode the representation into a string while implementing most of the features described in Section V.

For a given input, all or only some of these programs may be used, depending on the setting of control parameters. For example, a quick encoding of a

* Part of the Princeton University Computer Center Library.

rather smooth waveform into a string of symbols may be achieved by the sequence

$$(\text{INPUT:waveform}) \rightarrow (\text{FILTER}) \rightarrow (\text{SCAN}) \rightarrow (\text{RESULT: segments})$$

$$\rightarrow (\text{TRANSL}) \rightarrow (\text{RESULT: string}).$$

For a noisy waveform where prefiltering is undesirable, one might use:

$$(\text{INPUT:waveform}) \rightarrow (\text{INTAPP}) \rightarrow (\text{ARRANGE}) \rightarrow (\text{RESULT:segments})$$

$$\rightarrow (\text{EDITOR}) \rightarrow (\text{TRANSL}) \rightarrow (\text{RESULT:string}).$$

For data reduction purposes, one might use

$$(\text{INPUT:waveform}) \rightarrow (\text{APPREX}) \rightarrow (\text{LAWFIT}) \rightarrow (\text{RESULT:segments}).$$

ACKNOWLEDGMENTS

This work was supported by contract No. DAHCO4-69-C-0035 from the U.S. Army Research Office (Durham). The author would like to express his thanks to Messrs. R. J. Brachman, G. Staton, and M. Langan of the Frankford Arsenal, Philadelphia for supplying the engine-vibration and map records used in the examples of Section VI.

REFERENCES

1. Kirsch, R., "Computer Interpretation of English Text and Picture Patterns." *IEEE Trans. Electronic Computers* **EC-13**, 363–376 (1964).
2. Narasimhan, R., "Labeling Schemata and Syntactic Description of Pictures." *Information and Control* **7**, 151–179 (1964).
3. Bonner, R. E. *et al.*, "Computer Diagnosis of Electro-Cardiograms." *IBM Advance Systems Development Division Rep. No. 17–223.* IBM, Yorktown Heights, New York, 1967.
4. Feldman, J., "First Thoughts on Grammatical Inference," Memo No. 55. Stanford Univ., Stanford, California, 1968.
5. Minsky, M. *in* "IEEE Workshop on Pattern Recognition" (L. Kanal, ed.), pp. 183–185. Thomson, Washington, D.C., 1968.
6. Ahlberg, J. H., Nilson, E. N., and Walsh, J. L., "The Theory of Splines and Their Applications." Academic Press, New York, 1967.
7. Stone, H., "Approximation of Curves by Line Segments." *Math. Comp.* **15**, 40–47 (1961).
8. Bellman, R., "On the Approximation of Curves by Line Segments." *Comm. ACM* **4**, 284 (1961).
9. Gluss, B., "Further Remarks on Line Segment Curve-Fitting Using Dynamic Programming." *Comm. ACM* **5**, 441–443 (1962).
10. Frank, C. M., and Shear, R. E., "Function Approximation by a Polygonal Curve." Rep. No. 1363. U.S. Army Ballistic Res. Lab., Aberdeen Proving Ground, Maryland, 1967.
11. Lawson, C. L., "Characteristic Properties of the Segmented Rational Minimax Approximation Problem." *Numer. Math.* **6**, 293–301 (1964).
12. Esch, R. E., and Eastman, W. L., "Computational Methods for Best Approximation." Tech. Rep. SEG-TR-64-30. Sperry Rand Res. Center, Sudbury, Massachusetts, 1964.

13. Esch, R. E., and Eastman, W. L., "Computational Methods for Best Approximation and Associated Numerical Analyses," Tech. Rep. ASD-TR-68-37. Sperry Rand Res. Center, Sudbury, Massachusetts, 1968.

14. Fox, L., and Parker, I. B., "Chebyshev Polynomials in Numerical Analysis." Oxford Univ. Press, London and New York, 1968.

15. Davis, P. J., "Interpolation and Approximation." Ginn (Blaisdell), Boston, Massachusetts, 1963.

16. Isaacson, E., and Keller, H. B., "Analysis of Numerical Methods." Wiley, New York, 1966.

17. Hart, J. F. *et al.*, "Computer Approximations." Wiley, New York, 1968.

18. Rice, J. R., and Usow, K. H., "The Lawson Algorithm and Extensions." *Math. Comp.* **22**, 118–127 (1968).

19. Davisson, L. D., "The Theoretical Analysis of Data Compression Systems." *Proc. IEEE* **56**, 176–186 (1968).

20. "Computer Production of Terrain Models." *Comm. ACM* **6**, 190–191 (1963).

21. Jablinske, R., Scheihing, S., and Scott, J., "Numerical Mapping Applications." *Proc. Computerized Imaging Techniques Seminar, 1967, Washington, D.C.*, pp. I-1–I-16.

22. Pavlidis, T., "Computer Recognition of Figures through Decomposition." *Information and Control* **12**, 183–188 (1968).

23. Shaw, A. C., "The Formal Description and Parsing of Pictures." Ph.D. Thesis, Stanford Univ., Stanford, California, 1968.

24. McCormick, B. H., and Schwebel, J. C., "Consistent Formal Properties of Binary Relations." Rep. No. 762. Also "Properties of a Discrete Space Preserved by Image Processing Relations," Rep. No. 769. Univ. of Illinois, Urbana, Illinois, 1968.

25. Feder, J., "Languages of Encoded Line Patterns." *Information and Control* **13**, 230–244 (1968).

26. Aizerman, M. A., "Remarks on Two Problems Connected with Pattern Recognition." *In* "Methodologies of Pattern Recognition" (S. Watanabe, ed.). Academic Press, New York, 1969.

27. Resnikoff, H. L., and Sitton, G. A., "Linguistic Segmentation of Acoustic Speech Waveforms." *Meeting Acoustical Soc. of Amer., 25th, 1968, Ottawa, Canada.*

28. Patrick, E. A., Fischer, II, F. P., and Shen, L. Y. L., "Computer Analysis and Classification of Waveforms and Pictures: Pat. I—Waveforms," Tech. Rep. RADC-TR-69-279. Rome Air Develop. Center, Rome, New York, 1969.

A Grammar for Maps

Azriel Rosenfeld
UNIVERSITY OF MARYLAND
COLLEGE PARK, MARYLAND

and

James P. Strong
NATIONAL AERONAUTICS AND SPACE ADMINISTRATION
GREENBELT, MARYLAND

I. Introduction

"Grammars" whose "sentences" are not strings of symbols, but rather sets of symbols which can be interconnected in more general ways are of considerable interest in connection with the formal theory of picture processing and description [1]. One of the most general formalisms of this kind [2] deals with "sentences" which are labeled directed graphs ("webs").

Webs arise naturally in connection with descriptions of pictures; typically, a description will refer to relations among objects or regions in the given picture, so that (in the case of a binary relation) it can be represented by a web whose vertices represent regions and whose edges indicate related pairs of regions. (This suggests that it should be worthwhile to study webs in which not only the vertices, but also the edges, are labeled, with each edge label identifying a particular relation or degree of relatedness; but this generalization will not be considered in the present chapter.) Since pictures are planar, the webs that arise in this way will often be planar; there is so, for example, if the relation is that of adjacency. It is thus of interest for picture description applications, as well as for graph-theoretic reasons, to study web grammars whose languages consist of planar graphs; for the results of such a study, see the work of Montanari [3].

When a graph is used to represent the adjacency relation between regions in the plane, not all of the topological information about the regions is preserved. In particular, one cannot tell from the graph how many times two regions touch, or in what order (up to cyclic permutation) a region's neighbors are encountered as one traverses the region's boundaries. To represent this information, one can use graphs with multiple edges (in brief, *multigraphs*). The purpose of this chapter is to describe a grammar that has the set of such "adjacency multigraphs" as its language

II. Maps

Let C_0 be a simple closed curve in the plane; let C_0^+ and C_0^- denote the inside and outside of C_0, respectively. Let $C_1, \ldots, C_m$ be a (possibly empty, $m \geq 0$) set of simple closed curves no two of which intersect and each of which lies inside C_0. The set $\rho = C_0^+ \cap \bigcap_{i-1}^m C_i^-$ will be called a *bounded region*. Evidently, we can assume without loss of generality that no C_i lies inside any C_j (where $1 \leq i, j \leq m$), since, if it did, C_i^- could be eliminated from the intersection. It follows that the *boundary* of ρ [notation: $B(\rho)$] consists of just the union of the curves C_i, $0 \leq i \leq m$. The outside of C_0 will be called the outside of ρ, while the insides of $C_1, \ldots, C_m$ will be called *holes* in ρ.

Similarly, let $D_1, \ldots, D_n$ be simple closed curves each of which lies outside all the others; then the set $\rho = \bigcap_{i-1}^n D_i^-$ will be called an *unbounded region*. Readily, here $B(\rho)$ is just the union of the D's; the insides of the D's will be called *holes* in ρ.

By a *map* will be meant a finite set of regions such that

(a) No two of the regions intersect.
(b) The boundaries of any two of the regions meet in at most a finite set of arcs, each of nonzero length.†
(c) The closures of the regions cover the plane.

Clearly, by (a) and (c), any map contains exactly one unbounded region ρ_0; we shall further assume, for simplicity, that

(d) ρ_0 is the outside of a *single* simple closed curve.

The remaining regions are thus all inside this curve, i.e., they are all inside a hole in ρ_0. Note that, in particular, by this definition a map must have at least two regions.

It will be convenient in the remainder of this chapter to deal with maps in which no region other than ρ_0 has a hole; such maps will be called *nonseparable*. (To see the reason for this terminology, note that if a region $\rho \neq \rho_0$ has a hole, then ρ *separates* the plane into two nonempty parts, namely the part outside ρ and the part inside the hole.) Indeed, we can regard any map $\mathcal{M}$ as a hierarchy of nonseparable maps in the following sense: Let $\rho_1, \ldots, \rho_m$ be those regions of $\mathcal{M}$ that are not inside holes in other regions (expect ρ_0). If we were to fill up the holes in these ρ's (i.e., adjoin each hole to the region inside

† The implications of assumption (b) will be discussed in the next section.

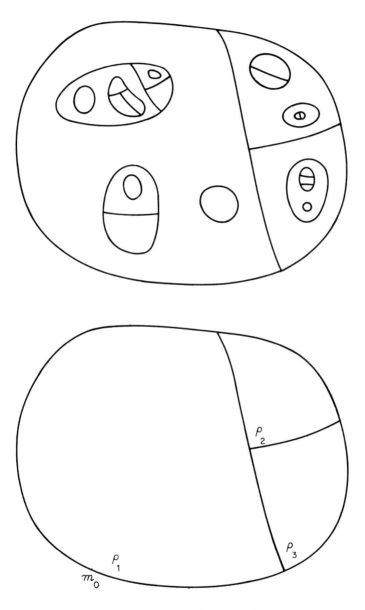

FIGURE 1a. Top: Original map $\mathcal{M}$.

FIGURE 1b. Bottom: Nonseparable map resulting when holes in the bounded regions of $\mathcal{M}$ are filled.

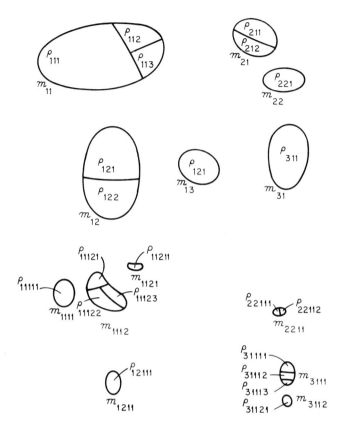

FIGURE 1c. Top: Nonseparable maps resulting when holes in these holes are filled.

FIGURE 1d. Bottom: Nonseparable maps contained in these secondary holes.

which it lies), we would have a nonseparable map. Now consider the regions $\rho_{11}, \ldots, \rho_{1n}$ of $\mathscr{M}$ that are inside a particular hole H_1 in (say) ρ_1, but that are not inside holes in other regions that lie inside H_1. If we fill up the holes in the ρ_{1j}'s, we have a nonseparable map inside H_1. This process can be repeated; it must terminate after finitely many steps, since $\mathscr{M}$ has only finitely many regions. In other words, $\mathscr{M}$ can be regarded as a "nonseparable" map in some of whose regions there are holes containing "nonseparable" maps, in some of whose regions in turn there are holes containing "non-separable" maps, and so on. Briefly: any map can be regarded as a *directed tree* of nonseparable maps.† An example of a map and its associated tree is shown in Figure 1.

† More precisely, we can think of this tree as a web having two types of vertices, one type representing holes, the other type representing regions. Each hole vertex is joined by

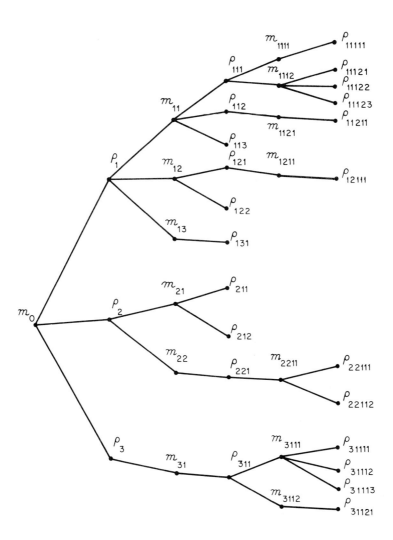

FIGURE 1e. Tree structure relating these nonseparable maps.

an edge to the vertices representing regions inside it (but not inside other holes inside it), and each region vertex is joined by an edge to the vertices representing holes in it. For a graph version of this concept, see Montanari [3].

III. Multigraphs

By a *multigraph*, we shall mean an ordered pair $\mathscr{G} = (S, E)$, where S is a finite set (its elements are called the *vertices* of $\mathscr{G}$) and E is an N-tuple of (unordered) pairs of elements of S (its terms are called the *edges* of $\mathscr{G}$).

For any $x \in S$, we denote by $E(x)$ the "subtuple" of E consisting of those pairs having x as a term [in other words: $E(x)$ consists of the edges at x]. Note that both in E and in $E(x)$, repetitions are allowed.

By an *m-multigraph*, we shall mean an ordered triple $\mathscr{G} = (S, E, C)$, where (S, E) is a multigraph, and $C = \{C_x \mid x \in S; C_x$ is a cyclic ordering of $E(x)\}$. Moreover, we shall assume that E contains no pair both of whose terms are the same. In other words, an m-multigraph is a multigraph with no "loops" and in which the edges at each vertex are cyclically ordered.

We shall now describe how one can associate an m-multigraph with any nonseparable map $\mathscr{M}$. Note first that any point on a region boundary in $\mathscr{M}$ must be on at least one other region boundary, since the inside and outside of a boundary curve cannot both contain points belonging to the same region. Thus, by part (b) of the definition of a map, as one traverses a boundary curve, one passes through a (finite) succession of nondegenerate arcs belonging to the boundaries of adjacent regions. (We call two regions *adjacent* or *neighbors* if their boundaries have a nonempty intersection.) Moreover, the interior of each of these arcs can only be on the boundary of *one* adjacent region, since the (open) arc is on only one of the original simple closed curves, and so can only be on the boundary of one region inside and one region outside this curve, Thus, traversing a boundary curve of a region uniquely determines a finite cyclically ordered sequence of neighboring regions (not necessarily all distinct). [Note that if we had allowed pairs of region boundaries to intersect in isolated points (i.e., arcs of zero length), it would have been more difficult to define an ordering of the adjacent regions, since many regions could share a single intersection point.]

Since $\mathscr{M}$ is nonseparable, any region $\rho \neq \rho_0$ of $\mathscr{M}$ has no holes, so that its boundary $B(\rho)$ is a single simple closed curve; while by (d), $B(\rho_0)$, too, is a single simple closed curve. Let us agree that the cyclic ordering of the neighbors of any $\rho \neq \rho_0$ will be that defined by traversing $B(\rho)$ counterclockwise, while that for ρ_0 will de defined by traversing $B(\rho_0)$ clockwise.† We can now define an m-multigraph $\mathscr{G}_{\mathscr{M}} = (S, E, C)$ as follows:

(a) $S = \mathscr{M}$ (i.e., we take the set of regions itself to be the set of vertices of $\mathscr{G}_{\mathscr{M}}$).

---

† This convention assures that, if c is any arc in which the boundaries of two regions σ, τ interesect, we traverse c in the opposite direction when we encounter it on $B(\sigma)$ than when we encounter it on $B(\tau)$.

(b) Let $A = \{a_1, \ldots, a_N\}$ be the set of arcs in which pairs of region boundaries intersect; then E is the N-tuple whose kth term is the pair of (distinct!) regions whose boundaries meet in the arc a_k.

(c) Each subtuple $E(x)$ is cyclically ordered as described just above.

An example of a nonseparable map and its associated multigraph is shown in Figure 2; here, the vertices of the multigraph are represented by dots and the edges by arcs joining the dots, while the cyclic orders are indicated (where necessary) by arrows.

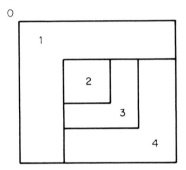

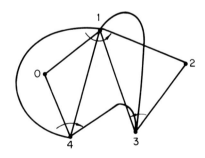

FIGURE 2. A nonseparable map and its multigraph.

IV. Splitting and Merging

Let $\mathcal{G} = (S, E, C)$ be an m-multigraph. We say that $\mathcal{G}' = (S', E', C')$ is a *split* of $\mathcal{G}$ if

(a) $S' = S - \{r\} \cup \{s, t\}$, where $r \in S$, and s, t are distinct elements not in S.

(b) $E' = E$ with the additional term (s, t), and with each term (r, x) replaced either by (s, x), (t, x), or both, according to the following criterion: Let $E(r)$ be the m-tuple $(r, r_1), \ldots, (r, r_m)$ (in that order, up to cyclic permutation); thus, if (r, x) is a term of E, we must have $x = r_k$ for some k, $1 \le k \le m$. Then there exist i, j, where $1 \le i \le j \le m$, such that (r, x) is replaced by (1) (s, x), if $i < k < j$; (2) (t, x), if $1 \le k < i$ or $j < k \le m$; (3) both, if $k = i$ or j and $i \ne j$, or if $k = i = j$ and $m = 1$; (4) (s, x) and two (t, x)'s, if $k = i = j$ and $m > 1$.†

(c) In each $E'(x)$ for which x is in S, the cyclic ordering corresponds to that of $E(x)$, i.e., each replacement term (or pair or triple of terms) has the same position as the term it replaces. When we replace $(r, x) = (r, r_k)$ by both (s, x) and (t, x), we put them in the order (s, x), (t, x) if $k = i$ or if $m = 1$; (t, x), (s, x) if $k = j$. In the case where $k = i = j$ and $m > 1$, the replacement terms are given the order (t, x), (s, x), (t, x). Finally, the cyclic ordering of $E'(s)$ is $(s, r_i), \ldots, (s, r_j), (s, t)$, while that of $E'(t)$ is $(t, r_j), \ldots, (t, r_m), (t, r_1), \ldots, (t, r_i), (t, s)$.

To see the geometrical significance of splitting, let $\mathcal{G} = \mathcal{G}_{\mathcal{M}}$ be the m-multigraph of the nonseparable map $\mathcal{M}$. Let $a_1, \ldots, a_m$ be (up to cyclic permutation) the arcs of $B(r)$ in which it meets the boundaries of $r_1, \ldots, r_m$. Imagine that a new arc b is drawn across r from the midpoint (or any interior point) of a_i to the midpoint of a_j, where $i \ne j$, splitting r into two regions s and t. It is easily verified that the arcs of $B(s)$ and $B(t)$ are, respectively, $a_{i1}, a_{i+1}, \ldots, a_{j1}, b$ and $a_{j2}, a_{j+1}, \ldots, a_m, a_1, \ldots, a_{i2}, b$, where a_{i1}, a_{i2} are the two halves of a_i and a_{j1}, a_{j2} are the two halves of a_j. Thus, the orders of the neighbors of s and t are $r_i, r_{i+1}, \ldots, r_j, t$ and $r_j, r_{j+1}, \ldots, r_m, r_1, \ldots, r_i$, s respectively. Moreover, if the region $x = r_k$ had r as a neighbor, it now has s as a neighbor if $i < k < j$; t if $1 \le k < i$ or $j < k \le m$; while in the neighbor sequences of r_i and r_j themselves, readily, r is replaced by s, t and by t, s, respectively. The discussion for the cases where $i = j$ is analogous. Evidently, splitting never creates a hole or a region that touches itself. Examples of splitting are shown in Figure 3.

We say that $\mathcal{G}^* = (S^*, E^*, C^*)$ is a *merge* of $\mathcal{G}$ if

(a) $S^* = S - \{u, v\} \cup \{w\}$, where w is not in S and (u, v) occurs exactly

---

† In other words: Vertex r is replaced by two vertices s, t, joined by an edge. Any x that was joined to r is now joined to s, if edge (r, x) was between i and j in the cyclic ordering of the edges at r; to t, if (r, x) was between j and i; to both, if (r, x) was the ith or jth edge (except that if $i = j$ and there was more than one edge at r, we join x to s by one edge and to t by *two* edges).

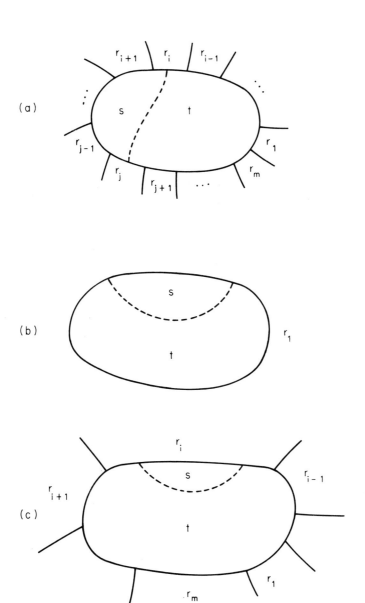

FIGURE 3. Examples of splitting. (a) $i \neq j$, $m > 1$; (b) $i = j$, $m = 1$; (c) $i = j$, $m > 1$.

once as a term of E, and where, if

$$E(u) = (u, v), (u, u_0), \ldots, (u, u_m)$$
$$E(v) = (v, u), (v, v_0), \ldots, (v, v_n)$$

(we require $m, n \geq 0$), then $u_0 = v_n$ and $u_m = v_0$.

(b) $E^* = E$ with the term (u, v) removed, and with each term (u, x) or (v, x) replaced by (w, x); except that the two terms $(u, u_0) = (u, v_n)$ and (v, v_n) are replaced by a single term (w, v_n), and the two terms (u, u_m) and $(v, v_0) = (v, u_m)$ are replaced by the single term (w, u_m). [If not all four of these terms are distinct, i.e., if $m = 0$ or $n = 0$, then these terms are all replaced by the single term $(w, u_m) = (w, v_n)$.]

(c) In each $E^*(x)$ for which x is in S, the cyclic ordering corresponds to that of $E(x)$, i.e., each replacement term occupies the same position as the term (or pair of terms) it replaces. The cyclic ordering of $E^*(w)$ is $(w, u_1), \ldots, (w, u_m), (w, v_1), \ldots, (w, v_n)$.

Note that any region of an m-multigraph can be split, and in many ways; while by contrast, only certain pairs of regions can be merged, and if so, only in one way.

The geometrical significance of merging is not difficult to see. In $\mathcal{M}$, let the regions u, v have only one boundary arc b in common. Readily, at each end point of this arc, u and v must have a common neighbor. If the arc b is deleted, u and v fuse into a single region w, whose neighbor sequence is obtained by combining those of u and v (deleting the repetitions of the common neighbors). Note that, if u and v have more than one boundary arc in common, and we delete just one such arc, the resulting region w touches itself; while if we delete two or more such arcs, it is not hard to see that the resulting w has holes. For this reason, we have defined merging only for pairs of regions that have exactly one common boundary arc (see Figure 4).

It follows readily from the definitions that *splitting and merging are inverses of one another*. Specifically, let $\mathcal{G}'$ be a split of $\mathcal{G}$ defined, as above, by splitting r into s and t, and let $(\mathcal{G}')^*$ be the merge of $\mathcal{G}'$ defined by merging s and t into r. [This is a legal merge, since, by definition of split, (s, t) does indeed occur exactly once in E', and

$$E'(s) = (s, t), (s, r_i), \ldots, (s, r_j)$$
$$E'(t) = (t, s), (t, r_j), \ldots, (t, r_i)$$

do indeed satisfy the conditions corresponding to $u_0 = v_n$, $u_m = v_0$.] Then it is straightforward to verify that $(\mathcal{G}')^* = \mathcal{G}$. Similarly, let $\mathcal{G}^*$ be the merge of $\mathcal{G}$

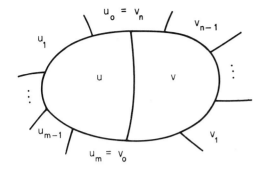

Figure 4. Examples of legal and illegal merging.

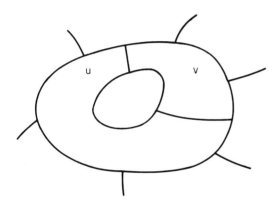

defined by merging u and v into w, and let $(\mathcal{G}^*)'$ be the split of $\mathcal{G}^*$ (splitting w into u and v) defined as follows: If

$$E(w) = (w, u_1), \ldots, (w, u_m), (w, v_1), \ldots, (w, v_n)$$
$$= (w, w_1), \ldots, (w, w_{m+n}),$$

we use the split for which $i = m, j = m + n$. Then, it is straightforward to verify that $(\mathcal{G}^*)' = \mathcal{G}$.

V. Map Multigraphs and Their Grammar

We call the m-multigraph $\mathcal{G}$ a *map multigraph* if there exists a nonseparable map $\mathcal{M}$ such that $\mathcal{G} = \mathcal{G}_{\mathcal{M}}$. As a very simple example, consider the *trivial multigraph* $\mathcal{G}_0 = (S_0, E_0, C_0)$, in which:

(a) S_0 has just two elements (call them a and b).

(b) E_0 has just one term (a, b).

(c) $E_0(a) = (a, b)$ and $E_0(b) = (b, a)$ have the trivial cyclic orderings.

Evidently, the trivial multigraph is a map multigraph; indeed, it is the multigraph of a map having just two regions a and b which are the inside and outside of a simple closed curve. Our goal in this section is to prove the following:

Theorem. $\mathscr{G}$ is a map multigraph if and only if it can be obtained from the trivial multigraph by a finite sequence of splits.

Since any trivial multigraph is a map multigraph, " if " follows immediately by induction from:

PROPOSITION 1. Any split of a map multigraph is a map multigraph.

Proof. Let $\mathscr{G}'$ be a split of $\mathscr{G}_\mathcal{M}$. By the remarks in Section IV about the geometrical significance of splitting, $\mathscr{G}'$ is the multigraph of a map $\mathcal{M}'$ obtained by "geometrically splitting" a region of $\mathcal{M}$; and $\mathcal{M}'$ is still nonseparable. ∎

[Similarly, it is easy to see that any (legal) merge of a map multigraph is a map multigraph.]

We next prove:

PROPOSITION 2. Let σ be any region of the nonseparable map $\mathcal{M}$; then there exists a region $\tau \in \mathcal{M}$ such that $B(\tau)$ has only one arc in common with $B(\sigma)$.

Proof. Let the sequence of neighbors of σ around $B(\sigma)$ be $\sigma_1, \ldots, \sigma_m$, whose boundaries meet $B(\sigma)$ in the sequence of arcs $a_1, \ldots, a_m$. Let $\sigma_i = \sigma_j$ have $|i - j|$ as small as possible (i.e., i and j as close together as possible in the cyclic order), where (say) $i < j$. We know that $j - i > 1$, since by definition of the neighbor sequence, consecutive neighbors are not the same; let $i < k < j$, and take $\tau = \sigma_k$. Since i and j were as close as possible, τ cannot occur twice among $\sigma_{i+1}, \ldots, \sigma_{j-1}$, and evidently τ is neither σ_i nor σ_j. On the other hand, suppose that we define a simple closed curve C by following $B(\sigma)$ through the arcs $a_{i+1}, \ldots, a_{j-1}$, and then continuing around $B(\sigma_i)$ until we reach the beginning of arc a_{i+1} again. It is not hard to see that $\tau = \sigma_k$ is inside C, but that none of the regions $\sigma_{j+1}, \ldots, \sigma_m, \sigma_1, \ldots, \sigma_{i-1}$ can be inside C. Thus, τ is not any of these regions, which proves that $B(\tau)$ has only one arc a_k in common with $B(\sigma)$. ∎

Note that Proposition 2 is not true for maps drawn on arbitrary surface. For example, consider the trivial map on a torus whose two regions are the upper and lower halves of the surface of the torus. This map is trivially non-separable, since it has only two regions; but its regions have two boundary curves in common, namely the "inside equator" and "outside equator" of the torus.

We can now prove the "only if" part of the theorem, using induction on the number n of regions in the map; if $n = 2$, the map evidently has a trivial multigraph. Suppose that "only if" holds for all maps having $n - 1$ regions (where $n \geq 3$), and let $\mathcal{M}$ have n regions. By Proposition 3, there exist two regions in $\mathcal{M}$ which can be "geometrically merged" (as described in Section IV) without creating holes; and, as indicated in Section IV, the multigraph $\mathcal{G}_{\mathcal{M}*}$ of the resulting map is a merge of $\mathcal{G}_{\mathcal{M}}$. Since the merged map has only $n - 1$ regions, by induction hypothesis, its multigraph $\mathcal{G}_{\mathcal{M}*}$ can be obtained from the trivial one by a succession of splits. But by the last part of Section IV, there exists a split $(\mathcal{G}_{\mathcal{M}*})'$ of $\mathcal{G}_{\mathcal{M}*}$ such that $(\mathcal{G}_{\mathcal{M}*})' = \mathcal{G}_{\mathcal{M}}$; thus, $\mathcal{G}_{\mathcal{M}}$ too can be obtained from the trivial multigraph by a succession of splits. ∎

If we rephrase our theorem, we can see that it describes an "m-multigraph grammar" whose language is exactly the set of map multigraphs. In fact, we can think of the splitting operation as defining a set of m-multigraph *rewriting rules*. Any split simply replaces one vertex ("r") of an m-multigraph by a pair of vertices ("s" and "t") joined by a single edge, and specifies which edges at r are to be transferred to s, which to t, and which to both (and which edge is to be replicated, in one case). In these terms, the theorem states that an m-multigraph $\mathcal{G}$ is "derivable," using these rewriting rules, from the trivial multigraph (which here plays the role of the initial graph of the grammar) if and only if $\mathcal{G}$ is a map multigraph. Conversely, since splitting and merging are inverse operations, we also see that $\mathcal{G}$ can be "parsed," by a sequence of merges (i.e., splits, in reverse), into the trivial multigraph if and only if $\mathcal{G}$ is a map multigraph.

ACKNOWLEDGMENTS

The support of the U.S. Atomic Energy Commission, under Contract AT-(40-1)-3662 with the University of Maryland, is gratefully acknowledged. This chapter is based on part of a Ph.D. dissertation now in preparation by J. P. Strong. The authors express their appreciation to John L. Pfaltz for many helpful and stimulating conversations.

REFERENCES

1. Miller, W. F., and Shaw, A. C., Linguistic methods in picture processing: A survey. *Proc. Fall Joint Comput. Conf., December 1968*, pp. 279–290.
2. Pfaltz, J. L., and Rosenfeld, A., Web grammars. *Proc. Internat. Joint Conf. on Artificial Intelligence, Washington, May 1969*, pp. 609–619.
3. Montanari, G. U., Separable graphs, planar graphs, and web grammars. *Inform. Control* **16**, 243–267 (May 1970).

A Software Engineering Approach to the Space Information System of the Future

T. P. Gorman

GORMAN COMPUTER SYSTEMS INC.
BOWIE, MARYLAND

I. The Space Information System of Today

A. THE SPACECRAFT

The space information system of today is a marvel of complex electronics. Orbiting high above the surface of the earth, an intricate assembly of scientific instruments makes observations on the environment through which it moves. Converted to currents or voltages or time periods, these observations are made into numbers by a special-purpose processor built to perform this feat, assembled, and, upon command from a data acquisition station below, transmitted to a waiting antenna.

B. THE GROUND STATION

At the station processing continues: More special-purpose equipment conditions the information streaming into the antenna and records it on magnetic tape. This operation demands the utmost from men and equipment. The signal is often so faint as to be nearly undetectable. The distances are great, the list of potential disruptions long, the need for precise timing necessarily acute, and the data volume enormous.

C. THE CONVERSION FACILITY

The tapes made at the data acquisition station find their way by land, sea, and air to a central facility for conversion to computer-acceptable digital tape. Now a third array of delicate, sophisticated electronic equipment does more careful exacting processing. All the problems collected by the data in their long journey from space must find identification here, and, if possible, correction as well.

D. The Quality Assurance Facility

These digital tapes are handled on a large-scale, general-purpose multi-processing computer. Involved calculations are performed to evaluate the quality of the data, to edit out or flag what can be recognized as noise, and to separate all the data by experiment onto more digital tapes for shipment to the waiting experimenter.

E. The Analysis Facility

Upon receipt of his data tapes, the experimenter's computing equipment begins the process of analysis, comparison, and interpretation of the data. Every datum has already been subjected to four separate processes, each one performed by unique, complex, and sophisticated electronic equipment, and only now, at the fifth and final step, is the real work of screening and inference under way.

II. Problems of the Current System

A. Delay of Inference

This system has worked surprisingly well during the first decade of the space age. But it has its drawbacks. The foremost of these is the postponement of inference to the last step of the process. This means a great many data which turn out to be of little importance have received a grossly uneconomical share of all the expensive steps preceding.

B. Fixed Data Collection Strategies

In addition there is not sufficient flexibility in the system to permit substantial changes in the overall processing strategy once it has been set in motion. This imposes the sometimes impossible burden on the space scientist or space engineer of anticipating his every requirement and objective from the very outset of his research effort.

C. Varying Reliability

Finally, since each spacecraft is a unique device used for one purpose one time, it is very difficult to improve reliability by experience. The last of a long series of very similar spacecraft is of course more likely to succeed than the first. But more standard parts and interchangeable units would mean much less work and worry.

These three flaws in today's space information system couple with each other to produce higher than desirable risks of overall mission failure.

III. The Space Information System of Tomorrow

A. In Space

The space information system of tomorrow will require hardware–software processors at all its major operating points. A spaceborne hardware–software processor will be needed to examine the space environment adaptively for events of relevance and significance.

B. At the Station

On the ground, a station hardware–software processor will be required for easy adjustment to changing information rates, signal characteristics, and data formats, not to mention rapid switching from spacecraft to spacecraft. The data will ordinarily be digitized here too and transmitted rather than shipped to a central facility.

C. At the Archive

At the central facility, where in the past the activities were data conversion and quality assurance, a data archive will be needed. This data archive will be operated by a hardware–software processor capable of editing, evaluating, and filing masses of data for quick future reference. All data taken will be available at different retrieval times under the automatic control of a usage-dependent algorithm.

D. At the Information Center

An information center will be needed at the central facility as well. This will be a massive hardware–software information "engine" capable of remotely-directed, largely self-organizing study of any or all of the archived data obtained in support of any research objective of any participant on any flight.

This processor must be capable of displaying these data in conceptually meaningful forms on selected hardware–software processors at locations possibly quite remote from the information center. It must also be capable of producing on demand not only the data to be studied but also programs to be executed on other processors in support of such study.

E. At the Experimenter's Laboratory

The final analysis of the data can be expected still to take place at the site of the space experimenter's hardware–software processor. There, under his supervision, software designed and developed in part at the central facility will be augmented, altered, and executed on the main volume of his data. The more sophisticated experimenter will probably gradually accumulate on his processor the text to be published as it is written, side by side with the results of the large-scale analysis as they are obtained.

IV. Problems of Tomorrow's System

It seems somehow ill-mannered and crude to speak of the problems expected with a system of the future. The general assumption always is that the system to be is a sink for today's problems but not a source for tomorrow's. It might help to remember that today's problem-plagued relic was once someone's bright hope for the future.

A. Delay of Readiness

In the first place the system whatever it is will not be ready for use on schedule. Most of the hardware will be in place and working on time. Most of the software will not. The space information system will be forced to evolve through several unplanned jury-rigged improvisations on the way to tomorrow's target. Many careers and corporate images will be damaged. Most unfortunate of all the sequence of desperate improvisations will distort the effort until what is actually achieved will be a caricature of what was planned.

B. Incomprehensibility

When the inevitable caricature of tomorrow's system has been thrust into operational use, a second era of troubles will begin. The innards of the system will have become, for all practical purposes, incomprehensible. No one will be able to speak with authority on how it works or what to do to effect a required change. All alterations will be made using the crude and ancient "cut and try" strategy. The most awkward and incongruous procedures, once adopted, will be left unchanged out of ignorant fear to make even trivial improvements in tomorrow's system. New and perhaps more numerous inflexibilities will replace the old.

C. UNCERTAIN PERFORMANCE

Tomorrow's system will bring its uncertain performance home to the entire community of users. This uncertainty will be made all the more frustrating because it will seem to admit of no correcting. Some will say there are not enough people to study the system; others will say that it was designed, implemented, or operated improperly; yet others will even say it was a foolish idea to start with. But no one will be able to make it work any better in time to make any real difference to any user.

These troubles can be predicted so confidently because they have appeared so faithfully in each of three succeeding generations of computers.

V. An Informal Description of Software Engineering

A. DEFINITION BY ANALOGY

Before I describe what I consider to be a software engineering approach to this challenge I will briefly describe what I mean by the words "software engineer."

Engineering is the profession that puts power and materials to work for man. It is more formally the application of knowledge of mathematical and physical sciences acquired by special education, training, and experience to the planning, design, and supervision of construction of public and private utilities, works, projects, structures, buildings, machines, electrical systems, etc. and I will add software systems.

B. BOUNDARIES OF THIS SPECIALIZED BRANCH

I will further characterize software engineering by describing it as the discipline which starts with the existence of a completed computing machine and ends with the conversion of that machine to a running, problem-solving processor. The effort that creates the computing machine lies outside this field, as does the effort that applies the problem-solving processor to some application in physics, mathematics, business, or indeed some other branch of engineering.

The software engineer with wisdom and art designs and directs the development of problem-solving processors and applies the principles of logic, mathematics, and systems theory to their production and modification. He demands from equipment technology firm high standards in reliability, efficiency, and utility in much the same way as the civil engineer demands the best from construction materials, equipment, and techniques. He makes no special use himself of a processor once he has produced it and it works, any more than an electrical engineer might make special use of a transmitter he produces.

VI. A Software Engineering Approach
to the Space Information System

Now to return to the task of designing the space information system of the future to minimize the three problems foreseen for it already: delay of readiness, incomprehensibility, and uncertain performance. I will assume these problems are caused not by the nature of things but by some factor subject to change, and will attempt to shed some light on what software engineering is by describing a software engineer's approach to the space information system of tomorrow.

The software engineer, because he is an engineer, aims to put power and materials to work for man. In this case he will be striving to put the power of computers to work for America's space effort. He will devise and submit ultimate design objectives for approval. He will consider several design approaches. He will recommend one with justification and stand ready to carry out his recommendation. He begins with comprehensive design objectives.

A. COMPREHENSIVE DESIGN OBJECTIVES

Clearly, tomorrow's space information system will involve not one hardware–software processor but several. As a matter of fact, the entire data handling system from spacecraft to published report will be evolving to a form at once more powerful and more complex. But some underlying substrate of simplicity must be prepared to support the coming complexity. Otherwise, it is highly likely that the real power of the complete system will never be realized.

Indeed, maximum use of the real capabilities of this system will depend heavily on the ease with which the space scientist and system engineer can manipulate and retrieve data with it. This implies the need for great programming convenience in each processor because it is by rapid programming and reprogramming that it can be "tuned" to yield the most meaningful transformation of the data under processing.

The immediate requirement is simply four processors: one to serve as a spaceborne unit, one to serve as a station controller, one as a data archivist, and one as a data analyst. But each must be simple enough to be mastered by a large number of people with varying backgrounds and different objectives, each must be easy to use, and all must work together.

B. THREE DESIGN APPROACHES

1. *A Family of Standard Processors*

The software engineer might consider first the design approach of using a family of off-the-shelf processors.

The seemingly endless complication which has attached itself to software development has been caused in part by an inexorable progression of hardware designs, each requiring a large amount of software support, each exerting a powerful influence on software configurations. It seems to follow that if one hardware design could be selected and held fixed, total system development effort could be substantially reduced.

This reasoning leads to the possibility of selecting an off-the-shelf hardware family for which the largest possible volume of needed software has already been produced and modifying specific family members for use at specific points in the space information system. There are a number of hardware manufacturer's product lines which lend themselves to this treatment.

Choice of a manufacturer would be based on the amount of software available as well as the appropriateness of this software to the space application.

This design approach is based on some assumptions: The main one is that there is really little to choose between machines so far as programming efficiency is concerned, and second, that this situation is deeply rooted in the nature of things.

2. *A Collection of Special-Purpose Processors*

A software engineer might take a different approach, starting as seems to be customary in hardware design, with the four problems to be handled. The best of today's electronic technology would be measured against each problem. A machine would be selected to simplify each application. Each memory would be organized in a way largely determined by the requirements of the latest memory devices and each processor selected to provide maximum efficiency in performing its own assignment.

Emerging from this process would be a hardware complex well suited to deal with all the predictable elements of the actual problems with which it will have to cope. Because of the special-purpose nature of the design however, it is unlikely that any quantity of prewritten programs would be at hand, and a large software effort would be needed.

Underlying this approach is the assumption that the most significant factor in the handling of the space information system problem is the character of the hardware. This approach tends to regard the production of needed software as a problem of less significance.

3. *A Family of Convenience Processors*

The software engineer might take yet a third approach. A single machine design might be selected with a special emphasis on the support of software development. This design would necessarily take into account the real hardware restrictions which apply to all equipment qualified for space information system use. It would, however, not be dominated by these, but rather by the single requirement that it be easy to program.

The type of system produced by this approach would lend itself not so much to the problem at hand as to the problem of adaptation to successive space problems yet to be encountered. Hardware or software "features," no matter how "powerful" for the application at hand, would count for nothing if they were likely to be hard to grasp or to be used infrequently. On the other hand, hardware or software capacities, no matter how time-consuming or memory-demanding to execute, would count for everything if only they contributed substantially to programming efficiency.

This approach assumes that the generation of the software is a computer problem at least as significant as the operation of the hardware. It also assumes that the speed with which software can be developed is largely determined by the suitability of the hardware for this purpose.

C. SELECTION OF APPROACH AND RATIONALE

The software engineer, I believe, would make and defend his choice among design approaches along the following lines.

It is now more than twenty years since the introduction of digital computers to the American technological scene. The machines of today are vastly different from their counterparts of the early fifties. Today's machines are far faster, much more reliable, much more easily built, and much cheaper per calculation than their forebearers.

In one respect, however, they have changed but little. They are about as difficult to program today as they ever were. All third generation manufacturers for instance, have found the problem of software development to be both acutely embarrassing and remarkably resistant to corrective pressures.

This clearly implies that the hardware of today runs so rapidly and is so simple to build only at the cost of becoming far too difficult to apply when built. It implies that the work of the hardware engineer has been organized and simplified to the point where it increases intolerably the work of the software engineer. It means that what is needed now is hardware which is a lot easier to program even, if necessary, because it is a little more difficult to build.

Following this reasoning the software engineer would reject the use of current off-the-shelf hardware. He would find the attractiveness of ready-made and available software more than overcome by the realization that the same old difficulties will be encountered in the production of all further software. He also would reject ad hoc, special-purpose hardware for the same reason. He would know better than to believe that any new design not especially aimed at simplifying the software development process would escape the problems which have plagued the large-scale third generation computer manufacturers.

The software engineer would advance a design approach based on the selection of hardware specifically designed to be simple and straightforward to program, even if this choice meant increased cost due to increased complexity in its construction or decreased speed in its execution of standard algorithms.

VII. Prospects for Software Engineering in Space and Elsewhere

Let it be noted here that such a recommendation made by anyone would stand small chance of adoption today. But software engineering must look to the future even if only to hope that it will be somehow different from the present. Would-be software engineers must approach the future in certain specific ways. They must believe that it will not be long before the consensus of computer users will accept the view that all their real computing needs can be reduced to the need to develop programs rapidly and reliably with only secondary concern for running speeds. They must have confidence that hardware which is easy to program can and will be produced to achieve any level of speed, power, and reliability for which a real requirement can be demonstrated.

A. Signs of the Times

In the world of computer technology these are turbulent times. Computers are successfully fomenting a world-wide revolution of methods and techniques. But all is far from well. Investment analysts have warned their clients that, while today it is next to impossible to buy a bad piece of computer hardware, it is still a rare company that does not run into some major programming problem. The melancholy fact is that the cost of executing a checked-out computer instruction has decreased to one-tenth of one percent of what it was in 1953, but the cost of producing such a checked-out instruction has more than tripled. A NASA subcommittee on information and data processing has complained that operational problems are magnified because no single manufacturer has complete systems responsibility for interfacing computer hardware, communications equipment, terminal devices, and system software.

B. PROGRAMMING AND THE ECONOMY OF WASTE

We are all familiar with a reproach that reads "Software historically has been about three years behind hardware." Suppose we restate that observation to read "Hardware has historically been about three years ahead of software." Suppose we now ask ourselves why should hardware be three years ahead?

One answer seems obvious. Software cannot be produced instantly and, since software depends on hardware characteristics, it must lag behind somewhat; it is only a question of how much. Three years does not seem excessive when compared with the lag between the development of a new kind of memory or circuit and its appearance in a computer. What seems to be needed is more hard work, better communication, clearer documentation, more and better trained programmers, wiser management, and so on. These obvious answers represent the accepted wisdom which has guided our largely fruitless efforts for the last twenty years or so.

Is this situation all that rooted in the nature of things? Why does software have to depend on hardware characteristics? Between IBM's 709, 7090, 7094, and 7094 mod 2, there were no significant software changes needed while the hardware components were changed enough to increase the speed of execution of such software by a factor of nine.

Hardware changes demand software changes because hardware manufacturers have decided it shall be so, because hardware engineers dabble in fields proper to software, because programmers would rather play with a new gadget than work with a familiar tool; but most of all because an upheaval like the introduction of a wholly different and new line of hardware which demands a whole reworking of every useful program *expands the market* for everything associated with computers. The so-called generations of computing machines are the cultural equivalent of the annual automobile model changes, the Paris fashion showings, the "new improved" household detergents.

Computing technology, as young as it is, has already achieved prominent status in the economy of waste which everywhere enriches and impoverishes modern life. Machines and programs, representing enormous investments of man-hours are scrapped and replaced, often at greater than original cost whenever the market is sold a new model.

This is one way to keep us all busy, but it is also the source of a species of pollution in the computing environment. This pollution takes the form of programs which do not quite work. It drives up the cost of what we buy or the time it takes to get what we want. It slows up our mails, our trains, and planes. It lengthens the queues we stand in. It will finally make our lives a nightmare of frustration if it cannot be controlled.

C. TOWARD AN ECONOMY OF CONSERVATION
WITH SOFTWARE ENGINEERING

Some years ago I proposed that we discard the name programmer in favor of the more proper software engineer. I said that this latter term describes the work the true programmer has always done—put the power of the finished computer hardware to work for mankind.

I favored the term software engineer then over programmer for other reasons as well. I believed it suggested a line of growth for software professionals and enhanced the possibility of a more productive division of labor between the hardware programmers we call engineers and the software engineers we call programmers who jointly produce today's computer systems.

These reasons still persuade me. I believe now that there is an even more important cause to be served by the creation of this new branch of engineering: The necessary cause of conservation. People called programmers are struggling now for the third time to make a generation of computer hardware finally useful. It is essential that these programmers be professionalized and organized to counterbalance the present dominance of marketing and electronic gadgetry over the computer field.

How would replacing the name programmer by software engineer help do this? In the first place not everyone called a programmer would be called a software engineer. There is a large mass of computer users properly called programmers because they write programs. But, since their aim is to put the computer to work for themselves in their pursuit of some extraneous but computer-dependent objective, they would not properly be called software engineers.

This distinction is not without its value: It should produce wiser counsel to management. The words of software engineers should carry an authority on computer subjects that the words of today's programmers of widely different levels of knowledge and experience can never have.

The main value to be achieved however by substitution of "software engineer" for "programmer" where appropriate would be the evocation of all that the creation of a branch of engineering implies: special academic preparation of those who work in the field, standards of quality and performance to guide them, a code of ethics to regulate professional conduct. The Institute of Software Engineers could be expected to oppose vociferously the destructive upheavals to which we have become so accustomed in the computer field. The software engineer would be enthusiastic about applying the fruits of computer science to the software field and about contributing to computer science software problems to be studied. The software engineer would free his hardware colleagues from the burden of speculating and deciding on things like byte sizes, order codes, and register configurations, and allow him to concentrate on essentially hardware questions like circuit speed, component size, system reliability, etc.

Most important, the software engineer's professional interests would coincide clearly with the neglected public interest in computing today. He would favor and lobby for steady, evolutionary change in hardware. He would oppose and frequently prevent the junking of the state of the art to boost sales.

I believe the public good demands that we move away from the present economy of waste in computing toward an economy of conservation. I favor the creation of a specialized branch of engineering which I have called software engineering as a step in that direction.

An Efficient Program for Real-Time Assignment of Jobs in a Hybrid Computer Network

I. T. Frisch

NETWORK ANALYSIS CORPORATION
GLEN COVE, NEW YORK

and

M. Malek-Zavarei†

UNIVERSITY OF CALIFORNIA
BERKELEY, CALIFORNIA

I. Introduction

From its infancy, the digital computer has been a boon to combinatorialists. For almost as long, combinatorics has, in turn, played a vital role in the optimization of both digital and analog computer usage [1]; this role has become even more important with the advent of time-shared computer networks [2–4]. One of the more recently developed areas of combinatorics deals with flows in networks. The purpose of this chapter is to apply some results of current research in network flows to a difficult problem arising in the study of hybrid computer networks.

We consider a network of digital and analog computers which are to participate in the simulation of control of some large-scale system such as a traffic network. The computers are in different geographic locations connected by data links. Data is to be fed into digital computers; the output of the digital computers is to be processed by analog computers, and the output returned to the users. For example, the digital computers might be controlling various analog simulations of traffic flow.

It is assumed that the speed of all the digital computers is the same although their memory capacities may differ radically. Users present inputs of data and instructions to the network (possibly after waiting on queues), which are to be processed by any of the digital computers. It is assumed that all jobs require

† Present affiliation: Bell Telephone Laboratories, Inc., Holmdel, New Jersey.

the same amount of digital computing time and that these computing times are long compared to the transmission times of commands over the links. However, different jobs may require significantly different amounts of computer memory. These are reasonable assumptions for a weakly interactive time-shared system in which jobs have already been subdivided into packets with identical, but fairly long computing times [4]. Because of interface problems and data requirements at the analog computers, the output of each digital computer is fed only to certain analog computers. Furthermore, at any time the outputs of different digital computers may require different numbers of amplifiers in a given analog computer. In general, these need not be correlated with memory requirements in the digital computers [5]. We consider the problem of formulating an efficient real-time computer program to assign packets to computers so as to maximize the number of packets handled by the computers at any time.

II. Graph-Theoretic Model

We model the computer network by a graph $G = (N, A)$, where N is a set of points, called nodes, and A is a set of directed lines, called arcs, joining the nodes. Let $\alpha(v_i)$ be the set of nodes to which an arc is directed from a node v_i, and $\beta(v_i)$ the set of nodes from which an arc is directed to v_i. Suppose there are jobs with k different memory requirements to be fed to the digital computers. There are n digital computers with finite memory capacities $c_1, \ldots, c_n$ and there are p analog computers, with the number of amplifiers per computer being $a_1, \ldots, a_p$. Then G has the appearance shown in Figure 1. The nodes in $\mathcal{M}$ labeled $v_{m_1}, \ldots, v_{m_k}$ represent the messages with memory requirements $m_1, \ldots, m_k$, respectively. The nodes in $\mathcal{C}$ represent digital computers and the nodes in $\mathcal{A}$ represent analog computers. We also add a source node v_s and a terminal node v_t.

We represent an arc by listing the variable associated with its initial node and the variable associated with its terminal node. The arcs in G are then defined as follows:

$(s, m_i) \in A$ for $i = i, \ldots, k$;

$(m_i, c_j) \in A$ if $m_i \leq c_j$;

$(c_j, a_l) \in A$ if the analog computer corresponding to a_l can handle output from the digital computers corresponding to c_j;

$(a_l, t) \in A$ for $l = 1, \ldots, p$.

We assign weights to the arcs as follows: $w(s, m_i) = Q_i$, the number of packets requiring m_i units of memory; $w(c_j, a_l) = r_{j,l}$ the number of amplifiers required from analog computer a_l to process an output from digital computer c_j. All other arcs are assumed to have infinite weights.

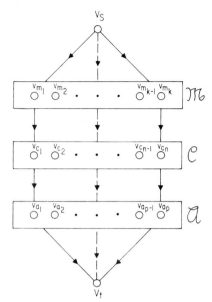

FIGURE 1. Graph representing a hybrid computer network.

Finally, we assign a nonnegative integer flow $f(i, j)$ to each arc (i, j). We can then formulate our original problems as the following constrained flow problem:

Problem 0: Maximize

$$v \triangleq \sum_{i=1}^{k} f(s, m_i)$$

subject to

$$\sum_{v_y \in \alpha(v_x)} f(x, y) - \sum_{v_y \in \beta(v_x)} f(y, x) = \begin{cases} v & \text{if } v_x = v_s \\ 0 & \text{if } v_x \neq v_s, v_t \\ -v & \text{if } v_x = v_t, \end{cases} \tag{1}$$

$$f(s, m_i) \leq Q_i \quad \text{for } i = 1, \ldots, k, \tag{2}$$

$$\sum_{(m_i, c_j) \in A} f(m_i, c_j) m_i \leq c_j \quad \text{for } j = 1, \ldots, n, \tag{3}$$

$$\sum_{(c_j, a_l) \in A} f(c_j, a_l) r_{j,l} \leq a_l \quad \text{for } l = 1, \ldots, p. \tag{4}$$

If constraints (3) and (4) are eliminated, Problem 0 reduces to a standard flow maximization [6]. If we neglect only constraint (4), then the problem reduces to determining flows in networks with gains, and has been treated by

Iri *et al.* [7] as reported by Berge and Ghouila-Houri [8]. The complete problem remained untreated until the recent results achieved by the present authors [9]. The remainder of this chapter gives a tutorial description of these results, and several comments on their computational feasibility.

III. Maximum Flows and Minimum-Cost Flows

In order to study the solution of Problem 0, we may remove some of the restrictions inherent in the constraints (1)–(4). In particular, there is no need to restrict the graph to have the form shown in Figure 1. Thus, we consider the following more general problem for a graph $G = (N, A)$, where $N = \{v_1, \ldots, v_n\}$ and A is arbitrary. We isolate one node, v_s, as a source and another, v_t, as a terminal.

Problem 1: Maximize

$$v = \sum_{v_i \in \alpha(v_s)} f(s, i)$$

subject to

$$\sum_{v_y \in \alpha(v_x)} f(x, y) - \sum_{v_y \in \beta(v_x)} f(y, x) = \begin{cases} v & \text{if } v_x = v_s \\ 0 & \text{if } v_x \neq v_s, v_t \\ -v & \text{if } v_x = v_t, \end{cases} \tag{1'}$$

$$0 \leq f(x, y) \leq U(x, y) \qquad \text{for all } (x, y) \in A, \tag{2'}$$

$$\sum_{v_x \in \beta(v_y)} f(x, y) \cdot k(x, y) \leq U(v_y) \qquad \text{for all } v_y \in \hat{N} \subseteq N, \tag{3'}$$

where $U(x, y)$, $U(v_y)$, and $k(x, y)$ are all greater than zero and $\hat{N}$ is a given subset of N.

Constraints (1') and (1) are identical; (2') is a capacity constraint which includes (2); and (3') is a linear constraint which includes (3) and (4).

Since $k(i, j) > 0$ for all (i, j), we can scale the constraints in (3') and order the $k(i, j)$ so that for each j

$$k(i_1, j) \leq 1 \leq k(i_2, j) \leq \cdots \leq k(i_{\gamma_j}, j),$$

where γ_j is the number of elements in $\beta(v_j)$. Further, let

$$A_j = \{(i, j) \mid v_j \in \hat{N} \quad \text{and} \quad (i, j) \in A\}$$

and

$$\hat{A} = \bigcup_{v_j \in \hat{N}} A_j.$$

We will evolve an approach to Problem 1 in three steps. We first consider the solution to Problem 1 with constraint (3') omitted. We then return to a simplified version of (3'). Finally we consider the solution to Problem 1 with all constraints included.

If we drop constraint (3'), then we simply wish to maximize the flow through a graph with capacitated arcs and flow conserved at the nodes.

Define an i_1–i_w path to be a sequence of distinct nodes

$$v_{i_1}, v_{i_2}, \ldots, v_{i_{w-1}}, v_{i_w}$$

and distinct arcs, such that, for all j in the range $2 \leq j \leq w$, either (i_j, i_{j-1}) or (i_{j-1}, i_j) is in the sequence.

Arcs of the form (i_j, i_{j-1}) are called backward arcs and arcs of the form (i_{j-1}, i_j) are called forward arcs.

Flow is said to be increased by an integer $\varepsilon > 0$ along an s–t path if, for every forward arc in the path, flow is increased by ε and, for every backward arc, flow is decreased by ε. An s–t path along which flow can be increased by an $\varepsilon > 0$, such that the resulting flow pattern still satisfies (2'), is said to be an ε augmentation path. The following algorithm can be used to find a maximum value of v, that is, a maximum flow from v_s to v_t [6].

Maximum Flow Algorithm. Repeat the following operation as often as possible: Increase the flow along an ε augmentation path by ε.

As an illustration of the use of the maximum flow algorithm, consider the graph in Figure 2. The integers associated with the arcs represent the arc capacities $U(x, y)$. We increase the flow along the paths $v_s(s, 1)v_1(1, 2)v_2(2, t)v_t$ by one unit, resulting in the flow pattern shown in Figure 3. The only remaining ε augmentation path is $v_s(s, 2)v_2(1, 2)v_1(1, t)v_t$. Note that $(1, 2)$ is a backward arc in the path. After increasing the flow along this path, the resulting maximum flow pattern is shown in Figure 4. Note that this maximum flow could also have been attained if our first selection had been the path $v_s(s, 1)v_1(1, t)v_t$. However, the algorithm is guaranteed to converge regardless

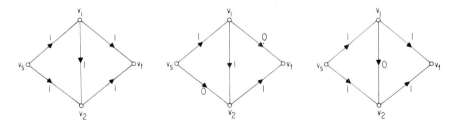

FIGURE 2. Left: Graph with arc capacities.

FIGURE 3. Center: Flow increase along an ε augmentation path.

FIGURE 4. Far right: Maximum flow pattern.

of which paths are actually chosen. As to whether this procedure is computationally efficient, this depends upon how easy it is to identify ε augmentation paths. As it happens, there are extremely efficient methods for locating these paths and therefore the suggested algorithm becomes the most efficient algorithm known for the solution of the maximum flow problem. A maximum flow can be found in a graph with several hundred nodes in less than a second and the computation time is observed to increase linearly with the number of nodes.

An interesting aspect of the maximum flow algorithm is that with a simple conceptual modification it yields an algorithm that gives a maximum flow at "minimum cost," that is, it yields a solution to Problem 2 below:

Problem 2: Maximize:

$$\sum_{v_i \in \alpha(v_s)} f(s, i) \triangleq v$$

subject to

$$\sum_{v_y \in \alpha(v_x)} f(x, y) - \sum_{v_y \in \beta(v_x)} f(y, x) = \begin{cases} v & \text{if} \quad v_x = v_s \\ 0 & \text{if} \quad v_x \neq v_s, v_t \\ -v & \text{if} \quad v_x = v_t, \end{cases} \tag{1'}$$

$$0 \le f(x, y) \le U(x, y) \qquad \text{for} \quad (x, y) \in A, \tag{2'}$$

$$\text{For the maximum value of} \quad v, \sum_{(x,y)\in A} f(x, y) \cdot c(x, y) \quad \text{is minimized} \tag{3''}$$

Problem 2 differs from Problem 1 in that (3′) is replaced by the constraint that a cost function is minimized. $c(x, y)$ is a constant cost per unit of flow in arc (x, y).

We define the cost $h(x, y)$ of an arc (x, y) relative to a given s–t path Π, or simply the "relative cost" of an arc, as follows:

(a) $h(x, y) = c(x, y)$ if (x, y) is a forward arc in the path and $f(x, y) < U(x, y)$.

(b) $h(x, y) = \infty$ if (x, y) is a forward arc in the path and $f(x, y) = U(x, y)$.

(c) $h(x, y) = -c(x, y)$ if (x, y) is a backward arc in the path and $f(x, y) > 0$.

(d) $h(x, y) = \infty$ if (x, y) is a backward arc in the path and $f(x, y) = 0$.

The cost of increasing the flow along an ε augmentation path Π is then

$$h(\Pi) \triangleq \sum_{(x,y)\,\text{in}\,\Pi} h(x, y),$$

where $h(\Pi)$ is called the cost of path Π.

To solve Problem 2, we can then use the following algorithm [10].

Minimum-Cost Flow Algorithm. Repeat the following operation as often as possible: Increase the flow by ε along the lowest-cost ε augmentation path.

Since there are efficient algorithms to find lowest-cost paths, the minimum-cost flow algorithm is itself an effective algorithm. We therefore seek to convert Problem 1 to Problem 2.

IV. Formulation of Computer Problem as a Minimum-Cost Flow Problem

We make the trivial observation that both Problems 1 and 2 can be modified as follows. Add a dummy source node $v_{s'}$ and a dummy terminal node $v_{t'}$. Next, add arcs (s', s) and (t, t') with infinite capacities. The constraints in Problems 1 and 2 are unchanged. However, the objective can be stated as maximizing $f(s', s)$, rather than v. Problem 2 can then be reformulated so that a solution of Problem 3 below will yield a solution to Problem 1:

Problem 3: Maximize $f(s', s)$ subject to

$$\sum_{v_y \in \alpha(v_x)} f(x, y) - \sum_{v_y \in \beta(v_x)} f(y, x) = 0 \qquad \text{for} \quad v_x \in N \qquad (1'')$$

$$0 \le f(x, y) \le U(x, y) \qquad \text{for} \quad (x, y) \in A. \qquad (2')$$

For the maximum value of $f(s', s)$,

$$-f(s', s) + \sum_{v_y \in \hat{N}} \lambda_y \sum_{v_x \in \beta(v_y)} k(x, y) \cdot f(x, y) \qquad (3''')$$

is minimized, where $\lambda_j \ge 0$ for all j.

The constraint set corresponding to $(1'')$ and $(2')$ is convex. Since $U(x, y)$ is finite for all (x, y), $-f(s', s)$ is bounded from below. Using these facts, the following theorem can be proved [9, 11]:

Theorem 1. If λ has nonnegative components and there is a set of $\bar{f}(x, y)$ solving Problem 3 such that

$$\lambda_y(U(v_y) - \sum_{v_x \in \beta(v_y)} k(x, y) \cdot \bar{f}(x, y)) = 0 \qquad \text{for} \quad v_y \in \hat{N} \qquad (5)$$

and

$$\sum_{v_x \in \beta(v_y)} k(x, y) \cdot \bar{f}(x, y) \le U(v_y) \qquad \text{for} \quad v_y \in N, \qquad (6)$$

then $\bar{f}(x, y)$ is a solution to Problem 1. Furthermore, such a λ exists.

That is, there is a solution of Problem 3 which gives a solution of Problem 1. But, for a given value of λ, Problem 3 is in the form of Problem 2, which is solvable by the minimum-cost flow algorithm. In particular, arc (s', s) has cost -1, the arcs in $\hat{A}$ have cost $\lambda_y k(x, y)$, and all other arcs have zero cost.

V. Solution

The only remaining difficulty therefore is in finding the proper vector λ, which essentially plays the role of Lagrange multipliers [12].

One obvious simplification is presented in Lemma 1.

Lemma 1. If, in Problem 1 for some $v_y \in \hat{N}$

$$\sum_{v_x \in \beta(v_y)} k(x, y)U(x, y) \leq U(v_y),$$

then we can set $\lambda_y = 0$ in Problem 3.

In order to actually order the lambdas, we can use the following theorem:

Theorem 2. Suppose $\bar{f}(x, y)$ and $\hat{f}(x, y)$ are solutions to Problem 3 for $\lambda = \bar{\lambda}$ and $\lambda = \hat{\lambda}$, respectively. If, for $j \neq y$,

$$\sum_{v_x \in \beta(v_y)} k(x, y) \cdot \bar{f}(x, y) = \sum_{v_x \in \beta(v_y)} k(x, y) \cdot \hat{f}(x, y) \tag{7}$$

and

$$\sum_{v_i \in \beta(v_j)} k(i, j) \cdot \bar{f}(i, j) < \sum_{v_i \in \beta(v_j)} k(i, j) \cdot \hat{f}(i, j), \tag{8}$$

then

$$\hat{\lambda}_j \leq \bar{\lambda}_j. \tag{9}$$

For Problem 2, this theorem can be interpreted as follows: If, for some $\lambda_j > 0$,

$$\sum_{v_i \in \beta(v_j)} k(i, j)f(i, j) < U(v_j), \tag{10}$$

then flow in the arcs A_j may be increased. Hence, λ_j must be decreased so the costs of the arcs in A_j will decrease and more flow can be allowed in them.

Hence, for the first trial, let $\lambda_j = \alpha$ for all $v_j \in \hat{N}$ and solve Problem 3. Since all λ_j are equal, the costs of the arcs in A_j can be assumed to be $k(i, j)$. Suppose in the solution the constraints for $v_j \in N_J$ become tight and the constraints for $v_j \in \bar{N}_J$ become loose, where $N_J \cup \bar{N}_J = \hat{N}$. Then, if $N_J = \varnothing$, i.e., if all the constraints are loose, let $\alpha = 0$. If $\bar{N}_J = \varnothing$, i.e., if all the constraints are tight, let $\alpha = 1$. Note that in both these cases (5) and (6) are satisfied. Hence, the solution is optimal. If $N_J \neq \emptyset$ and $\bar{N}_J \neq \emptyset$, then, by Theorem 2, λ_j for $v_j \in \bar{N}_J$ must be decreased. Let $\lambda_j = 1$ for $v_j \in N_J$ and $0 < \lambda_j < 1$ for $v_j \in \bar{N}_J$ and solve again. If still some constraints remain loose in the solution, decrease λ_j for those to zero (i.e., ignore those constraints) and solve again. If, in the new solution, all these constraints remain feasible and the rest are tight, then (5) and (6) are satisfied and the solution is optimal. Otherwise, λ_j must be increased for the constraints that are violated and decreased for those that are loose. Before illustrating the procedure with an example, we can point out one further simplification in the following theorem.

Theorem 3. In solving Problem 2 by using the minimum-cost flow algorithm, an arc in the set A is used in an ε augmentation path only if all ε augmentation paths using arcs only in $A - \hat{A}$ have already been used.

The theorem follows simply from the fact that all arcs in $A - \hat{A}$ have zero cost.

From Theorem 3, it is clear that, to solve Problem 1, one can first discard the arcs in the set A and find all the possible augmentation paths in the resulting partial graph $G' = (N, A - \hat{A})$. Then, we choose a set of λ_j for $v_j \in \hat{N}$ and introduce the arcs in $\hat{A}$ with costs $\lambda_j k(i, j)$. (We usually start with $\lambda_j = 1$ for all j.) Applying the minimum-cost flow algorithm, we then find a minimum-cost flow pattern. In augmenting the flow along the lowest-cost augmentation paths, constraints (2') and (3') are restricting. The flow must be so augmented that none of these constraints are violated.

VI. Example

We wish to maximize the flow from v_s to v_t in the graph $G = (N, A)$ given in Figure 5, where we require

$$f(s, 1) + 2f(2, 1) \leq 3, \tag{11}$$

$$f(3, 4) + 3f(2, 4) \leq 6, \tag{12}$$

and

$$f(1, 3) + 4f(2, 3) \leq 11. \tag{13}$$

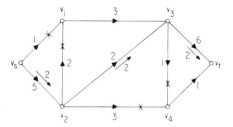

FIGURE 5. Graph G with arcs in A crossed and initial flow pattern indicated.

Since $c(1, 3) + 4c(2, 3) = 3 + 4 \times 2 = 11$, constraint (8) can be eliminated using Lemma 1. Using Theorem 3, we first discard the set of arcs $\hat{A} = \{(s, 1), (2, 1), (3, 4), (2, 4)\}$ to obtain $G' = (N, A - \hat{A})$. The maximum flow in G' is indicated in Figure 5 with crosses on the eliminated arcs. Now let $\lambda_1 = \lambda_2 = 1$. Hence, the arcs $(s, 1)$ and $(3, 4)$ will have cost 1 and the arcs $(2, 1)$ and $(2, 4)$ will have costs 2 and 3, respectively. The lowest-cost augmentation path is $v_s(s, 1)v_1(1, 3)v_3(3, t)v_t$ at cost 1 and $f(s, t)$ can be increased one unit as indicated (Figure 6). From (11),

$$2f(2, 1) \leq 3 - 1 \quad \text{or} \quad f(2, 1) \leq 1. \tag{14}$$

Now the lowest-cost augmentation path is

$$v_s(s, 2)v_2(2, 1)v_1(1, 3)v_3(3, t)v_t \quad \text{at cost 2.}$$

The resulting flow pattern is shown in Figure 7. The flow is increased by one unit since (11) is controlling. The lowest-cost augmentation path now is

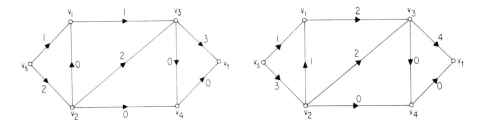

FIGURE 6. Left: Graph G with $V = 3$.

FIGURE 7. Right: Graph G with $V = 4$.

$v_3(s, 2)v_2(2, 4)v_4(4, t)v_t$ at cost 3 and $f(s, t)$ can be increased one unit. The resulting flow pattern is shown in Figure 8. The total flow now has value 5.

Note that constraint (11) is tight but (12) is loose. Hence, for the second trial, λ_2 must be decreased. Let $\lambda_1 = 1$ and $\lambda_2 = 0$, i.e., ignore constraint (12). In this case, the maximum s–t flow in G' has value 3 and is shown in Figure 9. Adding back $(s, 1)$ and $(2, 1)$, we can add two units of flow to achieve the flow in Figure 8. The flow is maximized with value 5 and (5) and (6) are satisfied. Hence, the solution is optimal.

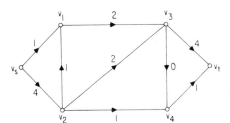

FIGURE 8. Graph G with $V = 5$.

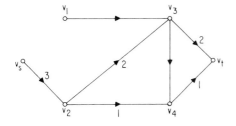

FIGURE 9. Maximum s–t flow in G' for $\lambda_1 = 1$ and $\lambda_2 = 0$.

VII. Conclusions

As we have seen in the example, the theorems in this chapter provide a heuristic method for solving a flow problem. If we specialize the structure of the graph for the flow problem, then we have a heuristic method for the assignment of jobs in a hybrid computer network. Because of the efficiency of flow algorithms, a calculation for a given set of lambdas in a network of up to fifty nodes takes less than 20 milliseconds on a CDC 6600 computer. Because of the special structure of the graph, in practice, only several possible values of λ need be tried before an optimum is reached. The entire computation therefore takes on the order of 100 milliseconds. Furthermore, the computation may be halted at any time and the best solution up to that time will yield an effective, if not optimal assignment.

ACKNOWLEDGMENT

Part of the work leading to this chapter was sponsored by the U.S. Army Research Office under Contract No. DAHCO 4–67–C–0046 at the University of California, Berkeley, California.

REFERENCES

1. Frank, H., "Matching on Graphs and the Interconnection of Digital Processors and Memories." *Conf. Record IEEE Internat. Conf. Comm., Boulder, Colorado, 1969*, pp. 21.2–21.9. IEEE, New York.
2. Frank, H., "Analysis and Optimization of Disk Storage Devices for Time Sharing Systems." *J. Assoc. Comput. Mach.* **16**, 602–620 (1969).
3. Kleinrock, L., "Models For Computer Networks." *Conf. Record IEEE Internat. Conf. Comm., Boulder, Colorado, 1969*, pp. 2.19–2.26.
4. Chu, W. W., "Optimal File Allocation in a Real Time Multicomputer Information System." *Int. Fed. Inf. Proc. Congr., Edinburgh, Scotland, 1968*.
5. Connelly, M. E., "Real Time Analog Digital Computation." *IRE Trans. Electronic Computers* **EC-11**, 31–41 (1962).
6. Ford, L. R., Jr., and Fulkerson, D. R., "Flows in Networks." Princeton Univ. Press, Princeton, New Jersey, 1962.
7. Iri, M., Amari, S., and Takata, M., R.A.A.G. Res. Notes, 3rd Ser., No. 47, Tokyo, 1961.

8. Berge, C., and Ghouila-Houri, M., "Programming, Games and Networks." Wiley, New York, 1965.
9. Malek-Zavarei, M., "Optimization on Directed Graphs," Ph.D. Dissertation, Univ. of California, Berkeley, California, 1970.
10. Busacker, R. G., and Gowen, P. J., "A Procedure for Determining a Family of Minimal Cost Network Flow Patterns." Operations Res. Office, Tech. Mcmo. No. 15, 1961.
11. Dantzig, G. B., "Linear Programming and Extensions." Princeton Univ. Press, Princeton, New Jersey, 1963.
12. Everett, III, H., "Generalized Lagrange Multiplier Method for Solving Problems of Optimum Allocation of Resources." *Operations Res.* **11**, 399–417 (1963).

An Algorithmic Approach to Sequential Automata Design

Chester C. Carroll
AUBURN UNIVERSITY
AUBURN, ALABAMA

William L. Oliver, Jr.
UNIVERSITY OF ILLINOIS
URBANA, ILLINOIS

and

William A. Hornfeck
AUBURN UNIVERSITY
AUBURN, ALABAMA

I. Introduction

The solution to most physical problems involves first formulating the problem in an exact manner and second, developing a suitable mathematical model of the problem. However, we are often limited in our choice of a mathematical model. This limitation stems from the fact that once we have chosen a model, we must possess the appropriate tools needed to manipulate our model so that we arrive at a solution to our problem. Fortunately, in most cases this limitation has been overcome by the development of efficient algorithms and techniques.

In particular many of the processes or systems which are encountered in engineering can be modeled successfully as sequential machines or sequential automata if the appropriate software is available. This software representation has been used to model problems in many different areas of engineering. Some of these are: sequential system design, models of learning systems and adaptive processes, artificial language problems, certain probabilistic processes, and models to study the efficiency of system simulation programs.

However, once we have modeled a given process or system as a sequential automaton, we are confronted with two basic questions: (1) Is the model we have devised the simplest model? (2) If we wish to implement the system under consideration, what is the best logical representation of our set of states Q?

Considering each of the above questions in turn, there exists an algorithm which solves the problem posed by question number one. The development of a computer program to perform the procedure greatly increases the effective utilization of the algorithm. The algorithm does not exist presently which solves the problem presented by question number two. Procedures do exist for obtaining a "fairly economical" implementation for sequential automata; however, a single algorithm for obtaining the optimum (i.e., lowest cost) implementation has not been found. As in the case of question number one, the existing algorithms for choosing a "good" logical representation of Q become even more effective when a digital computer is used to execute the procedures.

The following sections describe a particular type of programmed algorithm: the automated design of sequential automata. The procedure is designed to take sequential automata specifications and convert these specifications to Boolean functions from which an economical implementation of the machine can be made. Several subprograms are used in the automated procedure. Section II outlines the steps of the design procedure and indicates how information regarding automata specifications is entered into the procedure. Section III discusses the state-minimization algorithm used in the procedure and also discusses the programming of the algorithm. Section IV is a discussion of the algorithm and the program used in the state-assignment portion of the procedure.

II. Outline of Procedure

A. PROBLEM DEFINITION

Digital networks are classified into two categories: combinational networks and sequential networks. Combinational networks are those for which the output depends solely on the present input to the network. Sequential networks are those networks for which the output depends on both the present input and past inputs to the network. Thus a sequential network must "store" the "history" of its past inputs in its internal circuitry. The storage elements in a sequential network are often referred to as state variables, and it will be assumed in this work that the state variables are binary state variables; i.e., they can only be in the "on" and "off" conditions, represented by the binary values "1" and "0" respectively. Since each state variable has two possible conditions, for n state variables there are 2^n possible combinations of conditions in which the n state variables may be. Each of these 2^n possible combinations of conditions of the n state variables is called a "state" of the sequential network, and each state of the network serves to define a different history of inputs which the network may experience.

This work is concerned with an automated procedure for the design of sequential networks, or sequential machines as they are sometimes called, at a cost as low as possible. Since minimum cost is of primary importance, the automated procedure is necessarily concerned with the reduction of the number of storage elements needed by a given machine, i.e., state-minimization, and a method by which the states of the resulting minimum-state machine can be assigned to different combinations of the "0" and "1" conditions of the state variables such that the amount of combinational circuitry needed for the implementation is held to a minimum, i.e., state assignment.

Figure 1 is a block diagram of the organization of the automated sequential automata design procedure. The first block, labeled "Machine specifications," is the point at which information is entered into the program. There are many ways to represent desired machine characteristics, but the state-table type of specification was chosen to be used in this procedure. Thus, other types of machine specifications are transformed into state tables in block 2. Block 3 minimizes the number of states (and hence, storage elements) required by the

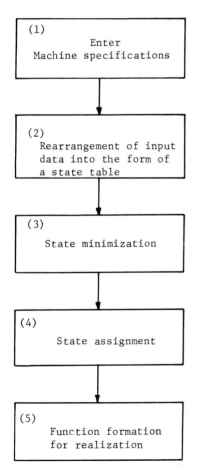

(1)
Enter
Machine specifications

(2)
Rearrangement of input
data into the form of
a state table

(3)
State minimization

(4)
State assignment

(5)
Function formation
for realization

FIGURE 1. Organization of the automated sequential automata design procedure.

machine; block 4 derives an economical state assignment for the minimum-state machine of block 3; and block 5 produces from the state assignment, Boolean equations from which an economical implementation of the machine can be constructed.

B. MODEL DEFINITION

Before further presentation of the procedure is given, a mathematical definition of "finite sequential machine" will be given to facilitate further discussion. This definition makes use of the concept of the "state" of a sequential machine developed earlier in this chapter.

DEFINITION. A *finite sequential machine M* is characterized by the following:

1. A finite set Q of states.
2. A finite set I of input symbols.
3. A finite set Z of output symbols.
4. A mapping δ of $I \times Q$ into Q called the next-state function.
5. A mapping ω of $I \times Q$ onto Z called the output function.

A sequential machine M is denoted by the five-tuple $M = \langle I, Q, Z, \delta, \omega \rangle$. If both mappings δ and ω are defined for all elements of $I \times Q$, then M is said to be a *completely specified sequential machine* (CSSM), while if either δ or ω is undefined for one or more elements of $I \times Q$, M is said to be an *incompletely specified sequential machine* (ISSM).

The next-state function δ and output function ω of a machine M contain all the information needed to specify the machine. There are several ways to compactly display these functions; the state table display will be used in this automated procedure because a state table can be conveniently represented in computer storage by two $n \times m$ arrays for an n-input, m-state machine. The general form of a state table is shown in Table I.

TABLE I

GENERAL FORM OF A STATE TABLE

	Present input		
I \ Q	i_1	$\ldots$	i_n
q_1	$\delta(i_1, q_1)/\omega(i_1, q_1)$	$\ldots$	$\delta(i_n, q_1)/\omega(i_n, q_1)$
Present state	. . .	Next state/present output	. . .
q_m	$\delta(i_1, q_m)/\omega(i_1, q_m)$	$\ldots$	$\delta(i_n, q_m)/\omega(i_n, q_m)$

III. State Minimization

After the required machine specifications are entered into the automated procedure, the next step in the design of a sequential machine is the minimization of the number of internal states required by the machine. This section describes the algorithm used for state minimization and the program written to apply the algorithm. Also, the capabilities and limitations of the program are discussed.

Before the state-minimization algorithm is presented, a few definitions must be made in order to facilitate discussion of the algorithm.

A. DEFINITIONS

1. *Output-sequence function.* For an input sequence $J_k = \langle i_1, i_2, \ldots, i_k \rangle$ and an initial state q_1 of a machine M, the *output-sequence function* $\omega(J_k, q_1)$ is defined to be

$$\omega(J_k, q_1) = \langle \omega(i_1, q_1), \omega(i_2, q_2), \omega(i_3, q_3), \ldots, \omega(i_k, q_k) \rangle,$$

where

$$q_2 = \delta(i_1, q_1), \qquad q_3 = \delta(i_2, q_2), \qquad \ldots, \qquad q_k = \delta(i_{k-1}, q_{k-1}).$$

2. *Output compatible.* Two entries $\omega(i_1, q_1)$ and $\omega(i_2, q_2)$ of the output function for a machine M are said to be *output compatible* if $\omega(i_1, q_1) = \omega(i_2, q_2)$ or either of $\omega(i_1, q_1)$ and $\omega(i_2, q_2)$ is undefined. Compatibility between entries of the output function will be denoted by the symbol $\sim$, $\omega(i_1, q_1) \sim \omega(i_2, q_2)$. Two output sequences of length k,

$$\omega(J_k, q_1) = \langle \omega(j_1, q_1), \omega(j_2, q_2), \ldots, \omega(j_k, q_k) \rangle$$

and

$$\omega(I_k, g_1) = \langle \omega(i_1, g_1), \omega(i_2, g_2), \ldots, \omega(i_k, g_k) \rangle$$

are said to be *output compatible* if $\omega(j_x, q_x) \sim \omega(i_x, g_x)$ for $1 \leq x \leq k$. Compatibility between output sequences also will be denoted by the symbol $\sim$.

3. *k-compatible states, compatible states.* States q_1 and q_2 of machine M are said to be *k-compatible states* if $\omega(J_k, q_1) \sim \omega(J_k, q_2)$ for all possible input sequences J_k of length k. If $\omega(J, q_1) \sim \omega(J, q_2)$ for all possible input sequences of any length, then q_1 and q_2 are said to be *compatible states*. Compatibility and k-compatibility between states will be denoted by the symbols $\sim$ and $\overset{k}{\sim}$ respectively.

4. *k-compatible set of states, compatible set of states.* A set of states S of a machine M is said to be a *k-compatible set of states* if $q_i \overset{k}{\sim} q_j$ for all $q_i, q_j \in S$. S is said to be a *compatible set of states* if $q_i \sim q_j$ for all $q_i, q_j \in S$.

5. *Maximum k-compatible set of states, maximum compatible set of states.* A k-compatible set of states is said to be a *maximum k-compatible set of states* if it is not a proper subset of some other k-compatible set of states. A compatible set of states is said to be a *maximum compatible set of states* if it is not a proper subset of some other compatible set of states.

6. *Final class.* The *final class* of a sequential machine M is the set of all maximum compatible sets of states of M.

7. *Next-state function for a set of states.* If i is an input of the input set I and B is a subset of the state set Q of a machine M, then the *next-state function for B under i* is defined to be the function $\delta(i, B)$ such that

$$\delta(i, B) = \{q \in Q \mid q = \delta(i, q_j) \quad \text{for} \quad q_j \in B \quad \text{and} \quad \delta(i, q_j) \quad \text{is defined}\}.$$

8. *Output function for a set of states.* If i is an input of the input set I and B is a subset of the output set Q of a machine M, then the *output function for B under i* is defined to be the function $\omega(i, B)$ such that

$$\omega(i, B) = \{z \in Z \mid z = \omega(i, q_j) \quad \text{for} \quad q_j \in B \quad \text{and} \quad q_j \text{ is defined}\}.$$

9. *Cover.* A set $B = \{B_1, B_2, \ldots, B_n\}$ of subsets of the state set Q of a machine M is said to be a *cover* for Q if

$$\sum_{i=1}^{n} B_i = Q \quad \text{and} \quad B_i \neq B_j \quad \text{if} \quad i \neq j.$$

10. *Closed cover.* A cover $B = \{B_1, B_2, \ldots, B_n\}$ for the state set Q of a machine M is said to be a *closed cover* for Q if for each input $i \in I$ and each $B_j \in B$ there exists a $B_k \in B$ such that $\delta(i, B_j)$ is a subset of B_k.

11. *C-class.* A *C-class* for a machine M is a closed cover C such that every element of C is a subset of a compatible set of M.

12. *Minimum C-class.* A *minimum C-class* for a machine M is a C-class C such that no other C-class has fewer elements than C.

13. *C-class machine.* A *C-class machine* S_c defined for a C-class $C = \{B_1, B_2, \ldots, B_r\}$ of a machine $M = \langle I, Q, Z, \delta, \omega \rangle$ is the five tuple $\langle I_c, Q_c, Z_c, \delta_c, \omega_c \rangle$ such that

1. $I_c = I$
2. $Z_c = Z$
3. $Q_c = \{b_1, b_2, \ldots, b_r\}$
4. If $\omega(i, B_j)$ is defined for $i \in I$ and $B_j \in C$, then $\omega_c(i, b_j) = \omega(i, q_j)$ for any $q_j \in B_j$ for which $\omega(i, q_j)$ is defined; if $\omega(i, B_j)$ is undefined, $\omega_c(i, b_j)$ is undefined.

5. If $\delta(i, B_j)$ is defined for $i \in I$ and $B_j \in C$, then $\delta_c(i, b_j) = b_k$ for some k such that $\delta(i, B_j)$ is a subset of B_k; if $\delta(i, B_j)$ is undefined, $\delta_c(i, b_j)$ is undefined.

14. *Minimum C-class machine.* A *minimum C-class machine* S_c for a machine M is a C-class machine of M derived from a minimum C-class for M.

Now that these definitions are available, the state-minimization program can be discussed. Since a minimum C-class machine is a minimum state representation of an original machine, it would be ideal if the design procedure would produce some minimum C-class machine from a given state table; unfortunately, this is not the case. The theory of machine minimization is not fully developed at the present time, and no algorithm that always produces a minimum C-class machine from any type of machine specifications is available, i.e., no method short of a completely exhaustive search until a solution is found. This exhaustive search is in most cases much too time consuming even for a computer for all but the smallest of machines. What is available is a well-defined algorithm for the calculation of the final class of a sequential machine, which is always a C-class but not necessarily a minimum C-class of the machine. This is the algorithm that has been programmed. The output of this program must be analyzed by hand to arrive at a reduced-state sequential machine, which hopefully will be close to a minimum-state machine. The final class algorithm will now be discussed.

B. Final Class Algorithm

Assume that it is desired to find the final class of a given machine $M = \langle I, Q, Z, \delta, \omega \rangle$. The final class algorithm consists of successively forming k covers of Q, $A_1, A_2, \ldots, A_k$, where A_i is the set of all maximum i-compatible sets of Q, until $A_k = A_{k-1}$. When a calculation yields $A_k = A_{k-1}$, this means that all maximum $(k-1)$-compatible sets are also maximum k-compatible sets and that application of the algorithm to A_k $(= A_{k-1})$ again will yield $A_{k+1} = A_k = A_{k-1}$. Thus it is intuitively seen, and it can be inductively proved, that if the sets of states of a class A_k are $(k+1)$-compatible sets, then these sets of states are indeed compatible. This last cover formed is the final class of M. Since each set of states in the final class is compatible, each set can be replaced by a single state if proper output and next-state conditions are imposed on the new state.

The formation of the covers $A_1, A_2, \ldots, A_k$ is accomplished by a recursive procedure consisting of four steps:

Step 1. From the output function ω form the 1-compatible class $A_1' = \{B_{1,1}', B_{1,2}', \ldots, B_{1,n_1}'\}$ such that each $B_{1,i}'$ contains only 1-compatible states and all sets of 1-compatible states are included by some $B_{1,j}'$.

Step 2. From the 1-compatible class A_1' form the maximum 1-compatible class $A_1 = \{B_{1,1}, B_{1,2}, \ldots, B_{1,n_1}\}$ by including in A_1 all maximum 1-compatible sets of A_1'.

Step 3. Assume that the j-compatible class $A_j = \{B_{j,1}, B_{j,2}, \ldots, B_{j,n_j}\}$ has been found. Each $B_{j,x} \in A_j$ is a j-compatible set. For each $B_{j,x} \in A_j$, calculate $(j+1)$-compatible sets such that each $(j+1)$-compatible set contains only groups of states of $B_{j,x}$ that, for each $i \in I$, either (1) have undefined images under the next-state mapping δ or (2) lead to any state of a particular element $B_{j,y}$ of A_j under the next state function δ. Also, each subset of each $B_{j,x} \in A_j$ that satisfies properties (1) and (2) above must be included in some $(j+1)$-compatible set. Call the set of all such $(j+1)$-compatible sets A_{j+1}'.

Step 4. From the $(j+1)$-compatible class A_{j+1}' form the maximum $(j+1)$-compatible class $A_{j+1} = \{B_{j+1,1}, B_{j+1,2}, \ldots, B_{j+1,n_{j+1}}\}$ by including in A_{j+1} all maximum $(j+1)$-compatible sets of A_{j+1}'. If $A_{j+1} = A_j$, then $A_j = A_{j+1}$ is the final class of M. If $A_{j+1} \neq A_j$, return to step 3.

This algorithm will terminate after a finite number of steps since the machines under consideration are finite. A flow chart illustrating the steps of the algorithm is given in Figure 2. An example illustrating the procedure will now be given.

EXAMPLE 1. FINAL CLASS. Find the final class of the machine described by the state table shown in Table IIa. The dashes in the table represent undefined outputs or next-states.

Step 1. Calculate 1-compatible sets:

$$B_{1,1}' = \{q_1, q_2, q_4, q_5, q_6\}: \quad \omega(i_1, B_{1,1}') \sim 0, \quad \omega(i_2, B_{1,1}') \sim 0.$$
$$B_{1,2}' = \{q_1, q_3, q_5, q_6\}: \quad \omega(i_1, B_{1,2}') \sim 0, \quad \omega(i_2, B_{1,2}') \sim 1.$$
$$B_{1,3}' = \{q_4, q_6\}: \quad \omega(i_1, B_{1,3}') \sim 1, \quad \omega(i_2, B_{1,3}') \sim 0.$$
$$B_{1,4}' = \{q_3, q_6\}: \quad \omega(i_1, B_{1,4}') \sim 1, \quad \omega(i_2, B_{1,4}') \sim 1.$$

Step 2. Pick out the maximum 1-compatible sets: the maximum 1-compatible sets are $B_{1,1}'$ and $B_{1,2}'$. Let $B_{1,1} = B_{1,1}'$, $B_{1,2} = B_{1,2}'$. Then $A_1 = \{B_{1,1}, B_{1,2}\}$. This data is conveniently displayed in Table IIb. This table gives the next state of each state of each set $B_{i,j}$, and also gives in parentheses beside each next state the numbers j identifying the sets $B_{1,j}$ in which these next states are contained. This diagram facilitates the forming of the 2-compatible sets $B_{2,j}$.

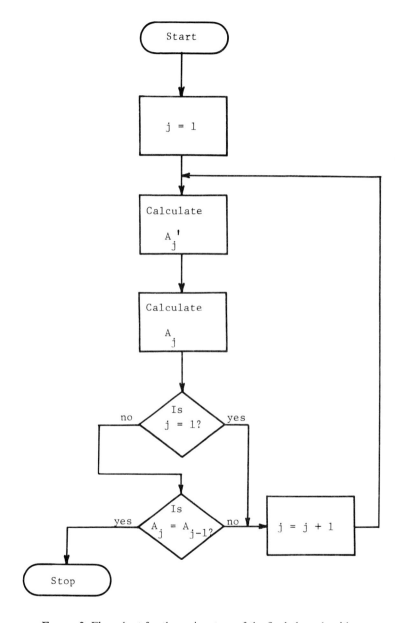

FIGURE 2. Flow chart for the major steps of the final class algorithm.

TABLE IIa

STATE TABLE FOR MACHINE
OF EXAMPLE 1

Q ⟍ I	i_1	i_2
q_1	$q_3/0$	$-/-$
q_2	$q_4/0$	$q_3/0$
q_3	$-/-$	$q_5/1$
q_4	$q_6/-$	$q_6/0$
q_5	$q_6/0$	$q_6/-$
q_6	$-/-$	$-/-$

TABLE IIb

MAXIMUM 1-COMPATIBLE CLASS A_1
FOR STATE TABLE IIa

B	Q ⟍ I	i_1		i_2	
	q_1	q_3	(2)	—	
	q_2	q_4	(1)	q_3	(2)
$B_{1,1}$	q_4	q_6	(1)(2)	q_6	(1)(2)
	q_5	q_6	(1)(2)	q_6	(1)(2)
	q_6	—		—	
	q_1	q_3	(2)	—	
$B_{1,2}$	q_3	—		q_5	(1)(2)
	q_5	q_6	(1)(2)	q_6	(1)(2)
	q_6	—		—	

TABLE IIc

MAXIMUM 2-COMPATIBLE CLASS A_2 FOR STATE
TABLE IIa

B	Q ⟍ I	i_1		i_2	
	q_2	q_3	(3)	—	
$B_{2,1}$	q_4	q_6	(1)(2)(3)	q_6	(1)(2)(3)
	q_5	q_6	(1)(2)(3)	q_6	(1)(2)(3)
	q_6	—		—	
	q_1	q_4	(1)(2)	q_3	(3)
$B_{2,2}$	q_4	q_6	(1)(2)(3)	q_6	(1)(2)(3)
	q_5	q_6	(1)(2)(3)	q_6	(1)(2)(3)
	q_6	—		—	
	q_1	q_3	(3)	—	
$B_{2,3}$	q_3	—		q_5	(1)(2)(3)
	q_5	q_6	(1)(2)(3)	q_6	(1)(2)(3)
	q_6	—		—	

Step 3. Calculate 2-compatible sets: From $B_{1,1}$:

$$B'_{2,1} = \{q_2, q_4, q_5, q_6\}: \quad \delta(i_1, B'_{2,1}) \sim B_{1,1}, \quad \delta(i_2, B'_{2,1}) \sim B_{1,2}.$$
$$B'_{2,2} = \{q_1, q_4, q_5, q_6\}: \quad \delta(i_1, B'_{2,2}) \sim B_{1,2}, \quad \delta(i_2, B'_{2,2}) \sim B_{1,2}.$$

From $B_{1,2}$:

$$B'_{2,3} = \{q_1, q_3, q_5, q_6\}: \quad \delta(i_1, B'_{2,3}) \sim B_{1,2}, \quad \delta(i_2, B'_{2,3}) \sim B_{1,2}.$$

Step 4. Pick out the maximum 2-compatible sets: The maximum 2-compatible sets are $B'_{2,1}$, $B'_{2,2}$, and $B'_{2,3}$. Let $B_{2,1} = B'_{2,1}$, $B_{2,2} = B'_{2,2}$, and $B_{2,3} = B'_{2,3}$. Then $A_2 = \{B_{2,1}, B_{2,2}, B_{2,3}\}$. This data is shown in Table IIc. Since $A_2 \neq A_1$, apply step 3 to A_2.

Step 5. Calculate 3-compatible sets: From $B_{2,1}$:

$$B'_{3,1} = \{q_2, q_4, q_5, q_6\}: \quad \delta(i_1, B'_{3,1}) \sim B_{2,1}, \quad \delta(i_2, B'_{3,1}) \sim B_{2,3}.$$

From $B_{2,2}$:

$$B'_{3,2} = \{q_1, q_4, q_5, q_6\}: \quad \delta(i_1, B'_{3,2}) \sim B_{2,3}, \quad \delta(i_2, B'_{3,2}) \sim B_{2,1}.$$

From $B_{2,3}$:

$$B'_{3,3} = \{q_1, q_3, q_5, q_6\}: \quad \delta(i_1, B'_{3,3},) \sim B_{2,3} \quad \delta(i_2, B'_{3,3}) \sim B_{2,1}.$$

Step 6. Pick out the maximum 3-compatible sets: The maximum 3-compatible sets are $B'_{3,1}$, $B'_{3,2}$, and $B'_{3,3}$. Let $B_{3,1} = B'_{3,1}$, $B_{3,2} = B'_{3,2}$, and $B_{3,3} = B'_{3,3}$. Then $A_3 = \{B_{3,1}, B_{3,2}, B_{3,3}\}$. By inspection $A_3 = A_2$. Therefore, $A_3 = A_2$ is the final class of M.

C. MINIMUM-STATE REPRESENTATION

The final class of a sequential machine groups together all states which may be merged into a single state. Since there can be many more maximum compatible sets in the final class than there are states in Q, we see that judicious mergings must be made. The selection of which states to merge in order to yield a minimum-state machine is a major problem in sequential automata theory. If a minimum-state machine is to be obtained, a minimum C-class must be found. This entails finding a minimum number of sets and subsets of the sets of the final class which form a preserved cover. This problem is largely unsolved at present, and there are but a few papers available [3, 4] which present any simplification to the procedure. An example will illustrate the principles involved in the selection of a minimum C-class machine.

EXAMPLE 2. C-CLASS MACHINES. Consider the example given earlier in which the final class for the state table of Table IIa was found. The maximum compatible sets of the final class along with the images of each set under the next-state function δ (definition 7) and the maximum compatible sets in which these images are contained are given in Table III(a). The table is arranged in such a way as to enable easy formation of a C-class machine (definition 12). There are three choices possible for the next state of B_1 under i_2, three choices for the next state of B_3 under i_2, two choices for the next state of B_2 under i_1, and only one choice for the remaining transitions. But all three sets B_1, B_2 and B_3 need not be chosen to represent states of the machine. B_2 and B_3 form a cover for $Q = \{q_1, q_2, q_3, q_4, q_5, q_6\}$, and since the next state function may be chosen such that $\delta(i_1, B_2) = B_2$ and $\delta(i_2, B_3) = B_2$ or B_3, the cover $\{B_2, B_3\}$

TABLE III

POSSIBLE C-CLASS MACHINES AND THEIR STATE TRANSITIONS FOR
THE MACHINE OF EXAMPLE 1

(a)

B \\ I	$\delta(i, B_j)$		$\delta(i, B_j) \subseteq B_k$	
	i_1	i_2	i_1	i_2
$B_1 = \{q_1, q_4, q_5, q_6\}$	$\{q_3, q_6\}$	$\{q_6\}$	B_3	B_1, B_2, B_3
$B_2 = \{q_2, q_4, q_5, q_6\}$	$\{q_4, q_6\}$	$\{q_3, q_6\}$	B_1, B_2	B_3
$B_3 = \{q_1, q_3, q_5, q_6\}$	$\{q_3, q_6\}$	$\{q_5, q_6\}$	B_3	B_1, B_2, B_3

(b)

B \\ I	i_1	i_2
B_2	B_2	B_3
B_3	B_3	B_2, B_3

(c)

B \\ I	i_1	i_2
B_2	B_2	D
D	D	B_2

is closed within itself. This choice for a C-class is shown in Table III (b). Another choice for a C-class machine is the set $\{B_2, D\}$, where $D = \{q_1, q_3, q_6\}$ is a subset of $B_3 = \{q_1, q_3, q_5, q_6\}$. The next-state mapping for this choice is shown in Table III(c). Thus, the original machine of six states can be reduced to a machine of two states. Table IV shows some possible C-class machines derived from the C-classes shown in Table III. Output specifications have been added by checking from the original state table the output requirements of the states of each set of each C-class. The C-class machines of Table IV (b) and (c) are minimum C-class machines.

TABLE IV

SOME C-CLASS MACHINES FOR THE C-CLASSES OF TABLE III

(a)			(b)			(c)		
Q \\ I	i_1	i_2	Q \\ I	i_1	i_2	Q \\ I	i_1	i_2
b_2	$b_2/0$	$b_3/0$	b_2	$b_2/0$	$b_3/0$	b_2	$b_2/0$	$d/0$
b_3	$b_3/0$	$b_2/1$	b_3	$b_3/0$	$b_3/1$	d	$d/0$	$b_2/1$
b_1	$b_3/0$	$b_1/0$						

D. Example Complete

There are generally many combinations of maximum compatible sets and subsets of maximum compatible sets of a final class which qualify as being covers. The next-state mappings of each of these covers must be checked to determine if the cover is closed. Since a minimum C-class machine is the object of the entire state-minimization procedure, the covers formed from the final class should be examined starting with the smallest covers first and then considering larger and larger covers until a closed cover is found. This can often be a quite lengthy process, even for a computer for large state machines. This is the main problem of the automated-design procedure, and it remains unsolved. Experience with machine minimization, however, often indicates how to pick the better solutions by hand.

E. Completely Specified Machines

When there are no unspecified entries in a state table, many simplifications can be made in the state-minimization procedure because each state can appear in only one maximum compatibility class. In fact, the compatibility relation becomes an equivalence relation, since the transitive property of the relation now holds. Complete machine minimization is so simple and well defined that it may be considered to be classic. Each resulting maximum equivalence class forms an essential state of the minimum-state machine, and thus, the final class is *the* minimum C-class. The incompletely specified machine program will minimize a completely specified machine, but a separate program for completely specified machine minimization was written because of the vast computer usage time and computer memory savings which can be realized with this specialized program.

IV. State Assignment

After the sequential machine specifications are entered into the automata design program and a reduced-state (preferably minimum state) representation of the machine has been decided on, the next step toward finding an economical realization of a sequential machine is the selection of the number of state variables which will be used and the assignment of each state of the minimum-state machine to some unique combination of these state variables. The number of state variables that may be used to realize a sequential machine has a lower bound, but is otherwise arbitrary. The choice of how many state variables to use may depend on several considerations, including facility of implementation, the type of physical elements available for implementation, and cost of implementation.

The cost of implementing a sequential machine is the sum total cost of the storage elements and the combinational elements used to implement the next-state and output functions of the machine. Many types of storage elements are in common use, and each type of element has a different purchasing cost. Storage elements, however, are generally more costly and more bulky than combinational elements, and for this reason the sequential automata design procedure is written to produce realization requiring the absolute minimum number of storage elements (state variables) possible. This does not imply that there are not cases for which the minimum state-variable approach is not the cheapest approach. But machines for which an increase in the number of state variables can reduce total cost occur infrequently, and therefore, they will not be considered in this procedure.

A. COMBINATIONAL COST CONSIDERATIONS

The amount of combinational circuitry needed to realize the next-state and output functions of a sequential machine depends on (1) the input and output coding of the machine, (2) the type of combinational elements to be used in the realization, and (3) the manner in which combinations of state variables are assigned to represent states of the machine. In order to simplify the calculations of combinational costs, two assumptions will be made about input and output coding. First, it will be assumed that the input coding is given, as is usually the case. Second, since the output interface requirements for a sequential machine may require a specific type of output coding, output circuitry costs are difficult to approximate from a state table representation of a sequential machine. For this reason, output circuitry costs are neglected in overall cost calculations; only the next-state equations for the state variables are considered in the cost evaluation. It should be noted that for a machine having many more states than outputs, this neglect of output circuitry is not of great importance, but for a machine having many more outputs than internal states, the output circuitry becomes the dominant cost factor, and the output coding must be known before realization costs can be reasonably evaluated. Since output circuitry costs will be neglected, this design procedure is of greater use in reducing realization costs for machines having small numbers of outputs.

Now that these assumptions concerning input and output codings have been made, the manner in which combinational costs will be evaluated will be discussed. The costs of implementing a Boolean function will be figured from its expression as a Boolean sum of Boolean products; i.e., from its two-level, and–or (or Nand–Nand) representation, assuming that the complements of all variables are available. A cost of "one" will be assessed to a function for each literal of each multiliteral product of the function, and a cost of "one" will also be assessed for each product in the function. For example, the function

$$F = abc + de + f$$

will be assessed a cost of "one" for each of the variables a, b, c, d, and e and also a cost of "one" for each of the products abc, de, and f. Thus, the cost of F is 8. This type of cost assessment corresponds closely to using transistor–transistor logic (T^2L) and corresponds somewhat less closely to using diode–transistor logic (DTL).

B. STATE-ASSIGNMENT PROBLEM

The major remaining cost factor to be considered for combinational circuitry is the manner in which combinations of the binary state variables are assigned to represent the different states of a sequential machine. The problem of finding the best assignment is known as the state-assignment problem. Since this procedure deals only with "finite"-state sequential machines, the number of state assignments possible for a given machine is finite. Consideration of every possible state assignment will indeed find a minimum-cost assignment, but the large number of state assignments which must be considered renders this exhaustive search infeasible. The number of distinct state assignments N possible for an n-state machine using the minimum number r of state variables is given by the formula

$$N = \frac{2^r!}{(2^r - n)!\,r!}.$$

This formula calculated for several values of n is shown in Table V. This table illustrates just how infeasible the exhaustive procedure is.

TABLE V. NUMBER OF DISTINCT STATE
ASSIGNMENTS FOR AN n-STATE SEQUENTIAL
MACHINE USING THE MINIMUM NUMBER r
OF BINARY STATE VARIABLES

n	$r = \log_2 n$	$N = \dfrac{2^r!}{(2^r - n)!\,r!}$
2	1	2
3	2	12
4	2	12
5	3	1,120
6	3	3,360
7	3	6,720
8	3	6,720
9	4	172,972,800

A considerable amount of literature has been written about the state-assignment problem. Much of this literature, however, deals with those special classes of machines for which certain state assignments result in "reduced-dependency" next-state equations, and while these reduced-dependency equations are usually very economical, these special types of machines form but a small class of sequential automata [5]. Also, great difficulty and lengthy calculations are often encountered when one attempts to find a state assignment which results in reduced-dependency equations, if such a state assignment exists. For these reasons, reduced-dependency techniques have not been considered here. Instead, cost-reduction techniques which are applicable to all machines are applied in this procedure.

C. COST-REDUCTION TECHNIQUES

The state-assignment techniques used in this procedure are directed toward producing minimum-cost next-state equations for the state variables used in a sequential machine realization. In particular, the techniques used attempt to make state assignments such that the resulting minterms of the next-state equations can be combined as extensively as possible into simpler Boolean expressions. An example will illustrate the principles involved.

EXAMPLE 3. STATE ASSIGNMENT. Consider the state transition table shown in Table VIa. The data from this table is rearranged in Table VIb into what is called an "inverse" state table. This inverse state table groups together all

TABLE VIa

STATE TRANSITION TABLE
FOR EXAMPLE 3

Q	$\bar{x}$	x
1	3	4
2	1	1
3	2	1
4	3	4

TABLE VIb

INVERSE STATE TABLE AND
STATE ASSIGNMENTS FOR EXAMPLE 3

| | | | Assignments | |
| | | | I | II |
$\bar{x}$	x	Q	$y_1\,y_2$	$y_1\,y_2$
2	2, 3	1	00	01
3	—	2	01	00
1, 4	—	3	10	10
—	1, 4	4	11	11

states from which a state may be entered under a specific input. For example, states 1 and 4 are entered in column 1, row 3 since both state 1 and state 4 lead to state 3 under a $\bar{x}$ input. Two state variables y_1 and y_2 are needed to represent this 4-state machine since $\log_2 4 = 2$. Also given in Table VIb are two possible state assignments for y_1 and y_2. The better state assignment is the one which yields the lower-cost next-state equations Y_1 and Y_2 for the state variables y_1 and y_2. The minterms for the next-state expressions Y_1 and Y_2 can be obtained by inspection from the inverse state table. For assignment I, y_1 represents states 3 and 4. States 3 and 4 are entered from states 1 and 4 under an $\bar{x}$ input and also from states 1 and 4 under an x input. Thus, the minterms for Y_1 are

$$\bar{x}\bar{y}_1\bar{y}_2, \quad \bar{x}y_1y_2, \quad x\bar{y}_1\bar{y}_2, \quad \text{and} \quad xy_1y_2,$$

or

$$Y_1 = \bar{x}\bar{y}_1\bar{y}_2 + \bar{x}y_1y_2 + x\bar{y}_1\bar{y}_2 + xy_1y_2,$$

where $\bar{y}_1\bar{y}_2$ is the state assignment for state 1 and y_1y_2 is the assignment for state 4. Similarly, the Y_2 equation becomes

$$Y_2 = \bar{x}y_1\bar{y}_2 + x\bar{y}_1\bar{y}_2 + xy_1y_2.$$

These equations can be simplified by multiple-output Boolean-algebra techniques to yield

$$Y_1 = y_1y_2 + \bar{y}_1\bar{y}_2$$

and

$$Y_2 = \bar{x}y_1\bar{y}_2 + x\bar{y}_1\bar{y}_2 + xy_1y_2.$$

These two equations have a combined cost of 18. State assignment II is a more judicious state assignment than is assignment I. The next-state equations for assignment 2 are $Y_1 = y_2$ and $Y_2 = x + \bar{y}_1\bar{y}_2$, a cost of 4.

The factors which affect the overall cost of next-state equations are complex; in fact, they are so complex that the state-assignment problem has never been solved. One very important factor, however, is illustrated by this example. In the inverse state table, note that the only multiple entries are the pair of states 2 and 3 under input $\bar{x}$ and the pair 1 and 4 under both inputs $\bar{x}$ and x. Now notice that for assignment I, the codes for states 2 and 3 differ in both positions. The same is true for states 1 and 4. Thus, whenever these multiple entries contribute minterms to a next-state expression, these minterms cannot be combined together into a simpler expression. For assignment II, however, both pairs of states (1–4 and 2–3) have codes differing only in one position. Thus, states 2 and 3 and states 1 and 4 are "adjacent" pairs of states. Now, when the pair of states 2 and 3, for example, contributes minterms to a next state equation, these minterms can be combined to yield a single product of two literals instead of the two products of three literals resulting from assignment I. The adjacencies between states 1 and 4 and states 2 and 3 are the main reason for the lower costs of assignment II.

D. STATE-ASSIGNMENT PROGRAM

The above example illustrates the principles used in the state-assignment program for this procedure. Two states which lead to the same next-state under any given input are identified as adjacent states. Adjacent states which produce minterms in the next-state equations are assigned codes differing in only one variable (adjacent codes) whenever possible. The only adjacent states which do not produce minterms in the next-state equations are those adjacent states leading to the state which has the "all-zero" state-assignment code. These adjacencies are neglected.

The state assignment program is begun by searching through the state table and finding which state is transferred to the largest number of times. This state is assigned the "all-zero" state assignment in order to reduce the number of minterms contained in the next-state equations (in case two or more states are equally transferred to the largest number of times, one of these states is chosen arbitrarily to have the all-zero assignment). This gives a starting point for making further assignments. States adjacent to this "reference" state are assigned codes containing only a single "1" until all codes with a single "1" are used or until all states adjacent to the reference state are assigned. Then, another state having an assigned code is designated as the "reference" state, and once again, unassigned states adjacent to this new reference state are assigned unused codes which are adjacent to the code of the reference state. Each state which has been assigned a code is in turn used as the "reference" state for making further assignments until all states have been assigned a code. If it happens that some states are left unassigned after this process, one of these unassigned states is assigned an arbitrarily-chosen unused code, and this state is then used as the reference state. Finally, all states will have codes assigned to them, and the procedure is finished. An example will be given to clarify this process.

EXAMPLE 4. STATE ASSIGNMENT. Consider the inverse state table shown in Table VIIa. The step-by-step procedure made by the state-assignment program is given below.

1. State 2 is transferred to most often; assign the code 000 to state 2.
2. State 2 is now the reference state.
3. Do not neglect the adjacency of states 3 and 6, since they occur in row 5 as well as row 2.
4. State 4 is adjacent to state 2; assign state 4 the code 001.
5. State 5 is adjacent to state 2; assign state 5 the code 010.
6. No other states are adjacent to state 2.
7. No other states are adjacent to state 4.
8. Set state 5 as the reference state.

9. State 1 is adjacent to state 5; assign to state 1 the code 011.
10. No other states are adjacent to state 5.
11. States 3 and 6 are left unassigned. Assign the code 100 to state 3; state 3 is the reference state.
12. State 6 is adjacent to state 3; assign to state 6 the code 101.
13. All states have codes.

TABLE VIIa

INVERSE STATE TABLE
FOR EXAMPLE 4

$\bar{x}$	x	Q
2, 4	—	1
3, 6	1	2
1, 5	—	3
—	2, 5	4
—	3, 6	5
—	4	6

TABLE VIIb

TWO STATE ASSIGNMENTS
FOR EXAMPLE 4

	Assignments	
Q	I	II
	$y_1\, y_2\, y_3$	$y_1\, y_2\, y_3$
1	0 1 1	0 0 0
2	0 0 0	0 0 1
3	1 0 0	0 1 0
4	0 0 1	0 1 1
5	0 1 0	1 0 0
6	1 0 1	1 0 1

For assignment I:
$$Y_1 = x\bar{y}_1\bar{y}_2 y_3 + \bar{x}y_2$$
$$Y_2 = \bar{x}\bar{y}_1\bar{y}_2 + xy_1$$
$$Y_3\, x\bar{y}_1\bar{y}_3 + \bar{y}_1\bar{y}_2$$

For assignment II:
$$Y_1 = xy_1y_3 + xy_2$$
$$Y_2 = x\bar{y}_1\bar{y}_2 y_3 + \bar{x}\bar{y}_2\bar{y}_3 + y_1\bar{y}_3$$
$$Y_3 = x\bar{y}_2\bar{y}_3 + \bar{x}y_1y_3 + \bar{x}y_2\bar{y}_3 + x\bar{y}_1y_3$$

The assignment obtained above and a "random" assignment are shown in Table VIIb. The next-state equations for each assignment are shown above. The cost of the "adjacency" state assignment is 22 while the cost of the random state assignment is 36–59% more. Despite the considerable savings made by the adjacency assignment, there is no evidence of optimality.

E. FUNCTION FORMATION FOR REALIZATION

Once a state assignment has been made for a sequential machine, it is a straightforward procedure to use the state table and state assignment to form combinational Boolean functions for the realization of a machine. Several methods for combinational minimization are in common use; the method used in conjunction with this procedure is the method presented by Jordan [6]. Since this is strictly a combinational problem and not a problem of sequential automata theory, this method of combinational minimization will not be discussed further.

V. Summary

This work has presented an automated procedure for the economical design of sequential machines. The automation of the procedure is a necessity for machines having more than a few states due to the large amount of calculation necessary.

The procedure consists of two main parts: the final class program and the state-assignment program. The final class program identifies all states of a sequential machine which may be combined into a single state. The best selection of which states to merge is at present an unsolved problem in automata theory, and this determination of a minimum-state machine from the final class is the only point in the procedure which is not automated. This problem, however, does not arise for completely specified machines and quite often does not arise for incompletely specified machines, and the procedure is fully automated for these cases.

State-assignment theory is also not fully developed at the present time, and minimum-cost state assignments are not guaranteed. Experimentation with the program indicates that the program makes assignments which are on the average 11% above minimum cost for machines not of the "reduced-dependency" type.

REFERENCES

1. Carroll, C. C., and Liner, M. Q., "Sequential Machine Realization of s-Domain Functions," Tech. Rep. No. 7, NAS8-20163. Auburn Res. Foundation, Auburn, Alabama, 1967.
2. Miller, R. E., "Switching Theory," Vol. II. Wiley, New York, 1965.
3. Grasselli, A., and Luccio, F., "A Method for Minimizing the Number of Internal States in Incompletely Specified Sequential Machines." *IEEE Trans. Electronic Computers* **EC-14**, 350–359 (1965).
4. Meisel, W. S., "A Note on Internal State Minimization in Incompletely Specified Sequential Networks." *IEEE Trans. Electronic Computers* **EC-16**, 508–509 (1967).
5. Dolotta, T. A., and McCluskey, E. J., "The Coding of Internal States of Sequential Circuits." *IEEE Trans. Electronic Computers* **EC-13**, 549–562 (1964).
6. Jordan, G. E., "A Fast Algorithm for Boolean Function Minimization." Masters Thesis, Auburn Univ., Auburn, Alabama, 1968.
7. Torng, H. C., "An Algorithm for Finding Secondary Assignments of Synchronous Sequential Circuits." *IEEE Trans. Computers*, **C-17**, 461–469 (1968).
8. Wood, P. E., Jr., "Switching Theory." McGraw-Hill, New York, 1968.
9. Krieger, M., "Basic Switching Circuit Theory." Macmillan, New York, 1967.
10. Hartmanis, J. and Stearns, R. E., "Algebraic Structure of Sequential Machines." Prentice-Hall, Englewood Cliffs, New Jersey, 1966.
11. Breuer, M. A., "General Survey of Design Automation of Digital Computers." *Proc. IEEE* **54**, 1708–1721 (1966).
12. Kuo, F. F., and Kaiser, J. F., "System Analysis by Digital Computers." Wiley, New York, 1966.

Behavioral Misconceptions Facing the Software Engineer

Richard H. Wilcox
EXECUTIVE OFFICE OF THE PRESIDENT
WASHINGTON, D.C.

Design of software for information systems usually proceeds on the basis of several tacit assumptions concerning behavioral patterns which are largely unjustified.

The first of these standard assumptions is an expectation that the intended user really wants a new information system, one different from what he uses currently. Although this expectation is usually implicit, it is sometimes based on statements made by potential customers—or by their bosses. Unfortunately, however, most information users have given very little thought to the sources they really use or the problems they actually face; they are basically disinterested, and they would prefer not to have to learn new procedures. Scientists, for example, are heavy participants in formal literature exchange, yet they learn of relevant work primarily from personal contacts and informal correspondence; traditional document retrieval systems can be of little help to them in this. Engineers, conversely, are notoriously light users of the formal literature, preferring trade journals for most of what professional reading they do. For one thing, reading and writing is not the kind of activity that the average engineer particularly enjoys doing—he would much rather solve a design problem successfully (even if unnecessarily) than hunt around to find some existing solution and copy it. Most technical managers are no better, even though they give frequent lip service to the importance of good information flow and are often the ones who call for new, automated systems. How often are managers seen browsing in the library? How many of them have used an interactive computer terminal? Do they ever ask for novel formats in standard reports? How frequently do they scan the technical literature themselves? Do they honestly know what specific benefits to expect of a sophisticated information system, other than prestige?

Note that while these observations apply to behavior patterns of the majority of scientists, engineers, and technical managers, there is a small but important group which is specifically excluded—and this leads to the second usual but unjustified assumption, namely that introspection provides legitimate guidance to the information system designer. The person who designs systems and writes systems software is highly atypical: He has great interest in information handling, he is neither confused nor frightened by computer systems, and he is by definition seeking something different and better. The reader of these proceedings, like the participant in the symposium which generated them, is almost *automatically* branding himself as nonstandard by this simple act of indulging in formal technical information usage. Thus his introspection will be a poor guide for design of information systems to serve the average scientist, engineer, or technical manager.

It is intriguing to speculate that negation of a third usual assumption might open the way to increased validity of the previous two, at least for technical literature systems. The standard approach specifies design of an information system to serve all members of a technical staff; as a corollary, when measures of effectiveness are tried a usual one involves counting the number of different staff members who use the facility. Yet some interesting recent research results by Thomas Allen, of the Sloan School of Management at Massachusetts Institute of Technology indicate that most technical communications with a group are carried on by a relatively small subset of group members comprised of what Allen calls information " gatekeepers." Perhaps it would make more sense (and dollars, too) to design information systems to serve the special needs and practices of these gatekeepers. The likelihood of substantial interest by such people in improved information handling should be considerably above the norm, and introspection on the part of the well-informed systems designer might be less suspect as a guide in this case because he himself is likely to be a gatekeeper type (for example, if he is reading this paper and others like it).

Another common but dubious assumption holds that the only important function of an information system is to provide information. Again, behavior patterns belie this. One need only visit a modern city or county library to discover that it serves an additional major function as a meeting place for school boys and girls—and after all, isn't that greatly preferable to many other possible meeting places? This, incidentally, is not a trivial library function; any library not designed to accommodate such meetings is doomed to discouragingly low usage rates by the young people it should be serving. In a similar vein, sophisticated computer based information systems are frequently installed partly on the basis of organizational status, whether that is actually admitted or not, and any such system which lacks demonstration packages to show off its capabilities easily is quite likely to have poor relationships with organization management. Again, addition of such seemingly minor services (in comparison with primary functions) as citation indices, for example, may provide scientific customers with a capability to show that their publications are frequently cited, which can be more important to them personally and professionally than the simple location of some new reference (it has been suggested that the phrase "publish or perish" is being replaced with "be cited or blighted").

One other erroneous assumption should not be necessary to mention, since everyone claims to be aware of its falsity, yet it is made so frequently that it must be included here. This is the assumption that an optimal information system will be designed the first time, or, equivalently, that the initial software package will do the job for which it was intended. The fact that user behavior patterns cannot be measured accurately to provide design standards, and—even more important—that a new information system or software package will by its very existence cause modification of user behavior patterns, should make it clear that all software designs must provide for subsequent modification and "tuning" after initial implementation. Note that this is entirely different from "debugging," which simply removes unintentional errors. Note too that this establishes a requirement for postimplementation monitoring to determine what additional changes are necessary or desirable. It is almost incredible that, with years of experience behind us now in programming computers, most programs are still written with seriously inadequate provision for subsequent modification.

In summary, software design and engineering is frequently based implicitly upon thoughtless misconceptions concerning user behavior. These may concern interest of the potential customer, validity of introspection as a design guide, identification of the primary user, absence of secondary system functions, and adequacy of initial design. Undoubtedly there are others. But the point should be clear: User behavior patterns will determine whether the system is ultimately successful or unsuccessful, regardless of technical excellence.

Index

A

Abbreviations, in natural languages, 107
Acronyms, 107
Add-substract-omit machine, 9
Adjacency multigraphs, 228
Admissible formula, 103
Algebraic language, 126
ALGOL, 115, 119–120
AMBIT/G, 120
AMPPL-II (Associative Memory Parallel
  Processing Language), 141
  description of, 143–152
Defined Entity in, 149
  Equivalence List in, 147
  memory matrix in, 144
  reverse relation in, 148
  Search and Flag operations in, 143, 147
Analog computer, in combinatorial net-
  works, 253
  see also Computer
AND feature, 7
  in ISL system, 63, 65
APPREX programs, 214, 223
ARRANGE programs, 214, 223
Array, symbolic question and, 98
Array manipulation, meaning and, 98
Artificial international languages, 109
Artificial language, defined, 105, 110
  see also Language
Associative memory
  content-addressable, 143
  defined, 142
  exact and nonexact, 141–153
Associative Memory Parallel Processing
  Language, see AMPPL-II
Atomic sentence, 91
Attributes, errors in assignment of, 76–79
Automata design
  block diagram of, 267
  combinatorial cost in, 278–279

completely specified machines for, 277
cost-reduction techniques in, 280–281
formal class algorithm in, 271
function formula for, 283
minimum-state representation in, 275–276
sequential, 265–284
state assignment in, 277–283
state minimization in, 269–277
Automata theory, syntactic analysis in, 179
Automatic classification, transcription
  errors in, 77
Automatic language processing, intermediate language for, 105–116
  see also Language
Available Space List (AVSL), 143
Average-slope approximation, proof of,
  221–222
AVSL, 143

B

Basic English, 108, 110
Bayesian procedure, enumerative, 186
Behavioral misconceptions, software
  engineer and, 285–287
Binary computer programs, computer-
  assisted documentation of, 1–17
  see also Computer
Binary translation, 113
Blank primitives, 167
BNF syntax, 119
Boolean function, cost of implementing, 278
Browsing
  by managers, 285
  as search strategy, 110

C

Cartesian indexing language, 26
C-class machines, in automata design,
  275–276